Dream Factories
and Radio Pictures

Dream Factories and Radio Pictures

Howard Waldrop

Dream Factories and Radio Pictures

Published by

🌾 **Wheatland Press**

http://www.wheatlandpress.com
P. O. Box 1818
Wilsonville, OR 97070

Contents

PREFACE

[Publisher's note: This preface was written for the electronic edition of Dream Factories and Radio Pictures published by Electric Story, 2001.]

What you are about to read is a collection of all my stories about movies (dream factories) and television (radio pictures) from my first four collections, plus an unpublished article and a new story. There'll be an introduction to each category. The movie part's divided into Dream Factories: The Past, stories about motion pictures from the beginning circa 1895 to one set in an alternate 1970s. Dream Factories: The Future is a couple of my 1980s stabs at where films and (well . . .) famous characters were going or could go. There's an Interlude for the new article; then we plunge together manfully forward into Radio Pictures, three stories dealing with television since before the beginning in the 1920s to now. (Well, June 2000 anyway, one that didn't happen.)

There'll be a new introduction to each story (I always do that, usually to give people who've read all the stories a reason to buy a collection of mine). My introductions usually deal with the actual writing, Strange But True facts uncovered while researching them; you know, writer stuff. . . . There'll be some of that here; mostly the new intros will be about the stories as they fit into (or outside or alongside) the history of motion pictures and television.

Why am I telling you this up front? First, I'm an upfront kind of guy. Second, this is my first eBook (and the far-seeing and astute Robert [Bob] Kruger at ElectricStory.com should be congratulated on his taste [and his quick contract and check]). I don't own a computer, a telephone, or, up until a year ago, a refrigerator; that being said, I do have a website (kind friends set it up) at http://www.sff.net/people/waldrop (last time I looked, the bibliography hadn't been updated since mid-'98, but any day now I hear . . .). This is also the first (mostly) retrospective collection of mine.

Stories here come from all four (Howard Who?, Doubleday 1986; All about Strange Monsters of the Recent Past, Ursus 1987; Night of the Cooters, Ursus/Zeising 1991; Going Home Again, Eidolon Press, Perth, Australia 1997/St. Martin's 1998, with various American paperback and foreign regroupings and additions and subtractions) of my previous short-story collections.

Most readers have the general impression of me (if they have any at all) of being a guy who writes about extinct species (only two stories), rock and roll (only three and a half stories), or alternate history (well, touché—a lot, including some overlap in all the other categories, including this one).

But as this collection shows, a lot of my stories have been about film and television; their evolution, their heights and depths, some side channels they could have or should have taken but didn't; actors, directors, technicians, hangers-on, all that Raymond Chandler/Nathaniel West Southern California stuff; other places, too, where movies and television evolved; what effect they have had and will have on us. These kinds of things will be in the individual sections.

There's more stuff from film, TV, etc., popping up in other stories of mine that aren't here. "The Sawing Boys," for instance, which is essentially the Bremen Town Musicians partly told in Damon Runyon style, set in the early 1920s, which allows a backwoods Kentucky musical-saw quartet to come on like a bunch of Beirut klezmorim because of the spread of mass communications (radio). But that's buried so deep in the story that when I tell most people what it's really about, they look at me funny. "It's the Bremen Town Musicians, with musical saws," they say. They could be right.

Anyhow: These are the stories that are directly (or mostly—see the individual intros) about movies and television; personalities, history, projections, alternatives, guesses, and the effects they had on everybody, especially me.

And, as John Barrymore said, after staggering up the center aisle, still in his street clothes, after they'd held the curtain for him thirty minutes, turning to the audience: "You sit right there. I'm going to give you the goddamndest King Lear you've ever seen. . . ."

Dream Factories: The Past

With humans, it goes like this:

1. You're born.
2. You learn to move.
3. You learn to talk.
4. You learn to tell stories and jokes.

The movies got it all wrong.

They were born. They learned to move. Then they learned to tell stories and jokes. Finally, they learned to talk.

The stories in this section are about film, from the beginnings to (some other) circa 1970. There's plenty of stuff here on grammar and orientation, on personalities and genres; all the stuff we love that the movies have done for the past 105 years.

Film was the first mass medium, one capable of taking a product to millions of people at the same time. (Music recording was first, but it took the product—mass-produced—to a few people at a time. Plays had large audiences, but someone seeing the same play in NYC and Cleveland is seeing two different plays; for that matter, someone seeing a matinee and an evening performance of the same play in the same theater with the same cast is seeing two different plays.) The movies—once past the Kinetoscope-card one-viewer-at-a-time penny-arcade version—showed the same thing every time to everyone who ever saw it, no matter where in the world. It was for forever (or as close to forever as celluloid nitrate stock could be), and because it was forever, it changed the way people looked at their transiently beautiful world. . . .

You'll see in my introductions to the individual stories what I call the Waldrop/Sennett universal plot [hereafter, "W/S u-plot"]: Tom Oakheart, Teddy the Keystone Dog, Oil Can Harry, Pearl. You can illustrate almost anything in film with the likes of *Teddy at the Throttle* (1916). Buddy movies? Tom and Teddy. Romance? Tom, Pearl. Drama? That plot itself. Psychodrama? Why does Oil Can Harry want to saw Pearl into wet kindling when she won't put out for him? Isn't that counterproductive? And so on. (If you think this is outdated: the film-within-the-film in *The Player*, the one that's always being pitched and talked about is the W/S u-plot: Tom Oakheart [Willis] with Teddy [his Land Rover] rescues Pearl [Julia Roberts] from the sawmill [gas chamber], where Oil Can Harry [The State of California] is killing her. Yes or no?)

These things are imprinted on you and me from childhood as surely as if we were baby ducks. The movies are as real (or more real) than the first grade or the SAT or your second car or 'Nam or whatever else we call life. They're part of it; they're escape from it. What I'm saying in all these stories is that they're beside life; a place we went that's better or worse than what we have here, now . . .

Remember this while you're reading these stories about the movies' past: How real they are.

Reporters waited outside the theater where the world premier of *The Robe* (1953 — the first movie using the Cinemascope screen) took place. It was over. Sam Goldwyn, always good for a mangled quote, came out.

"What was *The Robe* about, Mr. Goldwyn?" they asked him.

"It was about a guy with fourteen-foot lips," he said, and got in his limo, and left.

Introduction to

Fin de Cycle

Is this a story about bicycles, or is it about the beginnings of film? You tell me. I always give stories a reference title (before I give them a real one) by some private name—this I always thought of as "the velocipede story." But as I wrote it, it came to be as much or more about film as about two-wheeled vehicles.

The early history of film is about what is called grammar. At first, films were one- or two-minute pieces of life—trains arriving at stations, waves breaking on the coast, workers leaving a factory. Audiences would watch anything because it moved. The idea itself was astounding to them.

But then film started telling stories. (The Waterer Watered: gardener watering flowers; kid steps on hose; gardener looks in hose; kid steps off hose; gardener gets face-full; gardener beats shit out of kid. The End.) It was a minute long and it packed them in like *ET*. But to do that, the Lumière Bros. had to figure out how to tell it: Show the gardener watering. Show the kid stepping on the hose. Show the water flow stopping. Pretty simple. Cause and effect. Shot continuously, like you're watching a stage show. Gardener over here, kid over there, hose, flowers, etc.

It was a little later, when people tried to show simultaneous action that things got complicated. That's why to us early narrative film seems so slow moving. This happens. Then a title: Meanwhile, over at the sawmill . . . Oil Can Harry has Pearl tied to the log. Another title: Back at the Roundhouse . . . Teddy the Keystone Dog unties Tom Oakheart, who gets on a handcar to make for the sawmill. The titles had to do the early work.

3

There was no grammar of editing yet. It was only later that filmmakers (Griffith gets credit for a hundred other people) cut to: sawmill, Oil Can Harry, Pearl, the whirring saw blade. Cut to: the roundhouse, Teddy, Tom Oakheart, the bonds gnawed through, Tom and Teddy running to the handcar.

Also, you'll notice, in this (my and Mack Sennett's) universal scenario: Harry faces screen right; Pearl, in the middle, the whirring saw blade at the edge of the screen. When Tom's bonds are chewed through, he moves screen right (toward the screen sawmill) — and when Tom bursts in on Harry's plan to turn Pearl into red wet 2x4s, he'd damn well better come in from screen left, behind Harry (from the direction of the screen roundhouse).

This is screen orientation, part of the grammar of film movement and editing. (And the W/S u-plot is the kind of thing that was being done twenty years into film history — the kind of thing Sennett made fun of while he was making money from it.)

Nobody knew any of this stuff in the 1890s. They had to figure it out from Day One.

The other thing the early filmmakers (especially Méliès, who was a stage magician and illusionist) didn't realize was that MAGIC does not work on the screen; the screen is magic. In other words, you can do the most complicated illusion in the world, one that, if you did it outdoors, in broad daylight with two hundred thousand spectators, would be the most astounding thing ever seen. Let's say you make some behemoth of an elephant disappear. Bravo! Astounding! How'd he do it?

Now on film (and Méliès did discover this; he just never understood its impact): Daylight. Two hundred thousand spectators. Méliès waves his wand. We stop the camera. Europe holds still. We remove the elephant by walking it off to one side. We start the camera, Méliès finishes the wave. The elephant is gone. Bravo! (in the film) Astounding! (in the film) How'd he do it? (in the film) I can make an elephant disappear, so can you and so can your Aunt Minnie, on film. Méliès never understood this (beautiful as some of his tricks were). Houdini didn't, and neither did David Copperfield (the illusionist, not the Victorian journalist).

Elaborate tricks and trick photography have equal weight on the screen. Houdini could show his escape from a welded-shut, chained-up milk can on the bottom of the near-frozen Hudson River. You could see him do it; his contortions are amazing, his manipulations have never been equaled. BUT—

I can escape from a welded-shut, chained-up milk can on film, and so can you. Because it wouldn't be those things—it would be a cinematic milk can (one side cut away so I could be filmed); it wouldn't be welded shut. The chains would be papier-mâché; through the use of editing and with doubles hidden behind and under me (or now with the use of morphing) I could make my body move around like Plastic Man; and the damned thing wouldn't be at the bottom of the Hudson River (I'd be dropped in there, and swim out there, like Tony Curtis); it would be in some tank somewhere when it needed to be shown. (I'd be somewhere else high and dry doing the contortions.) Then I'd come out of the milk can in the tank and swim upward and then—again like Tony Curtis—I'd surface in the Hudson.

And, as in this story, the early filmmakers filmed in sequence, consecutively. It took awhile for them to realize they didn't have to; in fact, it was more costly to do it that way, even if you had time and space for standing sets. (You film Pearl's house; you film Tom at the roundhouse; you film Harry at the sawmill; you go back and forth to each set as needed, till the film is done. NO—WAIT! Hey, we can film all the scenes at Pearl's house, early, middle, late; all the scenes at the roundhouse, all at the sawmill, with appropriate costume changes—hence the industry need for script girls and continuity directors—and send the sets all back to the scene shop when we're through! We'll save a bundle!)

None of this stuff existed when this story starts. It was all out there, waiting—how to tell a story, how to edit it, how to make it work without confusing the audience.

I asked at the first of this whether this was about film or velocipedes.

It's mostly about Alfred Jarry, one of those truly unique people we are allowed to glimpse every century or so (we're overdue). He was the perfect counterpoint to the history of his times—in someone's phrase about someone else, he marched to the tune of a different kazoo, altogether. Some things in this story are a little exaggerated—but not the rancor of the Dreyfus Affair, and though some of the incidents are made up, Jarry did all the things here, or things far more—uh, individualistic. Go read a couple of books about him and his times, starting with Roger Shattuck's *The Banquet*

Years (1958 and rev. later).

This story was originally written in two goes, October 1989, the first half, and March through May 1990, the rest. It was the original in *Night of the Cooters*, was reprinted in the Mid-December 1991 issue of *Asimov's*, and was a Hugo nominee.

Back into the depths of the camera's mast, then . . .

FIN DE CYCLE

I. Humors in Uniform

A. Gentlemen, Start Your Stilts!

There was clanking and singing as the company came back from maneuvers.

Pa-chinka Pa-chinka, a familiar and comforting sound. The first of the two scouts came into view five meters in the air atop the new steam stilts. He storked his way into the battalion area, then paused.

Behind him came the second scout, then the cyclists in columns of three. They rode high-wheeled ordinaries, dusty now from the day's ride. Their officer rode before them on one of the new safety bicycles, dwarfed by those who followed behind.

At the headquarters he stopped, jumped off his cycle.

"Company! . . ." he yelled, and the order was passed back along by NCOs, ". . . company . . . company . . . company! . . ."

"Halt!" Again the order ran back. The cyclists put on their spoon-brakes, reached out and grabbed the handlebars of the man to the side. The high-wheelers stood immobile in place, 210 of them, with the two scouts standing to the fore, steam slowly escaping from the legs of their stilts.

"Company . . ." again the call and echoes, "Dis—" at the command, the leftward soldier placed his left foot on the step halfway down the spine of the bicycle above its small back wheel. The others shifted their weight backwards, still holding to the other man's handlebars.

" — mount!" The left-hand soldier dropped back to the ground, reached through to grab the spine of the ordinary next to him; the rider of that repeated the first man's motions, until all three men were on the ground beside their high-wheels.

At the same time the two scouts pulled the levers beside the knees of their metal stilts. The columns began to telescope down into themselves with a hiss of steam until the men were close enough to the ground to step off and back.

"Company C, 3rd Battalion, 11th Bicycle Infantry, Attention!" said the lieutenant. As he did so, the major appeared on the headquarters' porch. Like the others, he was dressed in the red baggy pants, blue coat and black cap with a white kepi on the back. Unlike them, he wore white gloves, sword, and pistol.

"Another mission well done," he said. "Tomorrow — a training half-holiday, for day after tomorrow, Bastille Day, the ninety-ninth of the Republic — we ride to Paris and then we roll smartly down the Champs-Élysées, to the general appreciation of the civilians and the wonder of the children."

A low groan went through the bicycle infantrymen.

"Ah, I see you are filled with enthusiasm! Remember — you are the finest Army in France — the Bicycle Infantry! A short ride of seventy kilometers holds no terrors for you! A mere ten kilometers within the city. An invigorating seventy kilometers back! Where else can a man get such exercise? And such meals! And be paid besides? Ah, were I a younger man, I should never have become an officer, but joined as a private and spent a life of earnest bodybuilding upon two fine wheels!"

Most of the 11th were conscripts doing their one year of service, so the finer points of his speech were lost on them.

A bugle sounded somewhere off in the fort. "Gentlemen: Retreat."

Two clerks came out of headquarters and went to the flagpole.

From left and right bands struck up the Retreat. All came to attention facing the flagpole, as the few sparse notes echoed through the quadrangles of the garrison.

From the corner of his eye the major saw Private Jarry, already placed on Permanent Latrine Orderly, come from out of the far row of toilets set halfway out toward the drill course. The major could tell Private Jarry was disheveled from this far away—even with such a job one should be neat. His coat was buttoned sideways by the wrong buttons, one pants leg in his boots, one out. His hat was on front-to-back with the kepi tied up above his forehead.

He had his toilet brush in his hand.

The back of the major's neck reddened.

Then the bands struck up "To the Colors"—the company area was filled with the sound of salutes snapping against cap brims.

The clerks brought the tricolor down its lanyard.

Private Jarry saluted the flag with his toilet brush.

The major almost exploded; stood shaking, hand frozen in salute.

The notes went on; the major calmed himself. This man is a loser. He does not belong in the Army; he doesn't deserve the Army! Conscription is a privilege. Nothing I can do to this man will ever be enough; you cannot kill a man for being a bad soldier; you can only inconvenience him; make him miserable in his resolve; the result will be the same. You will both go through one year of hell; at the end you will still be a major, and he will become a civilian again, though with a bad discharge. His kind never amount to anything. Calm yourself—he is not worth a stroke—he is not insulting France, he is insulting you. And he is beneath your notice.

At the last note the major turned on his heel with a nod to the lieutenant and went back inside, followed by the clerks with the folded tricolors.

The lieutenant called off odd numbers for cycle-washing detail; evens were put to work cleaning personal equipment and rifles.

Private Jarry turned with military smartness and went back in to his world of strong disinfectant soap and *merde*.

After chow that evening, Private Jarry retired behind the bicycle shop and injected more picric acid beneath the skin of his arms and legs.

In three more months, only five after being drafted, he would be released, with a medical discharge, for "chronic jaundice."

B. Cannons in the Rain

Cadet Marcel Proust walked into the company orderly room. He had been putting together his belongings; today was his last full day in the Artillery. Tomorrow he would leave active duty after a year at Orleans.

"Attention," shouted the corporal clerk as he came in. "At ease," said Marcel, nodding to the enlisted men who copied orders by hand at their desks. He went to the commanding officer's door, knocked. "*Entre.*" said a voice and he went in.

"Cadet Proust reporting, *mon capitaine*," said Marcel, saluting.

"Oh, there's really no need to salute in here, Proust," said Captain Dreyfus.

"Perhaps, sir, it will be my last."

"Yes, yes," said Captain Dreyfus. "Tea? Sugar?" The captain indicated the kettle. "Serve yourself." He looked through some papers absent-mindedly. "Sorry to bring you in on your last day—sure we cannot talk you into joining the officers corps? France has need of bright young men like you!—No, I thought not. Cookies? Over there; Madame Dreyfus baked them this morning." Marcel retrieved a couple, while stirring the hot tea in his cup.

"Sit, sit. Please!" Dreyfus indicated the chair. Marcel slouched into it.

"You were saying?" he asked.

"Ah! Yes. Inspections coming up, records, all that," said the captain. "You remember, some three months ago, August 19th to be exact, we were moving files from the old headquarters across the two quadrangles to this building? You were staff duty officer that day?"

"I remember the move, *mon capitaine*. That was the day we received the Maxim gun tricycles, also. It was—yes—a day of unseasonable rain."

"Oh? Yes?" said Dreyfus. "That is correct. Do you remember, perhaps, the clerks having to take an alternate route here, until we procured canvas to protect the records?"

"They took several. Or am I confusing that with the day we exchanged barracks with the 91st Artillery? That also was rainy. What is the matter?"

"Some records evidently did not make it here. Nothing important, but they must be in the files for the inspection, else we shall get a very black mark indeed."

Marcel thought. Some of the men used the corridors of the instruction rooms carrying files, some went through the repair shops. There were four groups of three clerks to each set of cabinets. . . .

"Which files?"

"Gunnery practice, instruction records. The boxes which used to be—"

"—on top of the second set of wooden files," said Marcel. "I remember them there. I do not remember seeing them here. . . . I am at a total loss as to how they could not have made it to the orderly room, *mon capitaine*."

"They were checked off as leaving, in your hand, but evidently, we have never seen them again."

Proust racked his brain. The stables? The instruction corridor; surely they would have been found by now. . . .

"Oh, we'll just have to search and search, get the 91st involved. They're probably in their files. This army runs on paperwork—soon clerks will outnumber the generals, eh, Proust?"

Marcel laughed. He drank at his tea—it was lemon tea, pleasant but slightly weak. He dipped one of the cookies—the kind called a madeline—in it and took a bite.

Instantly a chill and an aching familiarity came over him—he saw his Grandmother's house in Balbec, an identical cookie, the same kind of tea, the room cluttered with furniture, the sound of his brother coughing upstairs, the feel of the wrought iron dinner table chair against the back of his bare leg, his father looking out the far kitchen window into the rain, the man putting down the burden, heard his mother hum a tune, a raincoat falling, felt the patter of raindrops on the tool-shed roof, smelled the tea and cookie in a second overpowering rush, saw a scab on the back of his hand from eleven years before. . . .

"*Mon capitaine!*" said Marcel, rocking forward, slapping his hand against his forehead. "Now I remember where the box was left!"

II. Both Hands

Rousseau was painting a tiger.

It was not just any tiger. It was the essence of tiger, the apotheosis of *felis horribilis*. It looked out from the canvas with yellow-green eyes through which a cold emerald light shone. Its face was beginning to curve into a snarl. Individual quills of whiskers stood out from the black and gold jaws in rippling lines. The edge of the tongue showed around lips with a faint edge of white. A single flower, its stem bent, was the only thing between the face of the tiger and the viewer.

Henri Rousseau put down his brush. He stepped back from the huge canvas. To left and right, birds flew in fright from the charging tiger. The back end of a water buffalo disappeared through the rank jungle at the rear of the canvas. Blobs of gray and tan indicated where the rhinoceros and impala would be painted in later. A huge patch of bamboo was just a swatch of green-gold; a neutral tan stood in for the unstarted blue sky.

A pearl-disk of pure white canvas, with tree limbs silhouetted before it would later be a red-ocher sun.

At the far back edge of the sky, partially eclipsed by a yellow riot of bananas, rose the newly completed Eiffel Tower.

Rousseau wiped his hand against his Rembrandt beret. His eyes above his graying spade beard and mustache moved back and forth, taking in the wet paint.

Pinned to one leg of the easel was a yellowed newspaper clipping he kept there (its duplicate lay in a thick scrapbook at the corner of the room in the clutter away from the north light). He no longer read it; he knew the words by heart. It was from a review of the showing at the *Salon des Refusés* two years before.

"The canvases of Monsieur Rousseau are something to be seen (then again, they're not!). One viewer was so bold to wonder with which hand the artist had painted this scene, and someone else was heard to reply: 'Both, sir! Both hands! And both feet!' "

Rousseau walked back to the painting, gobbed his brush three times across the palette, and made a two-centimeter dot on the face of the tiger.

Now the broken flower seemed to bend from the foul breath of the animal; it swayed in the hot mammal wind.

Rousseau moved on to another section of the painting.

The tiger was done.

III. Supper for Four

Three young men walked quickly through the traffic of Paris on streets aclank with the sound of pedals, sprockets, and chains. They talked excitedly. Quadricycles and tricycles passed, ridden by women, older men, couples having quiet conversations as they pedaled.

High above them all, their heads three meters in the air, came young men bent over their gigantic wheels. They sailed placidly along, each pump of their legs covering six meters of ground, their trailing wheels like afterthoughts. They were aloof and intent; the act of riding was their life.

Occasionally a horse and wagon came by the three young men, awash in a sea of cyclists. A teamster kept pace with a postman on a hens-and-chickens pentacycle for a few meters, then fell behind.

There was a ringing of bells ahead and the traffic parted to each side; pedaling furiously came a police tricycle, a man to the front on the seat ringing the bell, another to the rear standing on the back pedals. Between them an abject-looking individual was strapped to the reclining seat, handcuffed and foot-manacled to the tricycle frame.

The ringing died away behind them, and the three young men turned a corner down toward the Seine. At a certain address they turned in, climbed to the third landing-and-a-half, and knocked loudly on the door.

"Enter Our Royal Chasublerie!" came the answer.

Blinking, the three tumbled into the dark room. The walls were covered with paintings and prints, woodcuts, stuffed weasels and hawks, books, papers, fishing gear and bottles. It was an apartment built from half a landing. Their heads scraped the ceiling. A huge ordinary lay on its side, taking up the whole center of the room.

"Alfred," said one of the young men. "Great news of Pierre and Jean-Paul!"

"They arrived in the Middle Orient on their world tour!" said the second.

"They've been sighted in Gaza and bombed in Gilead!" said the third.

"More bulletins soon!" said the first. "We have brought a bottle of wine to celebrate their joyous voyage."

The meter-and-a-quarter-tall Jarry brushed his butt-length hair back from his face. When they had knocked, he had just finished a bottle of absinthe.

"Then we must furnish a royal feast—that will be four in all for supper?" he asked. "Excuse our royal pardon."

He put on his bicycling cap with an emblem from the far-off League of American Wheelmen. He walked to the mantelpiece, where he took down a glass of water in which he had earlier placed 200 drops of laudanum, and ate the remains of a hashish cookie. Then he picked up his fly rod and fish basket and left, sticking his head back in to say, "Pray give us a few moments."

Two of the students began teasing one of Jarry's chameleons, putting it through an astonishing array of clashing color schemes, and then tossing one of his stuffed owls around like a football while the living one jumped back and forth from one side of its perch to the other, hooting wildly.

The second student watched through the single window.

This is what the student saw:

Jarry went through the traffic of bicycles and wheeled conveyances on the street, disappeared down the steps to the river, rigged up and made four casts — Bip bap bim bom — came up with a fish on each one — a tench, a gudgeon, a pickerel, and a trout, threw them in the basket, and walked back across the street, waving as he came.

What Jarry saw:

He was carrying a coffin as he left the dungeon and went into the roadway filled with elephants, and pigs on stilts. A bicycle ridden by a skeleton rose into the sky, the bony cyclist laughing, the sound echoing off itself, getting louder the further away it got.

He took a week getting down the twenty-seven-kilometer abyss of the steps, each step a block of antediluvian marble a hundred meters wide.

Overhead, the sun was alternate bands of green and brown, moving like a newly electric-powered barbershop sign. The words "raspberry jam teapot" whispered themselves over and over somewhere just behind his right ear.

He looked into the thousand-kilometer width of the river of boiling ether. The fumes were staggering — sweet and nausea-producing at the same time. A bird with the head of a Pekingese lapdog flew by the now purple and black orb of the sun.

Jarry pulled out his whip-coach made of pure silver with its lapis-lazuli guides and its skull of a reel. The line was an anchor chain of pure gold. He had a bitch of a time getting the links of chain through the eye of his fly. It was a two-meter-long, four-winged stained glass and pewter dragonfly made by Alphonse Mucha.

Jarry false-cast into the ether, lost sight of his fly in the roiling fumes, saw a geyser of water rise slowly into the golden air. The tug pulled his arm from its socket. He set the hook.

Good! He had hooked a kraken. Arms writhing, parrot beak clacking, it fought for an hour before he regained line and pulled it to the cobbles, smashing it and its ugly eyes and arms beneath his foot. Getting it into the steamer trunk behind him, he cast again.

There were so many geysers exploding into the sky he wasn't sure which one was his. He set the hook anyway and was rewarded with a Breughel monster; human head and frog arms with flippers, it turned into a jug halfway back and ended in a horse. As he fought it he tried to remember which painting it was from; *The Temptation of St. Anthony*, most likely.

The landing accomplished, he cast again just as the planet Saturn, orange and bloated like a pumpkin, its rings whirring and making a noise like a mill-saw, fell and flattened everything from Notre Dame to the Champ de Mars. Luckily, no one was killed.

Another strike. For a second, the river became a river, the fly rod a fly rod, and he pulled in a fish, a pickerel. Only this one had hands, and every time he tried to unhook it, it grabbed the hook and stuck it back in its own jaw, pulling itself toward Jarry with plaintive mewling sounds.

"*Merde!*" he said, taking out his fishing knife and cutting away the hands. More grew back. He cut them away, too, and tossed the fish into the mausoleum behind him.

Better. The ether-river was back. His cast was long. It made no sound as it disappeared. There was the gentlest tug of something taking the dragonfly—Jarry struck like a man possessed.

Something huge, brown and smoking stood up in the ether fumes, bent down and stared at Jarry. It had shoulders and legs. It was the Colossus of Rhodes. A fire burned through vents in the top of its head, the flames shone out the eyes. It could have reached from bank to bank; its first stride would take it to Montmartre.

Alfred gave another huge tug. The chain going from his rod to the lip of the Colossus pulled taut. There was a pause and a groan, the sound of a ship on a reef. With a boom and rattle, the bronze man tottered, tried to regain its balance, then fell, shattering itself on the bridges and quays, the fires turning to steam. The tidal wave engulfed the Île de la Cité and would no doubt wipe out everything all the way to the sea.

Painfully, Jarry gathered up the tons of bronze shards and put them in the wheelless stagecoach and dragged it up the attic stairs to the roadway.

The bicyclists and wolverines seemed unconcerned. Saturn had buried itself below its equator. Its rings still ran, but much more slowly; they would stop by nightfall. Pieces of the bronze Colossus were strewn all over the cityscape.

Jarry looked toward the Walls of Troy before him as he struggled with the sarcophagus. At one portal he saw his friends Hannibal, Hamilcar, and Odoacer waiting for him. If the meal weren't to their satisfaction, they were to kill and eat him. He put up his hand in acknowledgement of doom.

The sky was pink and hummed a phrase from Wagner, a bad phrase. The Eiffel Tower swayed to its own music, a gavotte of some kind. Jarry got behind the broken-down asphalt wagon and pushed it toward the drawbridge of despair that was the door of his building.

He hoped he could find the matches and cook supper without burning down the whole fucking city.

IV. Artfully Arranged Scenes

Georges Méliès rose at dawn in Montreuil, bathed, breakfasted, and went out to his home-office. By messenger, last night's accounts from the Théâtre Robert-Houdin would have arrived. He would look over those, take care of correspondence, and then go back to the greenhouse glass building that was his Star Films studio.

At ten, the workmen would arrive. They and Méliès would finish the sets, painting scenery in shades of gray, black, and white, each scene of which bore, at some place, the Star Films trademark to discourage film footage piracy. The mechanics would rig the stage machinery, which was Méliès' forte.

At eleven the actors would appear, usually from the *Folies Bergére*, and Méliès would discuss with them the film to be made, block out the movements, and with them improvise the stage business. Then there would be a jolly lunch, and a free time while Méliès and his technicians prepared the huge camera.

It was fixed on a track perpendicular to the stage, and could be moved from a position, at its nearest point, which would show the actors full-length upon the screen, back into the T-shaped section of the greenhouse to give a view encompassing the entire acting area. Today, the camera was to be moved and then locked down for use twice during the filming.

At two, filming began after the actors were costumed. The film was a retelling of Little Red Riding Hood. The first scene, of the girl's house, was rolled in, accessory wings and flies dropped, and the establishing scene filmed. The actresses playing the girl and her mother were exceptionally fine. Then the next scene, of the forest path, was dropped down; the camera moved back and locked in place.

The scene opened with fairies and forest animals dancing; then the Wolf (a tumbler from the *Folies*) came on in a very hideous costume, and hid behind a painted tree.

The forest creatures try to warn the approaching girl, who walks on the path toward the camera, then leave. She and the Wolf converse. The Wolf leaves.

The second scene requires eleven takes, minor annoyances growing into larger ones as filming progresses. A trap door needed for a later scene comes open at one point while the animals romp, causing a painted stump to fall into it.

The camera is moved once more, and the scenery for the grandmother's house is put in place, the house interior with an open window at the back. The Wolf comes in, chases the grandmother away, in continuous action, goes to the wardrobe, dresses, climbs in bed. Only then is the action stopped.

When filming begins again, with the same camera location, Red Riding Hood enters. The action is filmed continuously from this point to when the Wolf jumps from the bed. Then the Wolf chases the girl around the room, a passing hunter appears at the window, watches the action a second, runs in the door, shoots the Wolf (there is a flash powder explosion and the Wolf-actor drops through the trap door).

The grandmother appears at the window, comes in; she, the hunter, and Red Riding Hood embrace. *Fin*.

Méliès thanks the actors and pays them. The last of the film is unloaded from the camera (for such a bulky object it only holds sixteen meters of film per magazine) and taken to the laboratory building to be developed, then viewed and assembled by Méliès tomorrow morning.

Now 5:00 P.M., Méliès returns to the house, has early supper with his wife and children. Then he reads to them, and at 7:00 P.M. performs for them the magic tricks he is trying out, shows new magic lantern transitiontransfigurations to be incorporated into his stage act, gives them a puppet show or some other entertainment. He bids goodnight to his children, then returns to the parlor where he and his wife talk for an hour, perhaps while they talk he sketches her, or doodles scene designs for his films. He tells her amusing stories of the day's filming, perhaps jokes or anecdotes from the *Folies* the actors have told him at lunch.

He accompanies his wife upstairs, undresses her, opens the coverlet, inviting her in. She climbs into bed.

He kisses her sweetly goodnight.

Then he goes downstairs, puts on his hat, and goes to the home of his mistress.

V. We Grow Bored

The banquet was in honor of Lugné-Poe, the manager of the *Théâtre de l'Oeuvre*.

Jarry, in his red canvas suit and paper shirt with a fish painted on it for a tie, was late. The soup was already being served.

There were three hundred people, all male, attending. Alfred went to his seat; a bowl of soup, swimming with fish eyes, was placed before him. He finished it at once, as he had forgotten to eat for the last two days.

He looked left and right; to the right was a man known vaguely to him as a pederast and a frotteur, but whose social station was such that he would rather have swallowed the national tricolor, base, standard, and spike, than to have spoken to Jarry. To the left was a shabby man, with large spade beard and mustache, wearing an artist's beret and workman's clothes. He slowly spooned his soup while deftly putting all the bread and condiments within reach into the pockets of his worn jacket.

Then Jarry looked across the table and found himself staring into the eyes of a journalist for one of the right-wing nationalist Catholic cycling weeklies.

"Are you not Jarry?" asked the man, with narrowed eyes.

"We are," said Alfred. "Unfortunately, our royal personage does not converse with those who have forsaken the One True Means of Transportation."

"Ha. A recidivist!" said the reporter. "It is we who are of the future, while you remain behind in the lost past."

"Our conversation is finished," said Jarry. "You and Monsieur Norpois have lost our true salvation of the Wheel."

"Bi-cycle means two wheels," said the journalist. "When you and your kind realize that true speed, true meaning, and true patriotism depend on equal size and mighty gearing, this degenerate country will become strong once more."

The man to Jarry's left was looking back and forth from one to the other; he had stopped eating, but his left hand brought another roll to his pocket.

"Does not the First Citizen of our Royal Lands and Possessions to the East, the Lord Amida Buddha himself, speak of the Greater and Lesser Wheels?" asked Jarry. "Put that in your ghost-benighted, superstition-ridden censer and try to smoke it. Our Royal Patience becomes stretched. We have nothing against those grown weary, old, effete who go to three, four wheels or more; they have given up. Those, however, with equal wheels, riders of crocodiles and spiders, with false mechanical aids, we deem repugnant, unworthy; one would almost say, but would never, ever, that they have given in to . . . German ideas."

The conversation at the long table stopped dead. The man to Jarry's left put down his spoon and eased his chair back from the table ever so slightly.

The face of the reporter across the table went through so many color changes that Jarry's chameleon, at the height of mating season, would be shamed. The journalist reached under the table, lifted his heavy-headed cane, pushed it up through the fingers of his right hand with his left, caught it by the tip.

"Prepare yourself for a caning," said the turnip-faced man. No challenge to the field of honor, no further exchange of unpleasantries. He lifted his cane back, pushing back his sleeve.

"Monsieur," said Jarry, turning to the man on his left, "do us the honor of standing us upon our throne, here." He indicated his chair.

The man scooted back, picked up the one-and-a-quarter-meter-high Jarry and stood him on the seat of his chair in a very smooth motion. Then the man grabbed his soup bowl and stood away.

"I will hammer you down much farther before I am done," said the reporter, looking Jarry up and down. People from the banquet committee rushed toward them; Lugné-Poe was yelling who was the asshole who made the seating arrangements?

"By your red suit I take you for an anarchist. Very well, no rules," said the reporter. The cane whistled.

"By our Red Suit you should take us for a man whose Magenta Suit is being cleaned," said Jarry. "This grows tedious. We grow bored." He pulled his Navy Colt Model .41 from his waistband, cocked it and fired a great roaring blank which caught the reporter's pomaded hair on fire. The man went down yelling and rolling while others helpfully poured pitchers of water on him.

The committee members had stopped at the gun's report. Jarry held up his finger to the nearest waiter. "Check, please!" he said.

He left the hall out the front door as the reporter, swearing great oaths of vengeance and destruction, was carried back into the kitchen for butter to be applied to his burns.

Jarry felt a hand on his shoulder, swung his arm up, came around with the Colt out again. It was the man who had stood him on the chair.

"You talk with the accent of Laval," said the man.

"Bred, born, raised, and bored merdeless there," said Jarry.

"I, too," said the man.

"We find Laval an excellent place to be from, if you get our royal meaning," said Jarry.

"Mr. Henri-Jules Rousseau," said the man.

"Mr. Alfred-Henri Jarry." They shook hands.

"I paint," said Rousseau.

"We set people's hair afire," said Jarry.

"You must look me up; my studio is on the Boulevard du Port-Royal."

"We will be happy if a fellow Lavalese accompanies us immediately to drink, do drugs, visit the brothels, and become fast friends for life."

"Are you kidding?" said Rousseau. "They're getting ready to serve the cabbage back in there. Do look me up, though," he said, heading back in toward the banquet hall and putting his napkin back under his chin.

"We shall," said Jarry, and mounted his high-wheeler and was gone into the darkness.

VI. News from All Over
January 14, 1895 *Le Cycliste Français*
TRAITOR ON THE GENERAL STAFF!

ARREST AND TRIAL OF THE JEW CAPTAIN DREYFUS
DEGRADATION AND STRIPPING OF RANK
DEPORTATION TO GUIANA FOR LIFE

"Secrets vital to the Nation," says a General, "from which our Enemy will profit and France never recover. It is only the new lenient Jew-inspired law which kept the Tribunal from sentencing the human rat to Death!"

VII. Like the Spokes of a Luminous Wheel

The reporter Norpois rode a crocodile velocipede of singular aspect. Its frame was low and elongated. The seat was at the absolute center of the bicycle's length, making it appear as if its rider were disincorporated.

Though extremely modern in that respect, its wheels were anachronisms, heavily spoked and rimmed to the uncaring eye. On a close examination it was revealed the spokes were ironwork, eight to each wheel, and over them were wrought two overlapping semicircles, one of a happy, the other of a sad, aspect of the human face.

In unison, front and back, the wheels first smiled, then frowned at the world around them as they whirled their rider along the newly macadamized roads and streets.

In his sporty cap and black knickers, Norpois seemed almost to lean between the wheels of strife and fortune. Other bicyclists paused to watch him go spoking silently by, with an almost inaudible whisper of iron rim on asphalt. The crocodile frame seemed far too graceful and quiet for the heavy wheels on which it rode.

Norpois worked for *Le Cycliste Français*. His assignments took him to many *arrondissements* and the outlying parts of the city.

He was returning from interviewing a retired general before sunset one evening, when, preparatory to stopping to light his carbide handlebar-lamp, he felt a tickle of heat at his face, then a dull throbbing at his right temple. To his left, the coming sunset seemed preternaturally bright, and he turned his head to look at it.

His next conscious thought was of picking himself and his velocipede up from the side of the road where he had evidently fallen. He noticed he was several dozen meters down the road from where he had turned to look at the sunset. His heart hammered in his chest. The knees of his knickers were dusty, his left hand was scraped, with two small pieces of gravel embedded in the skin, and he had bitten his lip, which was beginning to swell. He absently dug the gravel from his hand. He had no time for small aches and pains. He had to talk to someone.

"Jules," he said to the reporter who shared the three-room apartment with him. As he spoke he filled a large glass with half a bottle of cognac and began sipping at it between his sentences. "I must tell you what life will be like in twenty years."

"You, Robida, and every other frustrated engineer," said Jules, putting down his evening paper.

"Tonight I have had an authentic vision of the next century. It came to me not at first as a visual illusion, a pattern on my eyes, some ecstatic vision. It came to me first through my nose, Jules. An overpowering, oppressive odor. Do you know what the coming years smell like, Jules? They smell of burning flesh. It was the first thing to come to me, and the last to leave. Think of the worst fire you ever covered. Remember the charred bodies, the popped bones? Multiply it by a city, a nation, a hemisphere! It was like that.

"The smell came; then I saw in the reddened clouds a line of ditches, miles, kilometers upon thousands of kilometers of ditches in churned earth, men like troglodytes killing each other as far as the eye could see, smoke everywhere, the sky raining death, the sky filled with aerial machines dropping explosives; detonations coming and going like giant brown trees which sprout, leaf, and die in an instant. Death everywhere, from the air, from guns, shells falling on all beneath them, the aerial machines pausing in their rain of death below only to shoot each other down. Patterns above the ditches, like vines, curling vines covered with thorns—over all a pattern formed on my retina—always the incessant chatter of machinery, screams, fire, death-agonies, men stomping each other in mud and earth. I could see it all, hear it all, above all else, smell it all, Jules, and . . ."

"Yes?"

"Jules, it was the most beautiful thing I have ever experienced." He stared at his roommate.

"There's some cold mutton on the table," said Jules. "And half a bottle of beer. He looked back down at his paper. After a few minutes he looked up. Norpois stood, looking out the window at the last glow of twilight, still smiling.

VIII. One Ordinary Day, with Anarchists

Alfred Jarry sailed along the boulevard, passing people and other cyclists right and left. Two and a half meters up, he bent over his handlebars, his cap at a rakish angle, his hair a black flame behind his head. He was the very essence of speed and grace, no longer a dwarfish man of slight build. A novice rider on a safety bicycle took a spill ahead of him. Jarry used his spoon-brake to stop a few centimeters short of the wide-eyed man who feared broken ribs, death, a mangled vehicle.

Then Jarry jumped up and down on his seat, his feet on the locked pedals, jerking the ordinary in small jumps a meter to the left until his path was clear; then he was gone down the road as if nothing had happened.

Riders who drew even with him dropped back—Jarry had a carbine slung across his back, carried bandoliers of cartridges for it on his chest, had two Colt pistols sticking from the waistband of his pants, the legs of which were tucked into his socks, knicker-fashion. Jarry was fond of saying firearms, openly displayed, were signs of peaceableness and good intentions, and wholly legal. He turned down a side street and did not hear the noise from the Chamber of Deputies.

A man named Vaillant, out of work, with a wife and children, at the end of his tether, had gone to the Chamber carrying with him a huge sandwich made from a whole loaf of bread. He sat quietly watching a debate on taxes, opened the sandwich to reveal a device made of five sticks of the new dynamite, a fuse and blasting cap, covered with one and a half kilos of #4 nails. He lit it in one smooth motion, jumped to the edge of the gallery balcony and tossed it high into the air.

It arced, stopped, and fell directly toward the center of the Chamber. Some heard the commotion, some saw it; Dreyfussards sensed it and ducked.

It exploded six meters in the air.

Three people were killed, forty-seven injured badly, more than seventy less so. Desks were demolished; the speaker's rostrum was turned to wood lace.

Vaillant was grabbed by alert security guards.

The first thing that happened, while people moaned and crawled out from under their splintered desks, was that the eight elected to the Chamber of Deputies on the Anarchist ticket, some of them having to pull nails from their hands and cheeks to do so, stood and began to applaud loudly. "Bravo!" they yelled, "Bravo! Encore!"

IX. The Kid from Spain

His name was Pablo, and he was a big-nosed, big-eyed Spanish kid who had first come to Paris with his mother two years before at the age of thirteen; now he was back on his own as an art student.

On this trip, the first thing he learned to do was fuck; the second was to learn to paint.

One day a neighbor pointed out to him the figure of Jarry tearing down the street. Pablo thought the tiny man on the huge bicycle, covered with guns and bullets, was the most romantic thing he had ever seen in his life. Pablo immediately went out and bought a pistol, a .22 single-shot, and took to wearing it in his belt.

He was sketching the River one morning when the shadow of a huge wheel fell on the ground beside him. Pablo looked up. It was Jarry, studying the sketch over his shoulder.

Pablo didn't know what to do or say, so he took out his gun and showed it to Jarry.

Jarry looked embarrassed. "We are touched," he said, laying his hand on Pablo's shoulder. "Take one of ours," he said, handing him a .38 Webley. Then he was up on his ordinary and gone.

Pablo did not remember anything until it was getting dark and he was standing on a street, sketchbook in one hand, pistol still held by the barrel in the other. He must have walked the streets all day that way, a seeming madman.

He was outside a brothel. He checked his pockets for money, smiled, and went in.

X. More Beans, Please

"Georges Méliès," said Rousseau, "Alfred Jarry."

"Pleased."

"We are honored."

"Erik Satie," said Méliès, "Henri Rousseau."

"Charmed."

"At last!"

"This is Pablo," said Satie. "Marcel Proust."

"'Lo."

"Delighted."

"Gentlemen," said Rousseau, "Mme. Méliès."

"Dinner is served," she said.

"But of course," said Marcel, "Everyone knows evidence was introduced in secret at the first trial, evidence the defense was not allowed to see."

"Ah, but that's the military mind for you!" said Rousseau. "It was the same when I played piccolo for my country between 1864 and 1871. What matters is not the evidence, but that the charge has been brought against you in the first place. It proves you guilty."

"Out of my complete way of thinking," said Satie, taking another helping of calamari in aspic, "having been unfortunate enough to be a civilian all my life. . . ."

"Hear, hear!" they all said.

". . . but is it not true that they asked him to copy the bordereau, the list found in the trash at the German Embassy and introduced that at the court-martial, rather than the original outline of our defenses?"

"More beans, please," said Pablo.

"That is one theory," said Marcel. "The list, of course, leaves off halfway down, because Dreyfus realized what was going to happen as they were questioning him back in December of '94."

"That's the trouble," said Rousseau. "There are too many theories, and of course, none of this will be introduced at the Court of Cassation next month. Nothing but the original evidence, and of course, the allegations brought up by Colonel Picquart, whose own trial for insubordination is scheduled month after next."

Méliès sighed. "The problem, of course, is that we shall suffer one trial after another; the generals are all covering ass now. First they convict an innocent man on fabricated evidence. Finding the spying has not stopped with the wrongful imprisonment of Dreyfus, they listen to Colonel Picquart, no friend of anyone, who tells them it's the Alsatian Esterhazy, but Esterhazy's under the protection of someone in the War Ministry, so they

send Picquart off to Fort Zinderneuf, hoping he will be killed by the Rifs;
when he returns covered with scars and medals, they throw him in jail on
trumped-up charges of daring to question the findings of the court-martial.
Meanwhile the public outcry becomes so great that the only way things can
be kept at *status quo* is to say questioning Dreyfus' guilt is to question
France itself. We can all hope, but of course, there can probably be only one
verdict of the court of review."

"More turkey, please," said Pablo.

"The problem, of course," said Satie, "is that France needs to be
questioned if it breeds such monsters of arrogance and vanity."

"Excuse me, Mr. Satie," said Madame Méliès, speaking for the first time
in an hour. "The problem, of course, is that Dreyfus is a Jew."

She had said the thing none of the others had yet said, the thing at base,
root, and crown of the Affair.

"And being so," said Jarry, "we are sure, Madame, if through our
actions this wronged man is freed, he will be so thankful as to allow Our
Royal Person to put him upon the nearest cross, with three nails, for
whatever period we deem appropriate."

"Pass the wine, please," said Pablo.

"It is a rough time for us," said Jarry, "what with our play to go into
production soon, but we shall give whatever service we can to this project."

"Agreed by all, then!" said Méliès. "Star Films takes the unprecedented
step of collaborating with others! I shall set aside an entire week, that of
Tuesday next, for the production of The Dreyfus Affair. Bring your pens,
your brushes, your ideas! Mr. Satie, our piano at Théâtre Robert-Houdin is
at your disposal for practice and for the première; begin your plans now.
And so, having decided the fate of France, let us visit the production
facilities at the rear of the property, then return to the parlor for cigars and
port!"

They sat in comfortable chairs. Satie played a medley of popular songs,
those he knew by heart from his days as the relief piano player at the Black
Cat; Méliès, who had a very good voice, joined Pablo and Rousseau (who
was sorry he had not brought his violin) in a rousing rendition of "The
Tired Workman's Song."

Jarry and Proust sat with unlit cigars in their mouths.

"Is it true you studied with Professor Bergson, at the Lycée Henri IV?" asked Marcel. "I was class of '91."

"We are found out," said Alfred. "We were class of all the early 1890s, and consider ourselves his devoted pupil still."

"Is it his views on time, on duration? His idea that character comes in instants of perception and memory? Is it his notion of memory as a flux of points in the mind that keeps you under his spell?" asked Proust.

"He makes us laugh," said Jarry.

They spent the rest of the evening—after meeting and bidding goodnight to the Méliès children, and after Madame Méliès rejoined them—playing charades, doing a quick round of Dreyfus Parcheesi, and viewing pornographic stereopticon cards, of which Georges had a truly wonderful collection.

They said their goodbyes at the front gate of the Montreuil house. Pablo had already gone, having a hot date with anyone at a certain street address, on his kangaroo bicycle; Rousseau walked the two blocks to catch an omnibus; Satie, as was his wont, strode off into the night at a brisk pace whistling an Aristide Bruant tune; he sometimes walked twenty kilometers to buy a piece of sheet music without a second thought.

Marcel's coachman waited. Jarry stood atop the Méliès wall, ready to step onto his ordinary. Georges and Madame had already gone back up the walkway.

Then Marcel made a Proposal to Alfred, which, if acted upon, would take much physical activity and some few hours of their time.

"We are touched by many things lately," said Jarry. "We fear we grow sentimental. Thank you for your kind attention, Our Dear Marcel, but we must visit the theater, later to meet with Pablo to paint scenery, and our Royal Drug Larder runs low. We thank you, though, from the bottom of our heart, graciously."

And he was gone, silently, a blur under each gas lamp he passed.

For some reason, during the ride back to Faubourg Ste.-Germain, Marcel was not depressed as he usually was when turned down. He too, hummed a Bruant song. The coachman joined in.

Very well, very well, thought Proust. We shall give them a Dreyfus they will never forget.

XI. The Enraged Umbrella

In the park, two days later, Marcel thought he was seeing a runaway carousel.

"Stop!" he yelled to the cabriolet driver. The brake squealed. Marcel leapt out, holding his top hat in his hand. "Wait!" he called back over his shoulder.

There was a medium-sized crowd, laborers, fashionable people out for a stroll, several tricycles and velocipedes parked nearby. Attention was all directed toward an object in the center of the crowd. There was a wagon nearby, with small machines all around it.

What Marcel had at first taken for a merry-go-round was not. It was round, and it did go.

The most notable feature looked like a ten-meter-in-diameter Japanese parasol made of, Marcel guessed, fine wire struts and glued paper. Coming down from the center of this, four meters long, was a central pipe, at its bottom was a base shaped like a plumb bob. Above this base, a seat, pedals and set of levers faced the central column. Above the seat, halfway down the pipe, parallel to the umbrella mechanism, was what appeared to be a weathervane, at the front end of which, instead of an arrow was a spiral, two-bladed airscrew. At its back, where the iron fletching would be, was a half-circle structure, containing within it a round panel made of the same stuff as the parasol. Marcel saw that it was rotatable on two axes, obviously a steering mechanism of some sort.

Three men in coveralls worked at the base; two holding the machine vertical while the third tightened bolts with a wrench, occasionally giving the pedal mechanism a turn, which caused the giant umbrella above to spin slowly.

Obviously the machine was very lightweight—what appeared to be iron must be aluminum or some other alloy, the strutwork must be very fine, possibly piano wire.

The workman yelled. He ran the pedal around with his hand. The paper-wire umbrella moved very fast indeed.

At the call, a man in full morning suit, like Marcel's, came out from behind the wagon. He walked very solemnly to the machine, handed his walking stick to a bystander, and sat down on the seat. He produced two bicyclist's garters from his coat and applied them to the legs of his trousers above his spats and patent-leather shoes.

He moved a couple of levers with his hands and began to pedal, slowly at first, then faster. The moving parasol became a flat disk, then began to strobe, appearing to move backwards. The small airscrew began a lazy revolution.

There was a soft growing purr in the air. Marcel felt gentle wind on his cheek.

The man nodded to the mechanics, who had been holding the machine steady and upright. They let go. The machine stood of its own accord. The grass beneath it waved and shook in a streamered disk of wind.

The man doffed his top hat to the crowd. Then he threw another lever. The machine, with no strengthening of sound or extra effort from its rider, rose three meters into the air.

The crowds gasped and cheered. *"Vive la France!"* they yelled. Marcel, caught up in the moment, had a terrible desire to applaud.

Looking to right and left beneath him, the aeronaut moved a lever slightly. The lazy twirling propeller on the weathervane became a corkscrewing blur. With a very polite nod of his head, the man pedaled a little faster.

Men threw their hats in the air; women waved their four-meter-long scarves at him.

The machine, with a sound like the slow shaking-out of a rug, turned and moved slowly off toward the Boulevard Haussmann, the crowd, and children who had been running in from all directions, following it.

While one watched, the other two mechanics loaded gear into the wagon. Then all three mounted, turned the horses, and started off at a slow roll in the direction of the heart of the city.

Marcel's last glimpse of the flying machine was of it disappearing gracefully down the line of an avenue above the treetops, as if an especially interesting woman, twirling her parasol, had just left a pleasant garden party.

Proust and the cabriolet driver were the only persons left on the field. Marcel climbed back in, nodded. The driver applied the whip to the air.

It was, Marcel would read later, the third heavier-than-air machine to fly that week, the forty-ninth since the first of the year, the one-hundred-twelfth since man had entered what the weeklies referred to as the Age of the Air late year-before-last.

XII. The Persistence of Vision

The sound of hammering and sawing filled the workshop. Rousseau painted stripes on a life-sized tiger puppet. Pablo worked on the silhouette jungle foliage Henri had sketched. Jarry went back and forth between helping them and going to the desk to consult with Proust on the scenario. (Proust had brought in closely written pages, copied in a fine hand, that he had done at home the first two days; after Jarry and Méliès drew circles and arrows all over them, causing Marcel visible anguish, he had taken to bringing in only hastily worded notes. The writers were trying something new — both scenario and title cards were to be written by them.)

"Gentlemen," said Satie, from his piano in the corner. "The music for the degradation scene!" His left hand played heavy bass notes, spare, foreboding. His right hit every other note from *La Marseillaise*.

"Marvelous," they said. "Wonderful!"

They went back to their paintpots. The Star Films workmen threw themselves into the spirit wholeheartedly, taking directions from Rousseau or Proust as if they were Méliès himself. They also made suggestions, explaining the mechanisms which would, or could, be used in the filming.

"Fellow collaborators!" said Méliès, entering from the yard. "Gaze on our Dreyfus!" He gestured dramatically.

A thin balding man, dressed in cheap overalls entered, cap in hand. They looked at him, each other, shifted from one foot to another.

"Come, come, geniuses of France!" said Méliès. "You're not using your imaginations!"

He rolled his arm in a magician's flourish. A blue coat appeared in his hands. The man put it on. Better.

"*Avec!*" said Méliès, reaching behind his own back, producing a black army cap, placing it on the man's head. Better still.

"*Voilà!*" he said, placing a mustache on the man's lip.

To Proust, it was the man he had served under seven years before, grown a little older and more tired. A tear came to Marcel's eye; he began to applaud, the others joined in.

The man seemed nervous, did not know what to do with his hands. "Come, come, Mr. Poulvain, get used to applause," said Méliès. "You'll soon have to quit your job at the chicken farm to portray Captain Dreyfus on the international stage!" The man nodded and left the studio.

Marcel sat back down and wrote with redoubled fury.

"Monsieur Méliès?" asked Rousseau.

"Yes?"

"Something puzzles me."

"How can I help?"

"Well, I know nothing about the making of cinematographs, but, as I understand, you take the pictures, from beginning to the end of the scenario, in series, then choose the best ones to use after you have developed them?"

"*Exactement!*" said Georges.

"Well, as I understand (if only Jarry and Proust would quit diddling with the writing), we use the same prison cell both for the early arrest scenes, and for Dreyfus' cell on Devil's Island?"

"Yes?"

"Your foreman explained that we would film the early scenes, break the backdrops, shoot other scenes, and some days or hours later reassemble the prison cell again, with suitable changes. Well, it seems to me, to save time and effort, you should film the early scenes, then change the costume and the makeup on the actor, and add the properties which represent Devil's Island, and put those scenes in their proper place when the scenes are developed. That way, you would be through with both sets, and go on to another."

Méliès looked at him a moment. The old artist was covered with blobs of gray, white, and black paint. "My dear Rousseau; we have never done it that way, since it cannot be done that way in the theater. But . . ."

Rousseau was pensive. "Also, I noticed that great care must be taken in moving the camera, and that right now the camera is to be moved many times in the filming. Why not also photograph all the scenes where the camera is in one place a certain distance from the stage, then all the others at the next, and so on? It seems more efficient that way, to me."

"Well," said Méliès. "That is surely asking too much! But your first suggestion, in the interest of saving time with the scenery. Yes. Yes, we could possibly do that! Thank you . . . as it is going now, the trial may very well be over before we even begin filming—if someone doesn't shoot Dreyfus as he sits in court since his return from Devil's Island even before that. Perhaps we shall try your idea . . ."

"Just thinking aloud," said Rousseau.

"Monsieur Director?" said Marcel.

"Yes?"

"Something puzzles me."

"Yes?"

"I've seen few Lumièreoscopes—"

"That name!" said Méliès, clamping his hands over his ears.

"Sorry . . . I've seen few films, at any rate. But in each one (and it comes up here in the proposed scenario) that we have Dreyfus sitting in his cell, on one side, the cutaway set of the hut with him therein; then the guard walks up and pounds on the door. Dreyfus gets up, goes to the door, opens it, and the guard walks in and hands him the first letter he is allowed to receive from France."

"A fine scene!" said Méliès.

"Hmmm. Yes. Another thing I have seen in all Lu—in moving pictures is that the actors are always filmed as if you were watching them on stage, their whole bodies from a distance of a few meters away."

"That is the only way it is done, my dear Marcel."

"Perhaps . . . perhaps we could do it another way. We see Dreyfus in his hut, in his chair. We show only his upper body, from waist to head. We could see the ravages of the ordeal upon him, the lines in his face, the circles under his eyes, the gray in his hair."

"But . . ."

"Hear me, please. Then you show a fist, as if it were in your face, pounding on the door. From inside the hut Dreyfus gets up, turns, walks to the door. Then he is handed the letter. We see the letter itself, the words of comfort and despair . . ."

Méliès was looking at him as if there were pinwheels sticking from his eye sockets.

". . . can you imagine the effects on the viewer?" finished Marcel.

"Oh yes!" said Méliès. "They would scream. Where are their legs? Where are their arms? What is this writing doing in my eye?!!!"

"But think of the impact! The drama?"

"Marcel, we are here to plead for justice, not frighten people away from the theater!"

"Think of it! What better way to show the impact on Dreyfus than by putting the impact on the spectator?"

"My head reels, Proust!"

"Well, just a suggestion. Sleep on it."

"I shall have nightmares," said Méliès.

Pablo continued to paint, eating a sandwich, drinking wine.

"Méliès?" said Jarry.

"(Sigh) Yes?"

"Enlighten us."

"In what manner?"

"Our knowledge of motio-kineto-photograms is small, but one thing is a royal poser to us."

"Continue."

"In our wonderful scene of the nightmares . . . we are led to understand that Monsieur Rousseau's fierce tigers are to be moved by wires, compressed air, and frantic stagehands?"

"Yes."

"Our mind works overtime. The fierce tigers are wonderful, but such movement will be seen, let us say, like fierce tigers moved by wires, air, and stage-labor."

"A necessary convention of stage and cinematograph," said Méliès. "One the spectator accepts."

"But we are not here to have the viewer accept anything but an intolerable injustice to a man."

"True, but pity . . ."

"Méliès," said Jarry. "We understand each click of the camera takes one frame of film. Many of these frames projected at a constant rate leads to the illusion of motion. But each is of itself but a single frame of film."

"The persistence of vision," said Méliès.

"We were thinking. What if we took a single click of the camera, taking one picture of our fierce tigers . . ."

"But what would that accomplish?"

"Ah . . . then, Méliès, our royal personage moves the tiger to a slightly different posture, but the next in some action, but only one frame advanced, and took another click of the camera?"

Méliès looked at him. "Then . . ."

"Then the next and the next and the next and so on! The fierce tiger moves, roars, springs, devours! But each frame part of the movement, each frame a still."

Méliès thought a second. "An actor in the scenes would not be able to move at all. Or he would have to move at the same rate as the tiger. He would have to hold perfectly still (we already do that when stopping the camera to substitute a skeleton for a lady or somesuch) but they would have to do it endlessly. It would take weeks to get any good length of film. Also, the tigers would have to be braced, strutted to support their own weight."

"This is our idea, Méliès; we are not technicians."

"I shall take it under advisement."

Méliès' head began to hurt. He had a workman go to the chemist's, and get some of the new Aspirin for him. He took six.

The film took three weeks to photograph. Méliès had to turn out three fairy tales in two days besides to keep his salesmen supplied with footage. Every day they worked, the Court of Cassation met to rehear the Dreyfus case, every day brought new evasions, new half-insinuations; Dreyfus' lawyer was wounded by a gunshot while leaving court. Every day the country was split further and further down the center: There was no middle ground. There was talk of a *coup d'état* by the right.

At last the footage was done.

"I hope," said Méliès to his wife that night, "I hope that after this I shall not hear the name of Dreyfus again, for the rest of my life."

XIII. The Elephant at the Foot of the Bed

Jarry was on stage, talking in a monotone as he had been for five minutes. The crowd, including women, had come to the *Theater of the Work* to see what new horrors Lugné-Poe had in store for them.

Alfred sat at a small folding table, which had been brought onstage, and a chair placed behind it, facing the audience. Jarry talked, as someone said, as a nutcracker would speak. The audience had listened but was growing restless—we have come for a play, not for someone dressed as a bicyclist to drone on about nothing in particular.

The last week had been a long agony for Jarry—working on this play, which he had started in his youth, as a puppet play satirizing a pompous teacher—it had grown to encompass all mankind's foibles, all national and human delusions. Then there had been the work on the Dreyfus film with Pablo and Rousseau and Proust and Méliès—it had been trying and demanding, but it was like pulling teeth, too collaborative, with its own limitations and ideas. Give a man the freedom of the page and boards!

Jarry ran down like a clock. He finished tiredly.

"The play takes place in Poland, which is to say, Nowhere." He picked up his papers while two stagehands took off the table and chair. Jarry left. The lights dimmed. There were three raps on the floor with Lugné-Poe's cane, the curtains opened in the darkness as the lights came up.

The walls were painted as a child might have—representing sky, clouds, stars, the sun, moon, elephants, flowers, a clock with no hands, snow falling on a cheery fireplace.

A round figure stood at one side, his face hidden by a pointed hood on which was painted the slitted eyes and mustache of a caricature bourgeoisie. His costume was a white canvas cassock with an immense stomach on which was painted three concentric circles.

The audience tensed, leaned forward. The figure stepped to the center of the stage, looked around.

"*Merde!*" he said.

The riot could be heard for a kilometer in all directions.

XIV. What He Really Thinks

"Today, France has left the past of Jew-traitors and degeneracy behind.

"Today, she has taken the final step toward greatness, a return to the True Faith, a way out of the German-Jew morass in which she has floundered for a quarter-century.

"With the second conviction of the traitor-spy Dreyfus, she sends a signal to all his rat-like kind that France will no longer tolerate impurities in its body-politic, its armies, its commerce. She has served notice that the Future is written in the French language; Europe, indeed the world, shall one day speak only one tongue, *Française*.

"The verdict of Guilty!—even with its softening of 'With extenuating circumstances'—will end this Affair, once and for all, the only way—short of public execution by the most excruciating means, which, unfortunately the law no longer allows—ah! but True Frenchmen are working to change that!—that it could be ended; with the slow passing of this Jew-traitor to rot in the jungle of Devil's Island—a man who should never have been allowed to don the uniform of this country in the first place.

"Let there be no more talk of injustice! Injustice has already been served by the spectacle of a thoroughly guilty man being given two trials; by a man not worth a sous causing great agitation—surely the work of enemies of the state.

"Let every True Frenchman hold this day sacred until the end of time. Let him turn his eyes eastward at our one Great Enemy, against that day when we shall rise up and gain just vengeance—let him not forget also to look around him, let him not rest until every Christ-murdering Jew, every German-inspired Protestant is driven from the boundaries of this country, or gotten rid of in an equally advantageous way—their property confiscated, their businesses closed, their 'rights'—usurped rights!—nullified.

"If this decision wakens Frenchmen to that threat, then Dreyfus will have, in all his evil machinations, his total acquiescence to our enemy's plans, done one good deed: He will have given us the reason not to rest until every one of his kind is gone from the face of the earth; that in the future the only place Hebrew will be spoken is in Hell." —Robert Norpois

XV. Truth Rises from the Well

Emile Zola stared at the white sheet of paper with the British watermark.

He dipped his pen in the bottle of Pelikan ink in the well and began to write.

As he wrote, the words became scratchier, more hurried. All his feelings of frustration boiled over in his head and out onto the fine paper. The complete cowardice and stultification of the Army, the anti-Semitism of the rich and the poor, the Church; the utter stupidity of the government, the treason of the writers who refused to come to the aid of an innocent man.

It was done sooner than he thought; six pages of his contempt and utter revulsion with the people of the country he loved more than life itself.

He put on his coat and hat and hailed a pedal cabriolet, ordering it to the offices of *L'Aurore*. The streets were more empty than usual, the cafés full. The news of the second trial verdict had driven good people to drink. He was sure there were raucous celebrations in every Church, every fort, and the basement drill-halls of every right-wing organization in the city and the country. This was an artist's quarter — there was no loud talk, no call to action. There would be slow and deliberate drunkenness and oblivion for all against the atrocious verdict.

Zola sat back against the cushion, listening to the clicking pedals of the driver. He wondered if all this would end with the nation, half on one side of some field, half on the other, charging each other in final bloodbath.

He paid the driver, who swerved silently around and headed back the other way. Zola stepped into the Aurora's office, where Clemenceau waited for him behind his desk. Emile handed him the manuscript.

Clemenceau read the first sentence, wrote, "Page One, 360 point RED TYPE headline — 'J'ACCUSE,' " called "Copy boy!", said to the boy, "I shall be back for a proof in three hours," put on his coat, and arm in arm he and Zola went off to the Théâtre Robert-Houdin for the first showing of Star Films' *The Dreyfus Affair*, saying not a word to each other.

XVI. Chamber Pots Shall Light Your Way

Zola and Clemenceau, crying tears of pride and exultation, ran back arm in arm down the Place de l'Opéra, turning into a side street toward the publisher's office.

Halfway down, they began to sing *La Marseillaise*; people who looked out their windows, not knowing the reason, assumed their elation for that of the verdict of the second trial, flung *merde* pots at them from second-story windows. "Anti-Dreyfussard scum!" they yelled, shaking their fists. "Wait till I get my fowling piece!"

Emile and Georges ran into the office, astonishing the editors and reporters there.

They went to Clemenceau's desk, where the page proof of Zola's article waited, with a separate proof of the red headline.

Zola picked up the proof.

"No need of this, my dear Georges?"

"I think not, my friend Emile."

Zola shredded it, throwing the strips on the pressman who was waiting in the office for word from Clemenceau.

"Rip off the front page!" Clemenceau yelled out the door of his office. "We print a review of a moving picture there! Get Veyou out of whatever theater watching whatever piece of stage-pap he's in and hustle him over to the Robert-Houdin for the second showing!"

Emile and Georges looked at each other, remembering.

"The Awful Trip to the Island!"

"The Tigers of the Imagination!"

"First News of Home!" said Emile

"Star Films," said Clemenceau.

"Méliès," said Zola.

"Dreyfus!" they said in unison.

Three days later, the President overturned the conviction of the second court, pardoned Dreyfus, and returned him to his full rank and privileges. The Ministry of War was reorganized, and the resignations of eleven generals received.

The President was, of course, shot down like a dog on the way home from a cabinet meeting that night. Three days of mourning were declared.

Dreyfus had been released the same night, and went to the country home of his brother Mathieu; he was now a drawn, shaken man whose hair had turned completely white.

XVII. Three Famous Quotes Which Led to Duels:

1. "The baron writes the kind of music a priest can hum while he is raping a choirboy."

2. "I see you carry the kind of cane which allows you to hit a woman eight or ten times before it breaks."

3. "Monsieur Jarry," said Norpois, "I demand satisfaction for your insults to France during the last three years."

"Captain Dreyfus is proved innocent. We have called attention to nothing that was not the action of madmen and cowards."

"You are a spineless dwarf masturbator with the ideas of a toad!" said Norpois.

"Our posture, stature, and habits are known to every schoolboy in France, Mister Journalist," said Jarry. "We have come through five years of insult, spittle, and outrage. Nothing you say will make Dreyfus guilty or goad our royal person into a gratuitous display of our unerring marksmanship."

Jarry turned to walk away with Pablo.

"Then, Monsieur Jarry, your bicycle . . ." said Norpois.

Jarry stopped. "What of Our Royal Vehicle?"

"Your bicycle eats *merde* sandwiches."

XVIII. The Downhill Bicycle Race
A. Prelims

The anemometer barely moved behind his head. The vane at its top pointed to the south; the windsock swelled and emptied slowly.

Jarry slowly recovered his breath. Below and beyond lay the city of Paris and its environs. The Seine curved like a piece of gray silk below and out to two horizons. It was just after dawn; the sun was a fat red beet to the east.

It was still cool at the weather station atop the Eiffel Tower, 300 meters above the ground.

Jarry leaned against his high-wheeler. He had taken only the least minimum of fortifying substances, and that two hours ago on this, the morning of the duel.

Proust had acted as his second (Jarry would have chosen Pablo—good thing he hadn't, as the young painter had not shown up with the others this morning, perhaps out of fear of seeing Jarry maimed or killed—but Proust had defended himself many times, with a large variety of weapons, on many fields of honor). Second for Norpois was the journalist whose hair Alfred had set afire at the banquet more than a year ago. As the injured party, Jarry had had choice of place and weapons.

The conditions were thus: weapons, any. Place: the Eiffel Tower. Duelists must be mounted on their bicycles when using their weapons. Jarry would start at the weather station at the top, Norpois at the base. After Jarry was taken to the third platform, using all three sets of elevators on the way up, and the elevator man — since this was a day of mourning, the tower was closed, and the guards paid to look the other way — returned to the ground, the elevators could not be used, only the stairways. Jarry had still had to climb the spiral steps from the third platform to the weather station, from which he was now recovering.

With such an arrangement, Norpois would, of course, be waiting in ambush for him on the second observation platform by the time Jarry reached it. Such was the nature of duels.

Jarry looked down the long swell of the south leg of the tower — it was gray, smooth, and curved as an elephant's trunk, plunging down and out into the earth. Tiny dots waited there; Norpois, the journalist, Proust, a few others, perhaps by now Pablo. The Tower cast a long shadow out away from the River. The shadow of the Trocadéro almost reached to the base of the Tower in the morning sun. There was already talk of painting the Tower again, for the coming Exposition of 1900 in a year and a half.

Alfred took a deep breath, calmed himself. He was lightly armed, having only a five-shot .32 revolver in his holster and a poniard in a sheath on his hip. He would have felt almost naked except for the excruciatingly heavy but comforting weapon slung across his shoulders.

It was a double-barreled Greener 4-bore Rhino Express which could fire a 130-gram bullet at 1200 meters per second. Jarry had decided that if he had to kill Norpois, he might as well wipe him off the face of the earth.

He carried four extra rounds in a bandolier; they weighed more than a kilo in all.

He was confident in his weapons, in himself, in his high-wheeler. He had oiled it the night before, polished it until it shone. After all, it was the insulted party, not him, not Dreyfus.

He sighed, then leaned out and dropped the lead-weighted green handkerchief as the signal he was starting down. He had his ordinary over his shoulder opposite the Greener and had his foot on the first step before he heard the weighted handkerchief ricocheting on its way down off the curved leg of the Tower.

B. The Duel

He was out of breath before he passed the locked apartment which

Gustave Eiffel had built for himself during the last phase of construction of the Tower, and which he sometimes used when aerodynamic experiments were being done on the drop-tube which ran down the exact center of the Tower.

Down around the steps he clanged, his bike brushing against the spiral railing. It was good he was not subject to vertigo. He could imagine Norpois' easy stroll to the west leg, where he would be casually walking up the broad stairs to the first level platform with four restaurants, arcades and booths, and its entry to the stilled second set of elevators. (Those between the ground and first level were the normal counterweighted kind; hydraulic ones to the second—American Otis had had to set up a dummy French corporation to win the contract—no one in France had the technology, and the charter forbade foreign manufacture; and tracked ones to the third— passengers had to change halfway up, as no elevator could be made to go from roughly 70° to 90° halfway up its rise.)

Panting mightily, Jarry reached the third platform, less than a third of the way down. Only 590 more steps down to sure and certain ambush. The rifle, cartridges, and high-wheeler were grinding weights on his back. Gritting his teeth, he started down the steep steps with landings every few dozen meters.

His footsteps rang like gongs on the iron treads. He could see the tops of the booths on the second level, the iron framework of the Tower extending all around him like a huge narrow cage.

Norpois would be waiting at one of the corners, ready to fire at either set of stairs. (Of course, he probably already knew which set Jarry was using, oh devious man, or it was possible he was truly evil and was waiting on the first level. It would be just like a right-wing nationalist Catholic safety-bicycle rider to do that.)

Fifteen steps up from the second level, in one smooth motion, Jarry put the ordinary down, mounted it holding immobile the pedals with his feet, swung the Rhino Express off his shoulder, and rode the last crashing steps down, holding back, then pedaling furiously as his giant wheel hit the floor.

He expected shots at any second as he swerved toward a closed souvenir booth: He swung his back wheel up and around behind him holding still, changing direction, the drainpipe barrels of the 4-bore resting on the handlebars.

Over at the corner of another booth the front wheel and handlebar of Norpois' bicycle stuck out.

With one motion Jarry brought the Greener to his cheek. We shall shoot the front end off his bicycle—without that he cannot be mounted and fire; ergo, he cannot duel; therefore, we have won; he is disgraced. *Quod Erat Demonstrandum.*

Jarry fired one barrel—the recoil sent him skidding backwards two meters. The forks of the crocodile went away—Fortune's smiling face wavered through the air like the phases of the Moon. The handlebars stuck in the side of another booth six meters away.

Jarry hung onto his fragile balance, waiting for Norpois to tumble forward or stagger bleeding with bicycle shrapnel from behind the booth.

He heard a noise behind him; at the corner of his eye he saw Norpois standing beside one of the planted trees—he had to have been there all along—with a look of grim satisfaction on his face.

Then the grenade landed directly between the great front and small back wheels of Jarry's bicycle.

C. High Above the City

He never felt the explosion, just a wave of heat and a flash that blinded him momentarily. There was a carnival ride sensation, a loopy feeling in his stomach. Something touched his hand; he grabbed it. Something tugged at his leg. He clenched his toes together.

His vision cleared.

He hung by one hand from the guardrail. He dangled over Paris. His rifle was gone. His clothes smelt of powder and burning hair. He looked down. The weight on his legs was his ordinary, looking the worse for wear. The rim of the huge front wheel had caught on the toe of his cycling shoe. He cupped the toe of the other one through the spokes.

His hand was losing its grip.

He reached down with the other for his pistol. The holster was still there, split up the middle, empty.

Norpois' head appeared above him, looking down, then his gun hand with a large automatic in it, pointing at Jarry's eyes.

"There are rules, Monsieur," said Jarry. He was trying to reach up with the other hand but something seemed to be wrong with it.

"Get with the coming century, dwarf," said Norpois, flipping the pistol into the air, catching it by the barrel. He brought the butt down hard on Jarry's fingers.

The second time the pain was almost too much. Once more and Alfred knew he would let go, fall, be dead.

"One request. Save our noble vehicle," said Jarry, looking into the journalist's eyes. There was a clang off somewhere on the second level.

Norpois' grin became sardonic. "You die. So does your crummy bike."

There was a small pop. A thin line of red, like a streak of paint slung off the end of a brush, stood out from Norpois' nose, went over Jarry's shoulder.

Norpois raised his automatic, then wavered, let go of it. It bounced off Alfred's useless arm, clanged once on the way down.

Norpois, still staring into Jarry's eyes, leaned over the railing and disappeared behind his head. There was silence for a few seconds, then:

Pif-Paf! Quel Bruit!

The sound of the body bouncing off the ironworks went on for longer than seemed possible.

Far away on the second level was the sound of footsteps running downstairs.

Painfully, Jarry got his left arm up next to his right, got the fingers closed, began pulling himself up off the side of the Eiffel Tower, bringing his mangled high-wheeler with him.

D. Code Duello

A small crowd had gathered, besides those concerned. Norpois' second was over by the body, with the police. There would of course be damages to pay for. Jarry carried his ordinary and the Greener, which he had found miraculously lying on the floor of the second level.

Proust came forward to shake Alfred's hand. Jarry gave him the rifle and ordinary, but continued to walk past him. Several others stepped forward, but Jarry continued on, nodding.

He went to Pablo. Pablo had on a long cloak and was eating an egg sandwich. His eyes would not meet Alfred's.

Jarry stepped in front of him. Pablo tried to move away without meeting his gaze. Alfred reached inside the cloak, felt around, ignoring the Webley strapped at Pablo's waist.

He found what he was looking for, pulled it out. It was the single-shot .22. Jarry sniffed the barrel as Pablo tried to turn away, working at his sandwich.

"Asshole," said Jarry, handing it back.

XIX. Fin de Cyclé

The bells were still ringing in the New Century.

Satie had given up composing and had gone back to school to learn music at the age of thirty-eight. Rousseau still exhibited at the *Salon des Refusés*, and was now married for the second time. Proust had locked himself away in a room he'd had lined with cork and was working on a never-ending novel. Méliès was still out at Montreuil, making films about trips to the Moon and the Bureau of Incoherent Geography. Pablo was painting; but so much blue; blue here, blue there, azure, cerulean, Prussian. Dreyfus was now a commandant.

Jarry lived in a shack over the Seine which stood on four supports. He called it Our Suitable Tripod.

There was noise, noise everywhere. There were few bicycles, and all those were safeties. He had not seen another ordinary in months. He looked over where his repaired one stood in the middle of the small room. His owl and one of his crows perched on the handlebars.

The noise was deafening—the sound of bells, of crowds, sharp reports of fireworks. Above all, those of motor-cycles and motor-cars.

He looked back out the window. There was a new sound, a dark flash against the bright moonlit sky. A bat-shape went over, buzzing, trailing laughter and gunshots, the pilot banking over the River. Far up the Seine, the Tower stood, bathed in floodlights, glorying in its blue, red, and white paint for the coming Exposition.

A zeppelin droned overhead, electric lights on the side spelling out the name of a hair pomade. The bat-shaped plane whizzed under it in near-collision.

Someone gunned a motor-cycle beneath his tiny window. Jarry reached back into the room, brought out his fowling piece filled with rock salt and fired a great tongue of flame into the night below. After a scream, the noise of the motor-cycle raced away.

He drank from a glass filled with brandy, ether, and red ink. He took one more look around, buffeted by the noise from all quarters and a motor launch on the River. He said a word to the night before slamming the window and returning to his work on the next Ubu play.

The word was *"merde!"*

INTRODUCTION TO

FLATFEET!

I have written about the genesis of this story twice, now, once for *Going Home Again*, my last collection (and while I'm at it, Shaun Tan's illustration for this story was wonderful—two feet propped up on a desk, candlestick, telephone, calendar on the wall opened to July. Tan was maybe eighteen when he illustrated the book . . .), and again in my first column, "Crimea River" in *Eidolon Magazine* in 1998, which was more or less a literary mash note to Constance Willis' story "In the Late Cretaceous," many of the effects of which I was trying for when I wrote this.

So I won't go through all that again. (When I wrote this one, it was October of 1994.) Where it started: I was reading a book on the first Red Scare, Sacco and Vanzetti, and the nationwide roundup of anarchists and socialists in 1920, and I suddenly realized it would have been done by guys like these . . . *Voilà!*

Hollywood is Hollywood because of an attempted American monopoly in 1910. Movies were being made in New Jersey, Philly, Long Island; all along the East Coast and Chicago. About 1910, all the people who owned major patents, and several production companies, got together and formed the Motion Picture Patents Company and said: Anybody who doesn't pay us for cameras, projectors, movies, etc., will be sued for patent infringement. It was an attempt to control the motion-picture business from raw film stock to the exhibition of the films. (A reverse Join-or-Die movement.) If you paid them, you could make movies; if you didn't, they'd hound you to the ends of the earth.

Well, almost. It was the last straw for small independent film companies, fed up with crooked distributors, conniving theater owners, sharpies and crooks — and the crummy East Coast weather that only let them shoot 150 days a year. (Arc lights were just coming in — most studios shot outdoors, or in glass-roofed buildings where you had to depend on sunlight — film wasn't fast enough for low light levels yet.)

The independents took off West. It could have been anywhere. (See "The Passing of the Western" later for another take on that.) As chance would have it, they ended up near Los Angeles — sunshine, cheap (at the time) real estate, plenty of people not doing much of anything. There was a thriving theater scene; vaudeville talent came through often. And, as chance would have it further, a small community (and Dry thirteen years before the rest of the country) called, by that time, Hollywood (and Culver City and Burbank, named for a guy who raised sweet potatoes . . .).

Things weren't easy at first. Cecil B. DeMille, in his autobiography, talks about having to wear a couple of pistols on his horseback ride each morning from town out to the lot where he was making *The Squaw Man*, because the Patents people hired guys to take potshots at the renegade filmmakers.

It took till the 1930s to finally kill film production on the East Coast — *Coconuts* (1929) and *Animal Crackers* (1930) with the Marxes were filmed on Long Island in the daytime while Harpo, Groucho, Chico, and Zeppo were in plays at night — even though the courts had ruled the MPPCo. was a Trust, and therefore illegal, by about 1915, ending that threat.

So it was, in trying to make millions, the MPPCo. did itself out of billions, and instead of having the thriving metropoli of the East as the centers of motion-picture production in the U.S. — and soon the world — they handed it, unconsciously, but with malice aforethought, to a sleepy crossroads on the edge of nowhere, and made its name stand for motion pictures for all time.

FLATFEET!

1912

Captain Teeheezal turned his horse down toward the station house just as the Pacific Electric streetcar clanged to a stop at the intersection of Sunset and Ivar.

It was just 7:00 A.M. so only three people got off at the stop. Unless they worked at one of the new moving-picture factories a little further out in the valley, there was no reason for someone from the city to be in the town of Wilcox before the stores opened.

The motorman twisted his handle, there were sparks from the overhead wire, and the streetcar belled off down the narrow tracks. Teeheezal watched it recede, with the official sign *No Shooting Rabbits from the Rear Platform* over the back door.

"G'hup, Pear," he said to his horse. It paid no attention and walked at the same speed.

By and by he got to the police station. Patrolman Rube was out watering the zinnias that grew to each side of the porch. Teeheezal handed him the reins to his horse.

"What's up, Rube?"

"Not much, Cap'n," he said. "Shoulda been here yesterday. Sgt. Fatty brought by two steelhead and a Coho salmon he caught, right where Pye Creek empties into the L.A. River. Big as your leg, all three of 'em. Took up the whole back of his wagon."

"I mean police business, Rube."

"Oh." The patrolman lifted his domed helmet and scratched. "Not that I know of."

"Well, anybody in the cells?"

"Uh, lessee . . ."

"I'll talk to the sergeant," said Teeheezal. "Make sure my horse stays in his stall."

"Sure thing, Captain." He led it around back.

The captain looked around at the quiet streets. In the small park across from the station, with its few benches and small artesian fountain, was the big sign *No Spooning by order of Wilcox P.D.* Up toward the northeast the sun was coming full up over the hills.

Sgt. Hank wasn't at his big high desk. Teeheezal heard him banging around in the squad room to the left. The captain spun the blotter book around.

There was one entry:

Sat. 11:20 P.M. Jimson H. Friendless, actor, of Los Angeles city, D&D. Slept off, cell 2. Released Sunday 3:00 P.M. Arr. off. Patrolmen Buster and Chester.

Sgt. Hank came in. "Oh, hello Chief."

"Where'd this offense take place?" He tapped the book.

"The Blondeau Tavern . . . uh, Station," said the sergeant.

"Oh." That was just inside his jurisdiction, but since the Wilcox village council had passed a local ordinance against the consumption and sale of alcohol, there had been few arrests.

"He probably got tanked somewhere in L.A. and got lost on the way home," said Sgt. Hank. "Say, you hear about them fish Sgt. Fatty brought in?"

"Yes, I did." He glared at Sgt. Hank.

"Oh. Okay. Oh, there's a postal card that came in the Saturday mail from Captain Angus for us all. I left it on your desk."

"Tell me if any big trouble happens," said Teeheezal. He went into the office and closed his door. Behind his desk was a big wicker rocking chair he'd had the village buy for him when he took the job early in the year. He sat down in it, took off his flat-billed cap, and put on his reading glasses.

Angus had been the captain before him for twenty-two years; he'd retired and left to see some of the world. (He'd been one of the two original constables when Colonel Wilcox laid out the planned residential village.) Teeheezal had never met the man.

He picked up the card—a view of Le Havre, France, from the docks. Teeheezal turned it over. It had a Canadian postmark, and one half had the address: *The Boys in Blue, Police HQ, Wilcox, Calif. U.S.A.* The message read:

Well, took a boat. You might have read about it. Had a snowball fight on deck while waiting to get into the lifeboats. The flares sure were pretty. We were much overloaded by the time we were picked up. (Last time I take a boat named for some of the minor Greek godlings.) Will write again soon.

—Angus

PS: Pretty good dance band.

Teeheezal looked through the rest of the mail; wanted posters for guys three thousand miles away, something from the attorney general of California, a couple of flyers for political races that had nothing to do with the village of Wilcox.

The captain put his feet up on his desk, made sure they were nowhere near the kerosene lamp or the big red bellpull wired to the squad room, placed his glasses in their cases, arranged his Farmer John tuft beard to one side, clasped his fingers across his chest, and began to snore.

The murder happened at the house of one of the curators, across the street from the museum.

Patrolman Buster woke the captain up at his home at 4:00 A.M. The Los Angeles County coroner was already there when Teeheezal arrived on his horse.

The door of the house had been broken down. The man had been strangled and then thrown back behind the bed where he lay twisted with one foot out the open windowsill.

"Found him just like that, the neighbors did," said Patrolman Buster. "Heard the ruckus, but by the time they got dressed and got here, whoever did it was gone."

Teeheezal glanced out the broken door. The front of the museum across the way was lit with electric lighting.

"Hmmm," said the coroner, around the smoke from his El Cubano cigar. "They's dust all over this guy's py-jamas." He looked around. "Part of a print on the bedroom doorjamb, and a spot on the floor."

Patrolman Buster said, "Hey! One on the front door. Looks like somebody popped it with a dirty towel."

The captain went back out on the front porch. He knelt down on the lawn, feeling with his hands.

He spoke to the crowd that had gathered out front. "Who's a neighbor here?" A man stepped out, waved. "He water his yard last night?"

"Yeah, just after he got off work."

Teeheezal went to the street and lay down.

"Buster, look here." The patrolman flopped down beside him. "There's some lighter dust on the gravel, see it?" Buster nodded his thin face. "Look over there, see?"

"Looks like mud, Chief." They crawled to the right to get another angle, jumped up, looking at the doorway of the museum.

"Let's get this place open," said the chief.

"I was just coming over; they called me about Fielding's death, when your ruffians came barging in," said the museum director, whose name was Carter Lord. "There was no need to rush me so." He had on suit pants but a pajama top and a dressing gown.

"Shake a leg, pops," said Patrolman Buster.

There was a sign on the wall near the entrance: *The Treasures of Pharaoh Rut-en-tut-en, April 20–June 13*.

The doors were steel; there were two locks Lord had to open. On the inside was a long push bar that operated them both.

"Don't touch anything, but tell me if something's out o' place," said Teeheezal.

Lord used a handkerchief to turn on the light switches.

He told them the layout of the place and the patrolmen took off in all directions.

There were display cases everywhere, and ostrich-looking fans, a bunch of gaudy boxes, things that looked like coffins. On the walls were paintings of people wearing diapers, standing sideways. At one end of the hall was a big upright wooden case. Patrolman Buster pointed out two dabs of mud just inside the door, a couple of feet apart. Then another a little further on, leading toward the back, then nothing.

Teeheezal looked around at all the shiny jewelry. "Rich guy?" he asked.

"Priceless," said Carter Lord. "Tomb goods, buried with him for the afterlife. The richest find yet in Egypt. We were very lucky to acquire it."

"How come you gettin' it?"

"We're a small, but a growing museum. It was our expedition — the best untampered tomb. Though there were skeletons in the outer corridors, and the outside seal had been broken, I'm told. Grave robbers had broken in but evidently got no further."

"How come?"

"Who knows?" asked Lord. "We're dealing with four thousand five hundred years."

Patrolman Buster whistled.

Teeheezal walked to the back. Inside the upright case was the gray swaddled shape of a man, twisted, his arms across his chest, one eye closed, a deep open hole where the other had been. Miles of gray curling bandages went round and round and round him, making him look like a cartoon patient in a lost hospital.

"This the guy?"

"Oh, heavens no," said Carter Lord. "The Pharaoh Rut-en-tut-en's mummy is on loan to the Field Museum in Chicago for study. This is probably some priest or minor noble who was buried for some reason with him. There were no markings on this case," he said, knocking on the plain wooden case. "The pharaoh was in that nested three-box sarcophagus over there."

Teeheezal leaned closer. He reached down and touched the left foot of the thing. "Please don't touch that," said Carter Lord.

The patrolmen returned from their search of the building. "Nobody here but us *gendarmerie*," said Patrolman Rube.

"C'mere, Rube," said Teeheezal. "Reach down and touch this foot."

Rube looked into the box, jerked back. "Cripes! What an ugly! Which foot?"

"Both."

He did. "So?"

"One of them feel wet?"

Rube scratched his head. "I'm not sure."

"I asked you to *please* not touch that," said Carter Lord. "You're dealing with very fragile, irreplaceable things here."

"He's conducting a murder investigation here, bub," said Patrolman Mack.

"I understand that. But nothing here has committed murder, at least not for the last four thousand five hundred years. I'll have to ask that you desist."

Teeheezal looked at the face of the thing again. It looked back at him with a deep open hole where one eye had been, the other closed. Just—

The hair on Teeheezal's neck stood up. "Go get the emergency gun from the wagon," said the chief, not taking his eyes off the thing in the case.

"I'll have to *insist* that you leave *now*!" said Carter Lord.

Teeheezal reached over and pulled up a settee with oxhorn arms on it and sat down, facing the thing. He continued to stare at it. Somebody put the big heavy revolver in his hand.

"All you, go outside, except Rube. Rube, keep the door open so you can see me. Nobody do anything until I say so."

"That's the last straw!" said Carter Lord. "Who do I call to get you to cease and desist?"

"Take him where he can call the mayor, Buster."

Teeheezal stared and stared. The dead empty socket looked back at him. Nothing moved in the museum, for a long, long time. The revolver grew heavier and heavier. The chief's eyes watered. The empty socket stared back, the arms lay motionless across the twisted chest. Teeheezal stared.

"Rube!" he said after a long time. He heard the patrolman jerk awake.

"Yeah, Chief?"

"What do you think?"

"Well, I think about now, Captain, that they've got the mayor all agitated, and a coupla aldermen, and five, maybe ten minutes ago somebody's gonna have figured out that though the murder happened in Wilcox, right now you're sitting in Los Angeles."

Without taking his eyes from the thing, Teeheezal asked, "Are you funnin' me?"

"I never fun about murder, Chief."

Three carloads of Los Angeles Police came around the corner on six wheels. They slammed to a stop, the noise of the hand-cranked sirens dying on the night. By now the crowd outside the place had grown to a couple of hundred.

What greeted the eyes of the Los Angeles Police was the Wilcox police wagon with its four horses in harness, most of the force, a crowd, and a small fire on the museum lawn across the street from the murder house.

Two legs were sticking sideways out of the fire. The wrappings flamed against the early morning light. Sparks rose up and swirled.

The chief of the Los Angeles Police Department walked up to where the captain poked at the fire with the butt end of a spear. Carter Lord and the Wilcox mayor and a Los Angeles city councilman trailed behind the L.A. chief.

"Hello, Bob," said Teeheezal.

With a pop and a flash of cinders, the legs fell the rest of the way into the fire, and the wrappings roared up to nothingness.

"Teeheezal! What the hell do you think you're doing!? Going out of your jurisdiction, no notification. It looks like you're burning up Los Angeles City property here! Why didn't you call us?"

"Didn't have time, Bob," said Teeheezal. "I was in hot pursuit."

They all stood watching until the fire was out; then all climbed into their cars and wagons and drove away. The crowd dispersed, leaving Carter Lord in his dressing gown. With a sigh, he turned and went into the museum.

1913

If southern California had seasons, this would have been another late spring.

Teeheezal was at his desk, reading a letter from his niece Katje from back in Pennsylvania, where all his family but him had been for six generations.

There was a knock on his door. "What? What?" he yelled.

Patrolman Al stuck his head in. "Another card from Captain Angus. The sergeant said to give it to you."

He handed it to Teeheezal and left swiftly. Patrolman Al had once been a circus acrobat, and the circus folded in Los Angeles city two years ago. He was a short thin wiry man, one of Teeheezal's few smooth-shaven patrolmen.

The card was a view of the Eiffel Tower, had a Paris postmark, with the usual address on the back right side. On the left:

Well, went to the Ballet last night. You would of thought someone spit on the French flag. Russians jumpin' around like Kansas City fools, frogs punching each other out, women sticking umbrellas up guys' snouts. I been to a rodeo, a country fair, six picnics, and I have seen the Elephant, but this was pretty much the stupidest display of art appreciation I ever saw. Will write again soon.

    — Angus

PS: Ooh-lah-lah!

"Hmmph!" said Teeheezal. He got up and went out into the desk area. Sergeant Hank had a stack of picture frames on his desk corner. He was over at the wall under the pictures of the mayor and the village aldermen. He had a hammer and was marking five spots for nails on the plaster with the stub of a carpenter's pencil.

"What's all this, then?" asked the Captain.

"My pictures got in yesterday, Chief," said Sgt. Hank. "I was going to put 'em up on this wall I have to stare at all day."

"Well, I can see how looking at the mayor's no fun," said Teeheezal. He picked up the top picture. It was a landscape. There was a guy chasing a deer in one corner, and some trees and teepees, and a bay, and a funny-shaped rock on a mountain in the distance.

He looked at the second. The hill with the strange rock was in it, but people had on sheets, and there were guys drawing circles and squares in the dirt and talking in front of little temples and herding sheep. It looked to be by the same artist.

"It's not just paintings," said Sgt. Hank, coming over to him. "It's a series by Thomas Cole, the guy who started what's referred to as the Hudson River School of painting way back in New York State, about eighty years ago. It's called *The Course of Empire*. Them's the first two — *The Savage State* and *The Pastoral or Arcadian State*. This next one's called *The Consummation of Empire* — see, there's this guy riding in a triumphal parade on an elephant, and there are these armies, all in this city like Rome or Carthage, it's been built here, and they're bringing stuff back from all over the world, and things are dandy."

Hank was more worked up than the chief had ever seen him. "But look at this next one, see, the jig is up. It's called *The Destruction of Empire*. All them buildings are on fire, and there's a rainstorm, and people like Mongols are killing everybody in them big wide avenues, and busting up statues and looting the big temples, and bridges are falling down, and there's smoke everywhere."

Teeheezal saw the funny-shaped mountain was over in one corner of those two paintings.

"Then there's the last one, number five, *The Ruins of Empire*. Everything's quiet and still, all the buildings are broken, the woods are taking back everything, it's going back to the land. See, look there, there's pelicans nesting on top of that broken column, and the place is getting covered with ivy and briers and stuff. I ordered all these from a museum back in New York City," said Hank, proudly.

Teeheezal was still looking at the last one.

"And look," said Sgt. Hank, going back to the first one. "It's not just paintings, it's philosophical. See, here in the first one, it's just after dawn. Man's in his infancy. So's the day. Second one—pastoral, it's midmorning. Consummation—that's at noon. First three paintings all bright and clear. But destruction—that's in the afternoon, there's storms and lightning. Like nature's echoing what's going on with mankind, see? And the last one. Sun's almost set, but it's clear again, peaceful, like, you know, Nature takes its time . . ."

"Sgt. Hank," said Teeheezal, "When a guy gets arrested and comes in here drunk and disorderly, the last thing he wants to be bothered by is some philosophy."

"But, Chief," said Sgt. Hank, "it's about the rise and fall of civilizations . . ."

"What the hell does running a police station have to do with civilization?" said Teeheezal. "You can hang one of 'em up. One at a time they look like nature views, and those don't bother anybody."

"All right, Chief," said Sgt. Hank.

That day, it was the first one. When Teeheezal arrived for work the next day, it was the second. And after that, the third, and on through the five pictures, one each day; then the sequence was repeated. Teeheezal never said a word. Neither did Hank.

1914

There had been murders three nights in a row in Los Angeles City when the day came for the Annual Wilcox Police vs. Firemen Baseball Picnic.

The patrolmen were all playing stripped down to their undershirts and uniform pants, while the firemen had on real flannel baseball outfits that said Hot Papas across the back. It was late in the afternoon, late in the game, the firemen ahead seventeen to twelve in the eighth.

They were playing in the park next to the observatory. The patrol wagon was unhitched from its horses; the fire wagon stood steaming with its horses still in harness. Everyone in Wilcox knew not to bother the police or fireman this one day of the year.

Patrolman Al came to bat on his unicycle. He rolled into the batter's box. Patrolman Mack was held on second, and Patrolman Billy was hugging third. The firemen started their chatter. The pitcher wound up, took a long stretch and fired his goof-ball from behind his back with his glove hand while his right arm went through a vicious fastball motion.

Al connected with a meaty *crack*; the outfielders fell all over themselves and then charged toward the Bronson place. Al wheeled down to first with blinding speed, swung wide ignoring the fake from the second baseman, turned between second and third, balancing himself in a stop while he watched the right fielder come up with the ball on the first bounce four hundred feet away.

He leaned almost to the ground, swung around, became a blur of pedals and pumping feet, passed third; the catcher got set, pounding his mitt, stretched out for the throw. The umpire leaned down, the ball bounced into the mitt, the catcher jerked around —

Al hung upside down, still seated on the unicycle, six feet in the air over the head of the catcher, motionless, sailing forward in a long somersault.

He came down on home plate with a thud and a bounce.

"Safe!" said the ump, sawing the air to each side.

The benches emptied as the catcher threw off his wire mask. Punches flew like they did after every close call.

Teeheezal and Sgt. Hank stayed on the bench eating a bag of peanuts. The people in the stands were yelling and laughing.

"Oh, almost forgot," said Sgt. Hank, digging in his pants pocket. "Here."

He handed Teeheezal a postcard. It had an illegible postmark in a language with too many Zs. The front was an engraving of the statue of a hero whose name had six Ks in it.

Well, was at a café. Bunch of seedy-looking students sitting at the table next to mine grumbling in Slavvy talk. This car come by filled with plumed hats, made a wrong turn and started to back up. One of the students jumped on the running board and let some air into the guy in the back seat — 'bout five shots I say. Would tell you more but I was already lighting out for the territory. Place filled up with more police than anywhere I ever seen but the B.P.O.P.C. convention in Chicago back in '09. This was big excitement last week but I'm sure it will blow over. Will write more soon.

— Angus

PS: Even here, we got the news the Big Ditch is finally open.

It was the bottom of the eleventh and almost too dark to see when the bleeding man staggered onto left field and fell down.

The man in the cloak threw off all six patrolmen. Rube used the emergency pistol he'd gotten from the wagon just before the horses went crazy and broke the harness, scattering all the picnic stuff everywhere. He emptied the revolver into the tall dark man without effect. The beady-eyed man swept Rube aside with one hand and came toward Teeheezal.

The captain's foot slipped in all the stuff from the ball game.

The man in the dark cloak hissed and smiled crookedly, his eyes red like a rat's. Teeheezal reached down and picked up a Louisville Slugger. He grabbed it by the sweet spot, smashed the handle against the ground, and shoved the jagged end into the guy's chest.

"*Merde!*" said the man, and fell over.

Rube stood panting beside him. "I never missed, Chief," he said. "All six shots in the space of a half-dime."

"I saw," said Teeheezal, wondering at the lack of blood all over the place.

"*That* was my favorite piece of lumber," said Patrolman Mack.

"We'll get you a new one," said the captain.

They had the undertaker keep the body in his basement, waiting for somebody to claim it. After the investigation, they figured no one would, and they were right. But the law was the law.

Sgt. Hank scratched his head and turned to the chief, as they were looking at the man's effects.

"Why is it," he asked, "we're always having trouble with things in boxes?"

1915

Teeheezal got off the streetcar at the corner of what used to be Sunset and Ivar, but which the village council had now renamed, in honor of a motion picture studio out to the northwest, Sunset and Bison. Teeheezal figured some money had changed hands.

The P.E. Street Railway car bell jangled rapidly as it moved off toward Mount Lowe and the Cawston Ostrich Farms, and on down toward San Pedro.

In the park across from the station, Patrolmen Chester and Billy, almost indistinguishable behind their drooping walrus mustaches, were rousting out a couple, pointing to the *No Sparking* sign near the benches. He stood watching until the couple moved off down the street, while Billy and Chester, pleased with themselves, struck noble poses.

He went inside. The blotter on the desk was open:

Tues. 2:14 A.M. Two men, Alonzo Partain and D. Falcher Greaves, no known addresses, moving-picture acting extras, arrested D&D and on suspicion of criminal intent, in front of pawn shop at Gower and Sunset. Dressed in uniforms of the G.A.R. and the Confederate States and carrying muskets. Griffith studio notified. Released on bond to Jones, business manager, 4:30 A.M. Ptlmn. Mack. R.D.O.T.

The last phrase officially meant Released until Day Of Trial, but was station house for Rub-Down with Oak Towel, meaning Patrolman Mack, who was 6'11" and 350 pounds, had had to use considerable force dealing with them.

"Mack have trouble?" he asked Sgt. Hank.

"Not that Fatty said. In fact, he said when Mack carried them in, they were sleeping like babies."

"What's this Griffith thing?"

"Movie company out in Edendale, doing a War Between the States picture. Mack figured they were waiting till the hock shop opened to pawn their rifles and swords. This guy Jones was ready to blow his top, said they sneaked off the location late yesterday afternoon."

Teeheezal picked up the newspaper from the corner of the sergeant's desk. He scanned the headlines and decks. "What do you think of that?" he asked. "Guy building a whole new swanky residential area, naming it for his wife?"

"Ain't that something?" said Sgt. Hank. "Say, there's an ad for the new *Little Tramp* flicker, bigger than the film it's playing with. That man's a caution! He's the funniest guy I ever seen in my life. I hear he's a Limey. Got a mustache like an afterthought."

"I don't think anybody's been really funny since Flora Finch and John Bunny," said Teeheezal. "This Brit'll have to go some to beat *John Bunny Commits Suicide*."

"Well, you should give him a try," said Sgt. Hank. "Oh, forgot yesterday. Got another from Captain Angus. Here go." He handed it to Teeheezal.

It had a view of Lisbon, Portugal, as seen from some mackerel-slapper church tower, the usual address, and on the other half:

Well, I had another boat sink out from under me. This time it was a kraut torpedo, and we was on a neutral ship. Had trouble getting into the lifeboats because of all the crates of howitzer shells on deck. Was pulled down by the suck when she went under. Saw airplane bombs and such coming out the holes in the sides while I was under water. Last time I take a boat called after the Roman name for a third-rate country. Will write again soon.

— Angus

PS: How about the Willard-Johnson fight?

The windows suddenly rattled. Then came dull booms from far away.

"What's that?"

"Probably the Griffith people. They're filming the battle of

Chickamauga or something. Out in the country, way past the Ince Ranch, even."

"What they using, nitro?"

"Beats me. But there's nothing we can do about it. They got a county permit."

"Sometimes," said Teeheezal, "I think motion picture companies is running the town of Wilcox. And the whole U.S. of A. for that matter."

1916

Jesus Christ, smoking a cigar, drove by in a Model T.

Then the San Pedro trolleycar went by, full of Assyrians, with their spears and shields sticking out the windows. Teeheezal stood on the corner, hands on hips, watching them go by.

Over behind the corner of Prospect and Talmadge the walls of Babylon rose up, with statues of bird-headed guys and dancing elephants everywhere, and big moveable towers all around it. There were scaffolds and girders everywhere, people climbing up and down like ants. A huge banner stretched across the eight-block lot: *D.W. Griffith Production – The Mother and the Law.*

He walked back to the station house. Outside, the patrolmen were waxing the shining new black box-like truck with *Police Patrol* painted on the sides. It had brass hand-cranked sirens outside each front door, and brass handholds along each side above the running boards. They'd only had it for three days, and had yet to use it for a real emergency, though they'd joy-rode it a couple of times, sirens screaming, with the whole force hanging on or inside it, terrifying the fewer and fewer horses on the streets. Their own draught-horses had been put out to pasture at Sgt. Fatty's farm, and the stable out back converted into a garage.

The village fathers had also wired the station house for electricity, and installed a second phone in Teeheezal's office, along with an electric alarm bell for the squad room on his desk.

The town was growing. It was in the air. Even some moving pictures now said *Made in Wilcox, U.S.A.* at the end of them.

The blotter, after a busy weekend, was blank.

The postcard was on his desk. It had an English postmark, and was a view of the River Liffey.

Well, with the world the way it is, I thought the Old Sod would be a quiet place for the holiday. Had meant to write you boys a real letter, so went to the Main Post Office. Thought I'd have the place to myself. Boy, was I wrong about that. Last time I look for peace and quiet on Easter Sunday. Will write more later.

— Angus

PS: This will play heck with Daylight Summer Time.

Teeheezal was asleep when the whole force burst into his office and Sgt. Hank started unlocking the rack with the riot guns and rifles.

"What the ding-dong?" yelled Teeheezal, getting up off the floor.

"They say Pancho Villa's coming!" yelled a patrolman. "He knocked over a coupla banks in New Mexico!"

Teeheezal held up his hand. They all stopped moving. He sat back down in his chair and put his feet back up on his desk.

"Call me when he gets to Long Beach," he said.

Sgt. Hank locked the rack back up; then they all tiptoed out of the office.

"Look out!" "Get 'im! Get him!" "Watch it!!"

The hair-covered man tore the cell bars away and was gone into the moonlit night.

"Read everything you can, Hank," said Teeheezal. "Nothing else has worked."

"You sure you know what to do?" asked the captain.

"I know exactly *what* to do," said Patrolman Al. "I just don't *like* it. Are you sure Sgt. Hank is right?"

"Well, no. But if you got a better idea, tell me."

Al swallowed hard. He was on his big unicycle, the one with the chain drive.

There was a woman's scream from across the park.

"Make sure he's after *you*," said Teeheezal. "See you at the place. And, Al . . ."

"Say 'break a leg,' Captain."

"Uh . . . break a leg, Al."

Al was gone. They jumped in the police patrol truck and roared off.

They saw them coming through the moonlight, something on a wheel and a loping shape.

Al was nearly horizontal as he passed, eyes wide, down the ramp at the undertaker's, and across the cellar room. Patrolman Buster closed his eyes and jerked the vault door open at the second before Al would have smashed into it. Al flew in, chain whizzing, and something with hot meat breath brushed Buster.

Patrolman Al went up the wall and did a flip. The thing crashed into the wall under him. As Al went out, he jerked the broken baseball bat out of the guy it had been in for two years.

There was a hiss and a snarl behind him as he went out the door that Buster, eyes still closed, slammed to and triple-locked; then Mack and Billy dropped the giant steel bar in place.

Al stopped, then he and the unicycle fainted.

There were crashes and thumps for two hours, then whimpering sounds and squeals for a while.

They went in and beat what was left with big bars of silver, and put the broken Louisville Slugger back in what was left of the hole.

As they were warming their hands at the dying embers of the double fire outside the undertaker's that night, it began to snow. Before it was over, it snowed five inches.

1917

The captain walked by the *No Smooching* sign in the park on his way to talk to a local store owner about the third break-in in a month. The first two times the man had complained about the lack of police concern, first to Teeheezal, then the mayor.

Last night it had happened again, while Patrolmen Al and Billy had been watching the place.

He was on his way to tell the store owner it was an inside job, and to stare the man down. If the break-ins stopped, it had been the owner himself.

He passed by a hashhouse with a sign outside that said "Bratwurst and Sauerkraut 15¢." As he watched, the cook, wearing his hat and a knee-length apron, pulled the sign from the easel and replaced it with one that said "Victory cabbage and sausage 15¢."

There was a noise from the alleyway ahead, a bunch of voices "get 'im, get 'im"; then out of the alley ran something Teeheezal at first thought was a rat or a rabbit. But it didn't move like either of them, though it was moving as fast as it could.

A group of men and women burst out onto the street with rocks and chunks of wood sailing in front of them, thirty feet behind it. It dodged, then more people came from the other side of the street, and the thing turned to run away downtown.

The crowd caught up with it. There was a single yelp, then the thudding sounds of bricks hitting something soft. Twenty people stood over it, their arms moving. Then they stopped and cleared off the street and into the alleyways on either side without a word from anyone.

Teeheezal walked up to the pile of wood and stones with the rivulet of blood coming out from under it.

The captain knew the people to whom the dachshund had belonged, so he put it in a borrowed toe sack, and took that and put it on their porch with a note. *Sorry. Cpt. T.*

When he got within sight of the station house, Patrolman Chester came running out. "Captain! Captain!" he yelled.

"I know," said Teeheezal. "We're at war with Germany."

A month later another postcard arrived. It had a view of the Flatiron Building in New York City, had a Newark New Jersey postmark, and the usual address. On the left back it said:

Well, went to the first Sunday baseball game at the Polo Grounds. New York's Finest would have made you proud. They stood at attention at the national anthem then waited for the first pitch before they arrested McGraw and Mathewson for the Blue Law violation. You can imagine what happened next. My credo is: When it comes to a choice between a religion and baseball, baseball wins every time. Last time I go to a ball game until they find some way to play it at night. Ha ha. Will write more later.

— Angus

PS: Sorry about Buffalo Bill.

1918

If every rumor were true, the Huns would be in the White House by now. Teeheezal had just seen a government motion picture (before the regular one) about how to spot the Kaiser in case he was in the neighborhood spreading panic stories or putting cholera germs in your reservoir.

Now, last night, one had spread through the whole California coast about a U-boat landing. Everybody was sure it had happened at San Pedro, or Long Beach, or maybe it was in Santa Barbara, or along the Sun River, or somewhere. And somebody's cousin or uncle or friend had seen it happen, but when the Army got there there wasn't a trace.

The blotter had fourteen calls noted. One of them reminded the Wilcox police that the President himself was coming to Denver Colorado for a speech—coincidence, or what?

"I'm tired of war and the rumors of war," said Teeheezal.

"Well, people out here feel pretty helpless, watching what's going on ten thousand miles away. They got to contribute to the war effort *somehows*," said walrus-mustached Patrolman Billy.

Innocently enough, Patrolmen Mack and Rube decided to swing down by the railroad yards on their way in from patrol. It wasn't on their beat that night, but Sgt. Fatty had told them he'd seen some fat rabbits down there last week, and, tomorrow being their days off, they were going to check it over before buying new slingshots.

The patrol wagon careened by, men hanging on for dear life, picked up Teeheezal from his front yard, and roared off toward the railroad tracks.

The three German sailors went down in a typhoon of shotgun fire and hardly slowed them down at all.

What they did have trouble with was the giant lowland gorilla in the spiked *pickelhaube* helmet, and the eight-foot-high iron automaton with the letter *Q* stenciled across its chest.

The Federal men were all over the place; in the demolished railyard were two huge boxes marked for delivery to the Brown Palace in Denver.

"Good work, Captain Teeheezal," said the Secret Service man. "How'd you get the lowdown on this?"

"Ask the two patrolmen," he said.

At the same time, Mack and Rube said, "Dogged, unrelenting police procedures."

The postcard came later than usual that year, after the Armistice.

It was a plain card, one side for the address, the other for the message.

Well, here in Reykjavik things are really hopping. Today they became an independent nation, and the firewater's flowing like the geysers. It's going to be a three-day blind drunk for all I can figure. Tell Sgt. Fatty the fish are all as long as your leg here. Pretty neat country; not as cold as the name. Last time I come to a place where nobody's at work for a week. Will write more later.

— Angus

PS: Read they're giving women over thirty in Britain the vote — can we be far behind? Ha ha.

PPS: I seem to have a touch of the flu.

1919

Sgt. Hank didn't look up from the big thick book in his hand when Teeheezal came out of his office and walked over and poured himself a cup of steaming coffee. Say whatever else about the Peace mess in Europe, it was good to be off rationing again. Teeheezal's nephew had actually brought home some butter and steaks from a regular grocery store and butcher's last week.

"What's Wilson stepping in today?"

No answer.

"Hey!"

"Huh?! Oh, gosh, Chief. Was all wrapped up in this book. What'd you say?"

"Asking about the President. Seen the paper?"

"It's here somewhere," said Sgt. Hank. "Sorry, Chief, but this is about the greatest book I ever read."

"Damn thick square thing," said Teeheezal. He looked closely at a page. "Hey, that's a kraut book!"

"Austria. Well, yeah, it's by a German, but not like any German you ever thought of."

Teeheezal tried to read it, from what he remembered of when he went to school in Pennsylvania fifty years ago. It was full of two-dollar words, the sentences were a mile long, and the verb was way down at the bottom of the page.

"This don't make a goddamn bit of sense," he said. "This guy must be a college perfesser."

"It's got a cumulative effect," said Sgt. Hank. "It's about the rise of cultures and civilizations, and how Third Century B.C. China's just like France under Napoleon, and how all civilizations grow and get strong, and wither and die. Just like a plant or an animal, like they're alive themselves. And how when the civilization gets around to being an empire it's already too late, and they all end up with Caesars and Emperors and suchlike. Gosh, Chief, you can't imagine. I've read it twice already, and every time I get more and more out of it . . ."

"Where'd you get a book like that?"

"My cousin's a reporter at the Peace Commission conference — somebody told him about it, and he got one sent to me, thought it'd be something I like. I hear it's already out of print, and the guy's rewriting it."

"What else does this prof say?"

"Well, gee. A lot. Like I said, that all civilizations are more alike than not. That everything ends up in winter, like, after a spring and summer and fall." He pointed to the Cole picture on the wall — today it was *The Pastoral State*. "Like, like the pictures. Only a lot deeper. He says, for instance, that Europe's time is over—"

"It don't take a goddamned genius to know *that*," said Teeheezal.

"No — you don't understand. He started writing this in 1911, it says. He already knew it was heading for the big blooie. He says that Europe's turn's over, being top dog. Now it's the turn of America . . . and . . . and Russia."

Teeheezal stared at the sergeant.

"We just fought a fuckin' war to get rid of ideas like that," he said. "How much is a book like that worth, you think?"

"Why, it's priceless, Chief. There aren't any more of them. And it's full of great ideas!"

Teeheezal reached in his pocket and took out a twenty-dollar gold piece (six weeks of Sgt. Hank's pay) and put it on the sergeant's desk.

He picked up the big book by one corner of the cover, walked over, lifted the stove lid with the handle, and tossed the book in.

"We just settled Germany's hash," said Teeheezal. "It comes to it, we'll settle Russia's too."

He picked up the sports section and went into his office and closed the door.

Sgt. Hank sat with his mouth open. He looked back and forth from the gold piece to the stove to the picture to Teeheezal's door.

He was still doing that when Patrolmen Rube and Buster brought in someone on a charge of drunk and disorderly.

1920

Captain Teeheezal turned his Model T across the oncoming traffic at the corner of Conklin and Arbuckle. He ignored the horns and sound of brakes and pulled into his parking place in front of the station house.

A shadow swept across the hood of his car, then another. He looked up and out. Two condors flew against the pink southwest sky where the orange ball of the sun was ready to set.

Sgt. Fatty was just coming into view down the street, carrying his big supper basket, ready to take over the night shift.

Captain Teeheezal had been at a meeting with the new mayor about all the changes that were coming when Wilcox was incorporated as a city.

Sgt. Hank came running out, waving a telegram. "This just came for you."

Teeheezal tore open the Western Union envelope.

TO: ALL POLICE DEPARTMENTS, ALL CITIES, UNITED STATES OF AMERICA

FROM: OFFICE OF THE ATTORNEY GENERAL

1. VOLSTEAD ACT (PROHIBITION) IS NOW LAW STOP ALL POLICE DEPARTMENTS EXPECTED TO ENFORCE COMPLIANCE STOP

2. ROUND UP ALL THE REDS STOP

PALMER

Teeheezal and the sergeant raced to punch the big red button on the sergeant's desk near the three phones. Bells went off in the squad room in the tower atop the station. Sgt. Fatty's lunch basket was on the sidewalk out front when they got back outside. He reappeared from around back, driving the black box of a truck marked *Police Patrol*, driving with one hand. And cranking the hand siren with the other, until Sgt. Hank jumped in beside him and began working the siren on the passenger side.

Patrolmen came from everywhere, the squad room, the garage, running down the streets, their nightsticks in their hands—Al, Mack, Buster, Chester, Billy, and Rube—and jumped onto the back of the truck, some missing, grabbing the back fender and being dragged until they righted themselves and climbed up with their fellows.

Teeheezal stood on the running board, nearly falling off as they hit the curb at the park across the street, where the benches had a *No Petting* sign above them.

"Head for the dago part of town," said Teeheezal, taking his belt and holster through the window from Sgt. Hank. "Here," he said to the sergeant, knocking his hand away from the siren crank. "Lemme do that!"

The world was a high screaming whine, and a blur of speed and nightsticks in motion when there was a job to be done.

Introduction to

Occam's Ducks

I'm glad Oscar Micheaux and other filmmakers of the separate "race," or black cinema of the teens through the fifties, are getting their due. They made films, sometimes on less than nothing, sometimes with a budget that would approach one for a regular-movie short subject; to be shown in theaters in black neighborhoods in the North, and at segregated showings throughout the South (where the black audience all sat in the balconies, even though they were the *only* ones there; it was the same place they sat when a regular Hollywood film was shown). Sometimes Micheaux would get some actors, shoot some photos for stills and lobby cards, and take them around the South, saying to theater owners, "This is knocking 'em dead in Harlem and Chicago, but I only have three prints. Give me twenty dollars and I'll guarantee you'll get it first when I get the new prints." With the money he and his coworkers got that way, he'd go and make the movies, sometimes with different actors than had appeared in the stills . . . (Roberts Townsend and Rodriguez didn't *invent* credit-card filmmaking — it was just that credit cards weren't around back then; if they had been, Micheaux could have saved lots of shoe leather . . .).

Starring in these race pictures (usually the entire cast was black, with a token Honky or two) were black entertainers from vaudeville, theater, the *real* movies (these were the only times they'd ever have leads in films and be top-billed); plus people who seem to *only* have acted in race movies (and who probably had day jobs). The films were comedies, dramas, horror movies, gangster films, backstage musicals, even Westerns (*Harlem on the*

Prairie, The Bronze Buckaroo). In other words, the same stuff as Hollywood, only different—all the actors were black and they weren't under the Production Code, the *bête noire* of regular filmmaking from 1934 through the late fifties.

Black actors hopped back and forth from playing comedy relief, singing convicts, elevator operators, musicians, and back-lot natives in real movies to these films.

This story is dedicated to two people; the one to Mr. Moreland is self-explanatory after you've read the story. I needed someone about five years older for my purposes, but I'm not making up much. Mantan Moreland's filmography is about as eclectic a one as you'll find, outside Andy Devine's, Lionel Stander's, and Kate Freeman's. He was everywhere, he did everything; this was besides vaudeville and service-station openings too, I assume. And unlike them, he was in a couple of dozen race movies besides.

The other dedicatee takes a little explaining. Icky Twerp was Bill Camfield, who worked for KTVT Channel 11 in Ft. Worth in the '50s and '60s. In the afternoons and on Saturday mornings he was Icky Twerp, with a pinhead cowboy hat, big glasses, and some truly Bad Hair; he showed the Stooges on *Slam-Bang Theater*, with the help of gorilla stagehands named Ajax and Delphinium, on a pedal-powered projector he mounted like a bicycle, from which sparks shot out. That's six days a week of live TV: But wait! There's more!—Saturday nights he was Gorgon, the host of *Horror Chiller Shocker Theater* (which ran the *Shock Theater* package of Universal classics plus some dreck). Unlike Count Floyd, he was *good*: Not only that, he did stuff with videotape, then in its infancy, that matched some of what Kovacs was doing. Since it *looked* real, kids would scream and yell, "How'd he do that?"

I think his real job, the one he'd been hired for, was as announcer and newsman. Besides all that, when Cap'n Swabbie (another newsman) had had too much spinach the night before, Camfield filled in for him on *Popeye Theater*, on just before *Slam-Bang. . . .*

What does that have to do with race pictures? Not much. But Camfield and Moreland are what it's all about; work where, when, and how you can. And be funnier than hell, which both of them were. They're both gone. I miss them.

Twist the dial on your Weibach Machine to just after WWI. . . .

OCCAM'S DUCKS

Producers Releasing Corporation Executive: Bill, you're forty-five minutes behind your shooting schedule.

Beaudine: You mean, someone's waiting to see this crap??

— William "One-Shot" Beaudine

For a week, late in the year 1919, some of the most famous people in the world seemed to have dropped off its surface.

The Griffith Company, filming the motion picture *The Idol Dancer*, with the palm trees and beaches of Florida standing in for the South Seas, took a shooting break.

The mayor of Fort Lauderdale invited them for a twelve-hour cruise aboard his yacht, the *Gray Duck*. They sailed out of harbor on a beautiful November morning. Just after noon a late-season hurricane slammed out of the Caribbean.

There was no word of the movie people, the mayor, his yacht, or the crew for five days. The Coast Guard and the Navy sent out every available ship. Two seaplanes flew over shipping lanes as the storm abated.

Richard Barthelmess came down to Florida at first news of the disappearance, while the hurricane still raged. He went out with the crew of the Great War U-boat chaser, the *Berry Islands*. The seas were so rough the captain ordered them back in after six hours.

The days stretched on; three, four. The Hearst newspapers put out extras, speculating on the fate of Griffith, Gish, the other actors, the mayor. The weather cleared and calm returned. There were no sightings of debris or oil slicks. Reporters did stories on the Marie Celeste mystery. Hearst himself called in spiritualists in an attempt to contact the presumed dead director and stars.

On the morning of the sixth day, the happy yachting party sailed back in to harbor.

First there were sighs of relief.

Then the reception soured. Someone in Hollywood pointed out that Griffith's next picture, to be released nationwide in three weeks, was called *The Greatest Question* and was about life after death, and the attempts of mediums to contact the dead.

W. R. Hearst was not amused, and he told the editors not to be amused, either.

Griffith shrugged his shoulders for the newsmen. "A storm came up. The captain put in at the nearest island. We rode out the cyclone. We had plenty to eat and drink, and when it was over, we came back."

The island was called Whale Cay. They had been buffeted by the heavy seas and torrential rains the first day and night, but made do by lantern light and electric torches, and the dancing fire of the lightning in the bay around them. They slept stacked like cordwood in the crowded belowdecks.

They had breakfasted in the sunny eye of the hurricane late next morning up on deck. Many of the movie people had had strange dreams, which they related as the far-wall clouds of the back half of the hurricane moved lazily toward them.

Nell Hamilton, the matinee idol who had posed for paintings on the cover of the *Saturday Evening Post* during the Great War, told his dream. He was in a long valley with high cliffs surrounding him. On every side, as far as he could see, the ground, the arroyos were covered with the bones and tusks of elephants. Their cyclopean skulls were tumbled at all angles. There were millions and millions of them, as if every pachyderm that had ever lived had died there. It was near dark, the sky overhead paling, the jumbled bones around him becoming purple and indistinct.

Over the narrow valley, against the early stars a strange light appeared. It came from a searchlight somewhere beyond the cliffs, and projected onto a high bank of noctilucent cirrus was a winged black shape. From somewhere behind him a telephone rang with a sense of urgency. Then he'd awakened with a start.

Lillian Gish, who'd only arrived at the dock the morning they left, going directly from the Florida Special to the yacht, had spent the whole week before at the new studio at Mamaroneck, New York, overseeing its completion and directing her sister in a comedy feature. On the tossing, pitching yacht, she'd had a terrible time getting to sleep. She had dreamed, she said, of being an old woman, or being dressed like one, and carrying a Browning semiautomatic shotgun. She was being stalked through a swamp by a crazed man with words tattooed on his fists, who sang hymns as he followed her. She was very frightened in her nightmare, she said, not by being pursued, but by the idea of being old. Everyone laughed at that.

They asked David Wark Griffith what he'd dreamed of. "Nothing in particular," he said. But he had dreamed: There was a land of fire and eruptions, where men and women clad in animal skins fought against giant crocodiles and lizards, much like in his film of ten years before, *Man's Genesis*. Hal Roach, the upstart competing producer, was there, too, looking older, but he seemed to be telling Griffith what to do. D. W. couldn't imagine such a thing. Griffith attributed the dream to the rolling of the ship, and to an especially fine bowl of turtle soup he'd eaten that morning aboard the *Gray Duck*, before the storm hit.

Another person didn't tell of his dreams. He saw no reason to. He was the stubby steward who kept them all rocking with laughter through the storm with his antics and jokes. He said nothing to the film people, because he had a dream so very puzzling to him, a dream unlike any other he'd ever had.

He had been somewhere; a stage, a room. He wore some kind of livery; a doorman's or a chauffeur's outfit. There was a big Swede standing right in front of him, and the Swedish guy was made up like a Japanese or a Chinaman. He had a big mustache like Dr. Fu Manchu on the book jackets, and he wore a tropical planter's suit and hat. Then this young Filipino guy had run into the room yelling a mile a minute, and the Swede asked, "Why number-three son making noise like motorboat?", and the Filipino yelled something else and ran to a closet door and opened it, and a white feller fell out of it with a knife in his back.

Then a voice behind the steward said, "Cut!" and then said, "Let's do it again," and the guy with the knife in his back got up and went back into the closet, and the Filipino guy went back out the door, and the big Swede took two puffs on a Camel and handed it to someone and then just stood there, and the voice behind the steward said to him, "Okay," and then, "This time, Mantan, bug your eyes out a little more." The dream made no sense at all.

After their return on the yacht, the steward had performed at the wrap party for the productions. An Elk saw him, and they hired him to do their next initiation follies. Then he won a couple of amateur nights, and played theaters in a couple of nearby towns. He fetched and carried around at the mayor's house in the daytime, and rolled audiences in the aisles at night.

One day early in 1920, he looked in his monthly pay envelope and found it was about a quarter of what he'd earned in the theater the last week.

He gave notice, hit the boards running, and never looked back.

So it was that two years later, on April 12, 1922, Mantan Brown found himself, at eight in the morning, in front of a large building in Fort Lee, New Jersey. He had seen the place the year before, when he had been playing a theater down the street. Before the Great War, it had been part of Nestor or Centaur, or maybe the Thantouser Film Company. The Navy had taken it over for a year to make toothbrushing and trench-foot movies to show new recruits, and films for the public on how to spot the Kaiser in case he was working in disguise on your block.

It was a commercial studio again, but now for rent by the day or week. Most film production had moved out to the western coast, but there were still a few — in Jersey, out on Astoria, in Manhattan itself — doing some kind of business in the East.

Mantan had ferried over before sunup, taken a streetcar, and checked in to the nearby hotel, one that let Negroes stay there as long as they paid in advance.

He went inside, past a desk and a yawning guard who waved him on, and found a guy in coveralls with a broom, which, Mantan had learned in two years in the business, was where you went to find out stuff.

"I'm looking for The Man with the Shoes," he said.

"You and everybody else," said the handyman. He squinted. "I seen you somewhere before."

"Not unless you pay to get in places I wouldn't," said Mantan.

"Bessie Smith?" said the workman. "I mean, you're not Bessie Smith. But why I think of her when I see you?"

Mantan smiled. "Toured with her and Ma Rainey last year. I tried to tell jokes, and people threw bricks and things at me till they came back on and sang. Theater Owners' Booking Agency. The TOBA circuit."

The guy smiled. "Tough On Black Asses, huh?"

"You got that right."

"Well, I thought you were pretty good. Caught you somewhere in the City. Went there for the jazz."

"Thank you—"

"Willie." The janitor stuck out his hand, shook Mantan's.

"Thank you, Willie. Mantan Brown." He looked around. "Can you tell me what the hoodoo's going on here?"

"Beats me. I done the strangest things I ever done this past week. I work here—at the studio itself, fetchin' and carryin' and ridin' a mop. Guy rented it two weeks ago—guy with the shoes is named Mr. Meister, a real yegg. He must be makin' a race movie—the waiting room, second down the hall to the left—looks like Connie's Club on Saturday night after all the slummers left. The guy directing the thing—Meister's just the watch chain—name's Slavo, Marcel Slavo. Nice guy, real deliberate and intense—somethin's wrong with him, looks like a jakeleg or blizzard-bunny to me—he's got some great scheme or somethin'. I been painting scenery for it. Don't make sense. You'd think they were making another *Intolerance*, but they only got cameras coming in Thursday and Friday, shooting time for a two-reeler. Other than that, Mr. Brown, I don't know a thing more than you do."

"Thanks."

The waiting room wasn't like Connie's; it was like a TOBA tent-show alumnus reunion. There was lots of yelling and hooting when he came in.

"Mantan!" "Why, Mr. Brown!" "Looky who's here!"

As he shook hands he saw he was the only comedian there.

There was a pretty young woman, a high-yellow he hadn't seen before, sitting very quietly by herself. She had on a green wool dress and toque, and a weasel-trimmed wrap rested on the back of her chair.

"Somethin', huh?" asked Le Roi Chicken, a dancer from Harlem who'd been in revues with both Moran and Mack and Buck and Bubbles. "Her name's Pauline Christian."

"Hey, Mr. Brown," said someone across the room. "I thought you was just a caution in *Mantan of the Apes!*"

Mantan smiled, pleased. They'd made the film in three days, mostly in the Authentic African Gardens of a white guy's plantation house in Sea Island, Georgia, during the mornings and afternoons before his tent-shows at night. Somebody had called somebody who'd called somebody else to get him the job. He hadn't seen the film yet, but from what he remembered of making it, it was probably pretty funny.

"I'm here for the five dollars a day, just like all of you," he said.

"That's funny," said fifteen people in unison, "us all is getting ten dollars a day!"

While they were laughing, a door opened in the far corner. A tough white mug who looked like an icebox smoking a cigar came out, yelled for quiet, and read names off a list.

Mantan, Pauline Christian, and Lorenzo Fairweather were taken into an office.

"Welcome, welcome," said Mr. Meister, who was a shorter version of the guy who'd called off the names on the clipboard.

Marcel Slavo sat in a chair facing them. Willie had been right. Slavo had dark spots under his eyes and looked like he slept with his face on a waffle iron. He was pale as a slug, and smoking a Fatima in a holder.

"The others, the extras, will be fitted today, then sent home. They'll be back Thursday and Friday for the shooting. You three, plus Lafayette Monroe and Arkady Jackson, are the principals. Mr. Meister here" — Meister waved to them and Marcel continued—"has got money to shoot a two-reeler race picture. His friends would like to expand their movie investments. We'll go on to the script later, rehearse tomorrow and Wednesday, and shoot for two days. I know that's unusual, not the way you're all used to working, but this isn't the ordinary two-reeler. I want us all to be proud of it."

"And I—and my backers—want it in the can by Friday night," said Mr.

Meister.

They laughed nervously.

"The two other principals will join us Wednesday. We can cover most of their shots Thursday afternoon," said Slavo.

He then talked with Lorenzo about the plays he'd been in, and with Mantan about his act. "*Mantan of the Apes* was why I wanted you," he said. "And Pauline," he turned to her, "you've got great potential. I saw you in *Upholding the Race* last week. A small part, but you brought something to it. I think we can make a funny satire here, one people will remember." He seemed tired. He stopped a moment.

"And —?" said Meister.

"And I want to thank you. There's a movie out there right now. It's the apotheosis of screen art —"

"What?" asked Lorenzo.

"The bee's knees," said Mantan.

"Thank you, Mr. Brown. It's the epitome of moviemaking. It's in trouble because it was made in Germany; veterans' groups picketing outside, all that stuff everywhere it plays. There's never been anything like it, not in America, France, or Italy. And it's just a bunch of bohunks keeping people away from it. Well, it's art, and they can't stop it."

"And," said Meister conspiratorially, "they can't keep us from sending it up, making a comedy of it, and making some bucks."

"Now," said Slavo, all business. "I'd like you to make yourselves comfortable, while I read through what we've got for you. Some of the titles are just roughs, you'll get the idea though, so bear with me. We'll have a title writer go over it after we finish the shooting and cutting. Here's the scene: We open on a shot of cotton fields in Alabama, usual stuff; then we come in on a sign: County Fair September 15–22. Then we come down on a shot of the side-show booths, the midway, big posters, et cetera."

And so it was that Mantan Brown found himself in the production of *The Medicine Cabinet of Dr. Killpatient.*

Mantan was on the set, watching them paint scenery.

Slavo was rehearsing Lafayette Monroe and Arkady Jackson, who'd come in that morning. They were still in their street clothes. Monroe must have been seven feet three inches tall.

"Here we go," said Slavo, "try these." What he'd given Lafayette were two halves of Ping-Pong balls with black dots drawn on them. The giant placed them over his eyes.

"Man, man," said Arkady.

Slavo was back ten feet, holding both arms and hands out, one inverted, forming a square with his thumbs and index fingers.

"Perfect!" he said. "Mantan?"

"Yes, Mr. Slavo?"

"Let's try the scene where you back around the corner and bump into him."

"Okay," said Brown.

They ran through it. Mantan backed into Lafayette, did a freeze, reached back, turned, did a double take, and was gone.

Arkady was rolling on the floor. The Ping-Pong balls popped off Lafayette's face as he exploded with laughter.

"Okay," said Slavo, catching his breath. "Okay. This time, Lafayette, just as he touches you, turn your head down a little and toward him. Slowly, but just so you're looking at him when he's looking at you."

"I can't see a thing, Mr. Slavo."

"There'll be holes in the pupils when we do it. And remember, a line of smoke's going to come up from the floor where Mr. Brown was when we get finished with the film."

"I'm afraid I'll bust out laughing," said Lafayette.

"Just think about money," said Slavo. "Let's go through it one more time. Only this time, Mantan . . ."

"Yes, sir?"

"This time, Mantan, bug your eyes out a little bit more."

The hair stood up on his neck.

"Yes sir, Mr. Slavo."

The circles under Slavo's eyes seemed to have darkened as the day wore on.

"I would have liked to have gone out to the West Coast with everyone else," he said, as they took a break during the run-throughs. "Then I realized this was a wide-open field, the race pictures. I make exactly the movies I want. They go out to 600 theaters in the North, and 850 in the South. They make money. Some go into state's rights distribution. I'm happy. Guys like Mr. Meister are happy—" He looked up to the catwalk overhead where Meister usually watched from, "The people who see the films are happy."

He put another cigarette in his holder. "I live like I want," he said. Then, "Let's get back to work, people."

"You tell her in this scene," said Slavo, "that as long as you're heeled, she has nothing to fear from the somnam—from what Lorenzo refers to as the Sleepy Guy."

He handed Mantan a slim straight razor.

Mantan looked at him. Pauline looked back and forth between them.

"Yes, Mr. Brown?" asked Slavo.

"Well, Mr. Slavo," he said. "This film's going out to every Negro theater in the U.S. of A., isn't it?"

"Yes."

"Well, you'll have everybody laughing at it, but not with it."

"What do you mean?"

"This is the kind of razor cadets use to trim their mustaches before they go down to the dockyards to wait for the newest batch of Irish women for the sporting houses."

"Well, that's the incongruity, Mr. Brown."

"Willie? Willie?"

The workman appeared. "Willie, get $2.50 from Mr. Meister, and run down to the drugstore and get a Double Duck Number 2 for me to use."

"What the hell?" asked Meister, who'd been watching. "A tree's a tree. A rock's a rock. A razor's a razor. Use that one."

"It won't be right, Mr. Meister. Mainly, it won't be as funny as it can be."

"It's a tiny razor," said Meister. "It's funny, if you think it can defend both of you."

Slavo watched and waited.

"Have you seen the films of Mr. Mack Sennett?" asked Brown.

"Who hasn't? But he can't get work now either," said Meister.

"I mean his earlier stuff. Kops. Custard. Women in bathing suits."

"Of course."

"Well, Mr. Sennett once said, if you bend it, it's funny. If you break it, it isn't."

"Now a darkie is telling me about the Aristophanic roots of comedy!" said Meister, throwing up his hands. "What about this theory of Sennett's?"

"If I use the little razor," said Mantan, "it breaks."

Meister looked at him a moment, then reached in his pocket and pulled three big greenbacks off a roll and handed them to Willie. Willie left.

"I want to see this," said Meister. He crossed his arms. "Good thing you're not getting paid by the hour."

Willie was back in five minutes with a rectangular box. Inside was a cold stainless steel thing, mother-of-pearl handled with a gold thumb-stop, half the size of a meat cleaver. It could have been used to dry-shave the mane off one of Mack Sennett's lions in fifteen seconds flat.

"Let's see you bend that!" said Meister.

They rehearsed the scene, Mantan and Pauline. When Brown flourished the razor, opening it with a quick look, a shift of his eyes each way, three guys who'd stopped painting scenery to watch fell down in the corner. Meister left.

Slavo said, "For the next scene . . ."

It was easy to see Slavo wasn't getting whatever it was that was keeping him going.

The first morning of filming was a nightmare. Slavo was irritable. They shot sequentially for the most part (with a couple of major scenes held back for the next day). All the takes with the extras at the carnival were done early that morning, and some of them let go, with enough remaining to cover the inserts with the principals.

The set itself was disorienting. The painted shadows and reflections were so convincing Mantan found himself squinting when moving away from a painted wall because he expected bright light to be in his eyes there. There was no real light on the set except that which came in from the old overhead glass roof of the studio, and a few arc lights used for fill.

The walls were painted at odd angles; the merry-go-round was only two feet tall, with people standing around it. The Ferris wheel was an ellipsoid of neon, with one car with people (two Negro midgets) in it, the others diminishingly smaller, then larger around the circumference. The tents looked like something out of a Jamaica ginger extract-addict's nightmare.

Then they filmed the scene of Dr. Killpatient at his sideshow, opening his giant medicine cabinet. The front was a mirror, like in a hotel bathroom. There was a crowd of extras standing in front of it, but what was reflected was a distant, windswept mountain (and in Alabama, too). Mantan watched them do the scene. As the cabinet opened, the mountain disappeared; the image revealed was of Mantan, Pauline, Lorenzo, and the extras.

"How'd you do that, Mr. Slavo?" asked one of the extras.

"Fort Lee magic," said Meister from his position on the catwalk above.

At last the morning was over. As they broke for lunch they heard loud voices coming from Meister's office. They all went to the drugstore across the street.

"I hear it's snow," said Arkady.

"Jake."

"Morphine."

"He's kicking the gong around," said another extra.

One guy who had read a lot of books said, "He's got a surfeit of the twentieth century."

"Whatever, this film's gonna scare the bejeezus out of Georgia, funny or not."

Mantan said nothing. He chewed at his sandwich slowly and drank his cup of coffee, looking out the window toward the cold façade of the studio. It looked just like any other warehouse building.

Slavo was a different man when they returned. He moved very slowly, taking his time setting things up.

"Okay . . . let's . . . do this right. And all the extras can go home early. Lafayette," he said to the black giant, who was putting in his Ping-Pong ball eyes, "carry . . . Pauline across to left. Out of sight around the pyramid. Then, extras. Come on, jump around a lot. Shake your torches. Then off left. Simple. Easy. Places. Camera. Action! That's right, that's right. Keep moving, Lafe, slow but steady. Kick some more, Pauline. Good. Now. Show some disgust, people. You're indignant. He's got your choir soloist from the

A.M.E. church. That's it. Take—"

"Stop it! Stop the camera thing. Cut!" yelled Meister from the catwalk.

"What?!" yelled Slavo.

"You there! You!" yelled Meister. "Are you blind?"

An extra wearing sunglasses pointed to himself. "Me?"

"If you ain't blind, what're you doing with sunglasses on? It's night!"

"How the hell would anybody know?" asked the extra, looking around at the painted square moon in the sky. "This is the most fucked-up thing I ever been involved with in all my life."

"You can say that again," said someone else.

"You," said Meister to the first extra. "You're fired. Get out. You only get paid through lunch." He climbed down as the man started to leave, throwing his torch with the papier-mâché flames on the floor. "Give me your hat," said Meister. He took it from the man. He jammed it on his head and walked over with the rest of the extras, who had moved back off-camera. "I'll do the damn scene myself."

Slavo doubled up with laughter in his chair.

"What? What is it?" asked Meister.

"If . . . if they're going to notice a guy . . . with sunglasses," laughed Slavo, "they're . . . damn sure gonna notice a white man!"

Meister stood fuming.

"Here go," said Mantan, walking over to the producer. He took the hat from him, pulled it down over his eyes, took off his coat. He got in the middle of the extras and picked up an unused pitchfork. "Nobody'll notice one more darkie," he said.

"Let's do it, then," said Slavo. "Pauline? Lafayette?"

"Meister," said a voice behind them. Three white guys in dark suits and shirts stood there. How long they had been watching no one knew. "Meister, let's go talk," said one of them.

You could hear loud noises through the walls of Meister's office. Meister came out in the middle of a take, calling for Slavo.

"Goddamnit to hell!" said Slavo. "Cut!" He charged into Meister's office. There was more yelling. Then it was quiet. Then only Meister was heard.

Lafayette Monroe took up most of the floor, sprawled out, drinking water from a quart jug. He wore a black body suit, and had one of the Ping-

Pong balls out of his eye socket. Arkady had on his doctor's costume—frock coat, hair like a screech owl, big round glasses, gloves with dark lines drawn on the backs of them. A big wobbly crooked cane rested across his knees.

Pauline fanned herself with the hem of her long white nightgown.

"I smell trouble," said Lorenzo. "Big trouble."

The guys with the dark suits came out and went past them without a look.

Meister came out. He took his usual place, clambering up the ladder to the walkway above the set. He leaned on a light railing, saying nothing.

After a while, a shaken-looking Marcel Slavo came out.

"Ladies and gentlemen," he said. "Let's finish this scene, then set up the next one. By that time, there'll be another gentleman here to finish up today, and to direct you tomorrow. I am off this film after the next scene . . . so let's make this take a good one, okay?"

They finished the chase setup, and the pursuit. Slavo came and shook their hands, and hugged Pauline. "Thank you all," he said, and walked out the door.

Ten minutes later another guy came in, taking off his coat. He looked up at Meister, at the actors, and said, "Another coon pitcher, huh? Gimme five minutes with the script." He went into Meister's office.

Five minutes later he was out again. "What a load of hooey," he said. "Okay," he said to Mantan and the other actors, "Who's who?"

When they were through the next afternoon, Meister peeled bills off a roll, gave each of the principals an extra five dollars, and said, "Keep in touch."

Mantan took his friend Freemore up to the place they told him Marcel Slavo lived.

They knocked three times before there was a muffled answer.

"Oh, Mr. Brown," said Slavo, as he opened the door. "Who's this?"

"This is Joe Freemore. We're just heading out on the 'chitlin circuit' again."

"Well, I can't do anything for you," said Slavo. "I'm through. Haven't you heard? I'm all washed up."

"We wanted to show you our act."

"Why me?"

"Because you're an impartial audience," said Mantan.

Slavo went back in, sat in a chair at the table. Mantan saw that along with bootleg liquor bottles and ashtrays full of Fatima and Spud butts, the two razors from the movie lay on the table. Slavo followed his gaze.

"Souvenirs," he said. "Something to remind me of all my work. I remember what you said, Mr. Brown. It has been a great lesson to me."

"Comfortable, Mr. Slavo?" asked Freemore.

"Okay. Rollick me."

"Empty stage," said Mantan. "Joe and I meet."

"Why, hello!" said Joe.

"Golly, hi," said Mantan, pumping his hand. "I ain't seen you since—"

"—it was longer ago than that. You had just—"

"—that's right. And I hadn't been married for more than—"

"—seemed a lot longer than that. Say, did you hear about—"

"—you don't say! Why, I saw her not more than—"

"—it's the truth! And the cops say she looked—"

"—that bad, huh? Who'd have thought it of her? Why she used to look—"

"—speaking of her, did you hear that her husband—"

"—what? How could he have done that? He always—"

"—yeah, but not this time. I tell you he—"

"—that's impossible! Why, they told me he'd—"

"—that long, huh? Well, got to go. Give my best to—"

"—I sure will. Goodbye."

"Goodbye."

They turned to Slavo.

"They'll love it down in Mississippi," he said.

It was two weeks later, and the South Carolina weather was the crummiest, said the locals, in half a century. It had been raining—a steady, continuous, monotonous thrumming—for three days.

Mantan stopped under the hotel marquee, looking out toward a gray two-by-four excuse for a city park, where a couple of ducks and a goose were kicking up their feet and enjoying life to its fullest.

He went inside and borrowed a Columbia newspaper from the catatonic day manager. He went up the four flights to his semiluxury room, took off his sopping raincoat and threw it over the three-dollar Louis Quatorze knock-off chair, and spread the paper out on the bed.

He was reading the national news page when he came across the story from New Jersey.

The police said that, according to witnesses, during the whole time of the attack, the razor-wielding maniac had kept repeating, "Bend, d–n it, don't break! Bend, d–n it, don't break!"

The names of the victims were unknown to Mantan, but the attacker's name was Meister.

Twenty years later, while he was filming *Mr. Pilgrim Progresses*, a lady brought him a War Bond certificate, and a lobby card for him to autograph.

The card was from *The Medicine Cabinet of Dr. Killpatient*, Breezy Laff Riot. There were no credits on it, but there on the card were Mantan, Pauline Christian, and Lorenzo Fairweather, and behind them the giant Lafayette Monroe in his medicine cabinet.

Mantan signed it with a great flourish with one of those huge pencils you get at county fairs when you knock down the Arkansas kitty.

He had never seen the film, never knew till now that it had been released.

As the lady walked away, he wondered if the film had been any good at all.

For Mr. Moreland, and for Icky Twerp.

INTRODUCTION TO

DER UNTERGANG DES ABENDLANDESMENSCHEN

This is an early story, and has had a remarkably long life (neither of its subjects ever gets stale); it was written in early 1975, and came out on that glorious day, the first one of MidAmericon, the 1976 World Science Fiction Convention in Kansas City, when six of my stories were on sale at once. (You tell that to kids nowadays, they won't believe you.) In fact, I'd made the editors of this one pay me in cash at the convention, because I knew I'd need it there. . . .

This is the most movie-movie of my stories — it takes place inside one, which none of the others do (well, does part of "French Scenes" or doesn't it?). The others are about making movies, or the results, or some sidebar. It takes a while to figure this out (but I just told you). It's about German Expressionist cinema, some years before Woody Allen's *Shadows and Fog*; it's about cowboy-heroes; it's got it all: action, adventure, humor, chills, the moral message.

This is the second time in the book (though the first in terms of when it was written) you'll run across Oswald Spengler in my stories; this time, the title. His book was an international bestseller (two volumes of truly heavy-going history/philosophy) current at about the time this story takes place. Spengler's title was translated over here as *The Decline of the West*; mine for the story comes out "The Undergoing of the Men of the Western Lands" or "Sunset of the Cowboy," if you will. It seemed to fit, from the first day I started work on this.

David J. Skal, in his *V Is for Vampire* (1995), an encyclopedic treatment of the subject, touches on some of the same matter in a couple of entries, without his ever having read this story. It was out there, all the time; I was just the first guy to have written about it.

Der Untergang des
Abendlandesmenschen

They rode through the flickering landscape to the tune of organ music.

Bronco Billy, short like an old sailor, and William S., tall and rangy as a windblown pine. Their faces, their horses, the landscape all darkened and became light; were at first indistinct, then sharp and clear as they rode across one ridge and down into the valley beyond.

Ahead of them, in much darker shades, was the city of Bremen, Germany.

Except for the organ and piano music, it was quiet in most of Europe.

In the vaults below the Opera, in the City of Lights, Erik the phantom played the *Toccata and Fugue* while the sewers ran blackly by.

In Berlin, Cesare the somnambulist slept. His mentor Caligari lectured at the University, and waited for his chance to send the monster through the streets.

Also in Berlin, Dr. Mabuse was dead and could no longer control the underworld.

But in Bremen . . .

In Bremen, something walked the night.

To the cities of china eggs and dolls, in the time of sawdust bread and the price of six million marks for a postage stamp, came Bronco Billy and William S. They had ridden hard for two days and nights, and the horses were heavily lathered.

They reined in, and tied their mounts to a streetlamp on the Wilhelmstrasse.

"What say we get a drink, William S.?" asked the shorter cowboy. "All this damn flickering gives me a headache."

William S. struck a pose three feet away from him, turned his head left and right, and stepped up to the doors of the *Gasthaus* before them.

With his high-pointed hat and checked shirt, William S. looked like a weatherbeaten scarecrow, or a child's version of Abraham Lincoln before the beard. His eyes were like shiny glass, through which some inner hellfires shone.

Bronco Billy hitched up his pants. He wore Levis, which on him looked too large, a dark vest, lighter shirt, big leather chaps with three tassels at hip, knee, and calf. His hat seemed three sizes too big.

Inside the tavern, things were murky gray, black, and stark white. And always, the flickering.

They sat down at a table and watched the clientele. Ex-soldiers, in the remnants of uniforms, seven years after the Great War had ended. The unemployed, spending their last few coins on beer. The air was thick with gray smoke from pipes and cheap cigarettes.

Not too many people had noticed the entrance of William S. and Bronco Billy.

Two had.

"Quirt!" said an American captain, his hand on his drinking buddy, a sergeant.

"What?" asked the sergeant, his hand on the barmaid.

"Look who's here!"

The sergeant peered toward the haze of flickering gray smoke where the cowboys sat.

"Damn!" he said.

"Want to go over and chat with 'em?" asked the captain.

"&%#*$ no!" cursed the sergeant. "This ain't our #%&*!*ing picture."

"I suppose you're right," said the captain, and returned to his wine.

"You must remember, my friend," said William S. after the waiter brought them beer, "that there can be no rest in the pursuit of evil."

"Yeah, but hell, William S., this is a long way from home."

William S. lit a match, put it to a briar pipe containing his favorite shag tobacco. He puffed on it a few moments, then regarded his companion across his tankard.

"My dear Bronco Billy," he said. "No place is too far to go in order to thwart the forces of darkness. This is something Dr. Helioglabulus could not handle by himself, else he should not have summoned us."

"Yeah, but William S., my butt's sore as a rizen after two days in the saddle. I think we should bunk down before we see this doctor fellow."

"Ah, that's where you're wrong, my friend," said the tall, hawk-nosed cowboy. "Evil never sleeps. Men must."

"Well, I'm a man," said Bronco Billy. "I say let's sleep."

Just then, Dr. Helioglabulus entered the tavern.

He was dressed as a Tyrolean mountain guide, in *Lederhosen* and feathered cap, climbing boots and suspenders. He carried with him an alpenstock, which made a large *clunk* each time it touched the floor.

He walked through the flickering darkness and smoke, and stood in front of the table with the two cowboys.

William S. had risen.

"Dr. —" he began.

"Eulenspiegel," said the other, an admonitory finger to his lips.

Bronco Billy rolled his eyes heavenward.

"Dr. Eulenspiegel, I'd like you to meet my associate and chronicler, Mr. Bronco Billy."

The doctor clicked his heels together.

"Have a chair," said Bronco Billy, pushing one out from under the table with his boot. He tipped his hat up off his eyes.

The doctor, in his comic opera outfit, sat.

"Helioglabulus," whispered William S., "whatever are you up to?"

"I had to come incognito. There are . . . others who should not learn of my presence here."

Bronco Billy looked from one to the other and rolled his eyes again.

"Then the game is afoot?" asked William S., his eyes more alight than ever.

"Game such as man has never before seen," said the doctor.

"I see," said William S., his eyes narrowing as he drew on his pipe. "Moriarty?"

"Much more evil."

"More evil?" asked the cowboy, his fingertips pressed together. "I cannot imagine such."

"Neither could I, up until a week ago," said Helioglabulus. "Since then, the city has experienced wholesale terrors. Rats run the streets at night, invade houses. This tavern will be deserted by nightfall. The people lock their doors and say prayers, even in this age. They are reverting to the old superstitions."

"They have just cause?" asked William S.

"A week ago, a ship pulled into the pier. On board was — one man!" He paused for dramatic effect. Bronco Billy was unimpressed. The doctor continued. "The crew, the passengers were gone. Only the captain was aboard, lashed to the wheel. And he was — drained of blood!"

Bronco Billy became interested.

"You mean," asked William S., bending over his beer, "that we are dealing with — the undead?"

"I am afraid so," said Dr. Helioglabulus, twisting his mustaches.

"Then we shall need the proper armaments," said the taller cowboy.

"I have them," said the doctor, taking cartridge boxes from his backpack.

"Good!" said William S. "Bronco Billy, you have your revolver?"

"What!? Whatta ya mean, 'Do you have your revolver?' Just what do you mean? Have you ever seen me without my guns, William S.? Are you losing your mind?"

"Sorry, Billy," said William S., looking properly abashed.

"Take these," said Helioglabulus.

Bronco Billy broke open his two Peacemakers, dumped the .45 shells on the table. William S. unlimbered his two Navy .36s and pushed the recoil rod down in the cylinders. He punched each cartridge out onto the tabletop.

Billy started to load up his pistols, then took a closer look at the shells, held one up and examined it.

"Goddamn, William S.," he yelled. "Wooden bullets! Wooden bullets?"

Helioglabulus was trying to wave him to silence. The tall cowboy tried to put his hand on the other.

Everyone in the beer hall had heard him. There was a deafening silence, all the patrons turned toward their table.

"Damn," said Bronco Billy. "You can't shoot a wooden bullet fifteen feet and expect it to hit the broad side of a corncrib. What the hell we gonna shoot wooden bullets at?"

The tavern began to empty, people rushing from the place, looking back in terror. All except five men at a far table.

"I am afraid, my dear Bronco Billy," said William S., "that you have frightened the patrons, and warned the evil ones of our presence."

Bronco Billy looked around.

"You mean those guys over there?" he nodded toward the other table. "Hell, William S., we both took on twelve men one time."

Dr. Helioglabulus sighed. "No, no, you don't understand. Those men over there are harmless; crackpot revolutionists. William and I are speaking of *nosferatu* . . ."

Bronco Billy continued to stare at him.

". . . the undead . . ."

No response.

". . . er, ah, vampires. . . ."

"You mean," asked Billy, "like Theda Bara?"

"Not vamps, my dear friend," said the hawk-nosed wrangler. "Vampires. Those who rise from the dead and suck the blood of the living."

"Oh," said Bronco Billy. Then he looked at the cartridges. "These kill 'em?"

"Theoretically," said Helioglabulus.

"Meaning you don't know?"

The doctor nodded.

"In that case," said Bronco Billy, "we go halfies." He began to load his .45s with one regular bullet, then a wooden one, then another standard.

William S. had already filled his with wooden slugs.

"Excellent," said Helioglabulus. "Now, put these over your hatbands. I hope you never have to get close enough for them to be effective."

What he handed them were silver hatbands. Stamped on the shiny surface of the bands was a series of crosses. They slipped them on their heads, settling them on their hat brims.

"What next?" asked Bronco Billy.

"Why, we wait for nightfall, for the *nosferatu* to strike!" said the doctor.

"Did you hear them, Hermann?" asked Joseph.

"Sure. You think we ought to do the same?"

"Where would we find someone to make wooden bullets for pistols such as ours?" asked Joseph.

The five men sitting at the table looked toward the doctor and the two cowboys. All five were dressed in the remnants of uniforms belonging to the war. The one addressed as Hermann still wore the Knight's Cross on the faded splendor of his dress jacket.

"Martin," said Hermann. "Do you know where we can get wooden bullets?"

"I'm sure we could find someone to make them for the automatics," he answered. "Ernst, go to Wartman's; see about them."

Ernst stood, then slapped the table. "Every time I hear the word vampire, I reach for my Browning!" he said.

They all laughed. Martin, Hermann, Joseph, Ernst most of all. Even Adolf laughed a little.

Soon after dark, someone ran into the place, white of face. "The vampire!" he yelled, pointing vaguely toward the street, and fell out.

Bronco Billy and William S. jumped up. Helioglabulus stopped them. "I'm too old, and will only hold you up," he said. "I shall try to catch up later. Remember . . . the crosses. The bullets in the heart!"

As they rushed out past the other table, Ernst, who had left an hour earlier, returned with two boxes.

"Quick, Joseph!" he said as the two cowboys went through the door, "Follow them! We'll be right behind. Your pistol!"

Joseph turned, threw a Browning automatic pistol back to Hermann, then went out the doors as hoofbeats clattered in the street.

The other four began to load their pistols from the boxes of cartridges.

The two cowboys rode toward the commotion.

"Yee-haw!" yelled Bronco Billy. They galloped down the well-paved streets, their horses' hooves striking sparks from the cobbles.

They passed the police and others running toward the sounds of screams and dying. Members of the Free Corps, ex-soldiers, and students swarmed the streets in their uniforms. Torches burned against the flickering black night skies.

The city was trying to overcome the *nosferatu* by force.

Bronco Billy and William S. charged toward the fighting. In the center of a square stood a coach, all covered in black crêpe. The driver, a plump, cadaverous man, held the reins to four black horses. The four were rearing high in their traces, their hooves menacing the crowd.

But it was not the horses which kept the mob back.

Crawling out of a second-story hotel window was a vision from nightmare. Bald, with pointed ears, teeth like a rat, beady eyes bright in the flickering night, the vampire climbed from a bedroom to the balcony. The front of his frock coat was covered with blood, his face and arms were smeared. A man's hand stuck halfway out the window, and the curtains were spattered black.

The *nosferatu* jumped to the ground, and the crowd parted as he leaped from the hotel steps to the waiting carriage. Then the driver cracked his whip over the horses—there was no sound—and the team charged, tumbling people like leaves before the night wind.

The carriage seemed to float to the two cowboys who rode after it. There was no sound of hoofbeats ahead, no noise from the harness, no creak of axles. It was as if they followed the wind itself through the nighttime streets of Bremen.

They sped down the flickering main roads. Once, when Bronco Billy glanced behind him, he thought he saw motorcycle headlights following. But he devoted most of his attention to the fleeing coach.

William S. rode beside him. They gained on the closed carriage.

Bronco Billy drew his left-hand pistol (he was ambidextrous) and fired at the broad back of the driver. He heard the splintery clatter of the wooden bullet as it ricocheted off the coach. Then the carriage turned ahead of them.

He was almost smashed against a garden wall by the headlong plunge of his mount; then he recovered, leaning far over in the saddle, as if his horse were a sailboat and he a sailor heeling against the wind.

Then he and William S. were closing with the hearse on a long broad stretch of the avenue. They pulled even with the driver.

And for the first time, the hackles rose on Bronco Billy's neck as he rode beside the black-crêpe coach. There was no sound but him, his horse, their gallop. He saw the black-garbed driver crack the long whip, heard no *snap*, heard no horses, heard no wheels.

His heart in his throat, he watched William S. pull even on the other side. The driver turned that way, snapped his whip toward the taller cowboy. Bronco Billy saw his friend's hat fly away, cut in two.

Billy took careful aim and shot the lead horse in the head, twice. It dropped like a ton of cement, and the air was filled with a vicious, soundless image—four horses, the driver, the carriage, he, his mount, and William S. all flying through the air in a tangle. Then the side of the coach caught him and the incessant flickering went out.

He must have awakened a few seconds later. His horse was atop him, but he didn't think anything was broken. He pushed himself out from under it.

The driver was staggering up from the flinders of the coach—strange, thought Bronco Billy, now I hear the sounds of the wheels turning, the screams of the dying horses. The driver pulled a knife. He started toward the cowboy.

Bronco Billy found his right-hand pistol, still in its holster. He pulled it, fired directly into the heart of the fat man. The driver folded from the recoil, then stood again.

Billy pulled the trigger.

The driver dropped as the wooden bullet turned his heart to giblets.

Bronco Billy took all the regular ammo out of his pistol and began to cram the wooden ones in.

As he did, motorcycles came screaming to a stop beside him, and the five men from the tavern climbed from them or their sidecars.

He looked around for William S. but could not see him. Then he heard the shooting from the rooftop above the street—twelve shots, quick as summer thunder.

One of William S.'s revolvers dropped four stories and hit the ground beside him.

The Germans were already up the stairs ahead of Bronco Billy as he ran.

When the carriage had crashed into them, William S. had been thrown clear. He jumped up in time to see the vampire run into the doorway of the residential block across the way. He tore after it while the driver pulled himself from the wreckage and Bronco Billy was crawling from under his horse.

Up the stairs he ran. He could now hear the pounding feet of the living dead man ahead, unlike the silence before the wreck. A flickering murky hallway was before him, and he saw the door at the far end close.

William S. smashed into it, rolled. He heard the scrape of teeth behind him, and saw the rat-like face snap shut inches away. He came up, his pistols leveled at the vampire.

The bald-headed thing grabbed the open door, pulled it before him.

William S. stood, feet braced, a foot from the door and began to fire into it. His colt .36 inches in front of his face, he fired again and again into the wooden door, watching chunks and splinters shear away. He heard the vampire squeal, like a rat trapped behind a trashcan, but still he fired until both pistols clicked dry.

The door swung slowly awry, pieces of it hanging.

The *nosferatu* grinned, and carefully pushed the door closed. It hissed and crouched.

William S. reached up for his hat.

And remembered that the driver had knocked it off his head before the collision.

The thing leaped.

One of his pistols was knocked over the parapet.

Then he was fighting for his life.

The five Germans, yelling to each other, slammed into the doorway at the end of the hall. From beyond, they heard the sounds of scuffling, labored breathing, the rip and tear of cloth.

Bronco Billy charged up behind them.

"The door! It's jammed," said one.

"His hat!" yelled Bronco Billy. "He lost his hat!"

"Hat?" asked the one called Joseph, in English. "Why his hat?" The others shouldered against the gaped door. Through it, they saw flashes of movement and the flickering night sky.

"Crosses!" yelled Bronco Billy. "Like this!" he pointed to his hatband.

"Ah!" said Joseph. "Crosses."

He pulled something from the one called Adolf, who hung back a little, threw it through the hole in the door.

"*Cruzen!*" yelled Joseph.

"The cross!" screamed Bronco Billy. "William S. The cross!"

The sound of scuffling stopped.

Joseph tossed his pistol through the opening.

They continued to bang on the door.

The thing had its talons on his throat when the yelling began. The vampire was strangling him. Little circles were swimming in his sight. He was down beneath the monster. It smelled of old dirt, raw meat, of death. Its rat eyes were bright with hate.

Then he heard the yell, "A cross!" and something fluttered at the edge of his vision. He let go one hand from the vampire and grabbed it up.

It felt like cloth. He shoved it at the thing's face.

Hands let go.

William S. held the cloth before him as breath came back in a rush. He staggered up, and the *nosferatu* put its hands over its face. He pushed toward it.

Then the Browning automatic pistol landed beside his foot, and he heard noises at the door behind him.

Holding the cloth, he picked up the pistol.

The vampire hissed like a radiator.

William S. aimed and fired. The pistol was fully automatic.

The wooden bullets opened the vampire like a zipper coming off.

The door crashed outward, the five Germans and Bronco Billy rushed through.

William S. held to the doorframe and caught his breath. A crowd was gathering below, at the site of the wrecked hearse and the dead horses. Torchlights wobbled their reflection on the houses across the road. It looked like something from Dante.

Helioglabulus came onto the roof, took one look at the vampire and ran his alpenstock, handle first, into its ruined chest.

"Just to make sure," he said.

Bronco Billy was clapping William S. on the back. "Shore thought you'd gone to the last roundup," he said.

The five Germans were busy with the vampire's corpse.

William S. looked at the piece of cloth still clenched tightly in his own hand. He opened it. It was an armband.

On its red cloth was a white circle with a twisted black cross.

Like the decorations Indians used on their blankets, only in reverse.

He looked at the Germans. Four of them wore the armbands; the fifth, wearing an old corporal's uniform, had a torn sleeve.

They were slipping a yellow armband over the arm of the vampire's coat. When they finished, they picked the thing up and carried it to the roof edge. It looked like a spitted pig.

The yellow armband had two interlocking triangles, like the device on the chest of the costumes William S. had worn when he played *Ben-Hur* on Broadway. The Star of David.

The crowd below screamed as the corpse fell toward them.

There were shouts, then.

The unemployed, the war-wounded, the young, the bitter, the disillusioned. Then the shouting stopped . . . and they began to chant.

The five Germans stood on the parapet, looking down at the milling people. They talked among themselves.

Bronco Billy held William S. until he caught his breath.

They heard the crowds disperse, fill in again, break, drift off, reform, reassemble, grow larger.

"Well, pard," said Bronco Billy. "Let's mosey over to a hotel and get some shut-eye."

"That would be nice," said William S.

Helioglabulus joined them.

"We should go by the back way," he said.

"I don't like the way this crowd is actin'," said Bronco Billy.

William S. walked to the parapet, looked out over the city.

Under the dark flickering sky, there were other lights. Here and there, synagogues began to flicker.

And then to burn.

INTRODUCTION TO

SAVE A PLACE IN THE LIFEBOAT FOR ME

Again the question: Is this about rock and roll? Is this about funny people of the movies? You tell me.

This is the second-earliest story in the collection. It was written in September and October of 1974, a heady personal time for me; a fairly disastrous one for my career. I'd been living for six months in Bryan, Texas, in the Monkey House, what would have been called in earlier days a Slan Shack; a house full of SF fans. I wrote and wrote and wrote while I lived there. Absolutely nothing I wrote in those six months while living there sold. I moved to Austin in late October 1974. *Everything* I owned, plus a medium-sized dog, fit in a friend's VW Beetle.

I hadn't been in Austin a week before all that stuff I'd written in Bryan started to sell, and it all sold in the next few months. Why? I don't know. I don't give a damn! Third Base!

Comedians. Everybody loves them; nobody, as Dangerfield says, gives them any respect. When people make a list of the greatest actors — male and female — of all time in the movies — hey! Where's the funny folks?

From the silents to *right now*, the comedians are there; they're appreciated, loved; they're in the feel-good movie of the year; everybody knows them and goes to see them. But to get any respect, they've got to go against type, get serious, deal with a heavy subject in a heavy way.

Chaplin knocked the blocks out from under his career that way. Langdon, as Capra said, never knew what hit him after he started directing himself, instead of listening to people who knew *exactly* what he could and couldn't do (like Capra) and could tell him how to do it, and roll the audiences in the aisles.

Did Tom Hanks win an Academy Award for *Joe vs. The Volcano*? No, it was for *Philadelphia*, after he'd been knocking himself out for ten years doing some of the best acting ever seen. *In comedies . . .*

So then, a story about 1959, but with characters from the history of film scattered all through it, in parts they couldn't have gotten in life, and true to their art.

This being an early story, I hear you ask: Would you like to rewrite this now, knowing what you do? Of course, but as someone said once, that would be confusing literature with journalism, wouldn't it? Would I do it differently? *You bet*, but you can say that about almost anything, once you see it in print. I could rewrite this: better construction, some tightening, places to be more subtle, places not to. I know how to do *all that stuff* now, twenty-six years later.

But if I did, I don't think it would be as good a story. I was writing then to show how much I liked all those people, and how many guts they'd made me bust over the years, and I think that comes through, and that's what I wanted to say. *So there.*

SAVE A PLACE IN THE LIFEBOAT FOR ME

The hill was high and cold when they appeared there, and the first thing they did was to look around.

It had snowed the night before, and the ground was covered about a foot deep.

Arthur looked at Leonard and Leonard looked at Arthur.

"Whatsa matter you? You wearin' funny clothes again!" said Leonard.

Arthur listened, his mouth open. He reached down to the bulbhorn tucked in his belt.

Honk Honk went Arthur.

"Whatsa matter us?" asked Leonard. "Look ata us! We back inna vaudeville?"

Leonard was dressed in pants two sizes too small, and a jacket which didn't match. He wore a tiny pointed felt hat which stood on his head like a roof on a silo.

Arthur was dressed in a huge coat which dragged the ground, balloon pants, big shoes, and above his moppy red hair was a silk top hat, its crown broken out.

"It's a fine-a mess he's gots us in disa time!"

Arthur nodded agreement.

"Quackenbush, he's-a gonna hear about this!" said Leonard.

Honk Honk went Arthur.

The truck backed into the parking lot and ran into the car parked just inside the entrance. The glass panels which were being carried on the truck fell and shattered into thousands of slivers in the snowy street. Cars slushing down the early morning swerved to avoid the pieces.

"Ohh, Bud, Bud!" said the short baby-faced man behind the wheel. He was trying to back the truck over the glass and get it out of the way of the dodging cars.

A tall thin man with a rat's mustache ran from the glass company office and yelled at the driver.

"Look what you've done. Now you'll make me lose this job, too! Mr. Crabapple will . . ." He paused, looked at the little fat man, swallowed a few times.

"Uh . . . hello, Lou," he said, a tear running into his eye and brimming down his face. He turned away, pulled a handkerchief from his coveralls and wiped his eyes.

"Hello, Bud," said the little man, brightly. "I don' . . . don' . . . understand it either, Bud. But the man said we got something to do, and I came here to get you." He looked around him at the littered glass. "Bud, I been a baaad boy!"

"It doesn't matter, Lou," said Bud, climbing around to the passenger side of the truck. "Let's get going before somebody gets us arrested."

"Oh, Bud?" asked Lou, as they drove through the town. "Did you ever get out of your contract?"

"Yeah, Lou. Watch where you're going! Do I have to drive myself?"

They pulled out of Peoria at eight in the morning.

The two men beside the road were dressed in black suits and derby hats. They stood; one fat, the other thin. The rotund one put on a most pleasant face and smiled at the passing traffic. He lifted his thumb politely, as would a gentleman, and held it as each vehicle roared past.

When a car whizzed by, he politely tipped his hat.

The thin man looked distraught. He tried at first to strike the same pose as the larger man, but soon became flustered. He couldn't hold his thumb right, or let his arm droop too far.

"No, no, no, Stanley," said the larger, mustached man, as if he were talking to a child. "Let me show you the way a man of gentle breeding asks for a ride. Politely. Gently. Thus."

He struck the same pose he had before.

A car bore down on them doing eighty miles an hour. There was no chance in the world it would stop.

Stanley tried to strike the same pose. He checked himself against the larger man's attitude. He found himself lacking. He rubbed his ears and looked as if he would cry.

The car roared past, whipping their hats off.

They bent to pick them up and bumped heads. They straightened, each signaling that the other should go ahead. They simultaneously bent and bumped heads again.

The large man stood stock still and did a slow burn. Stanley looked flustered. Their eyes were off each other. Then they both leaped for the hats and bumped heads once more.

They grabbed up the hats and jumped to their feet.

They had the wrong hats on. Stanley's derby made the larger man look like a tulip bulb. The large derby covered Stanley down to his chin. He looked like a thumbtack.

The large man grabbed the hat away and threw Stanley's derby to the ground.

"MMMMMM-MMMMMM-MMMMM!" said the large man.

Stanley retrieved his hat. "But Ollie . . ." he said, then began whimpering. His hat was broken.

Suddenly Stanley pulled Ollie's hat off and stomped it. Ollie did another slow burn, then turned and ripped off Stanley's tie.

Stanley kicked Ollie in the shin. The large man jumped around and punched Stanley in the kneecap.

A car stopped, and the driver jumped out to see what the trouble was.

Ollie kicked him in the shin. He ripped off Stanley's coat.

Twenty minutes later, Stanley and Ollie were looking down from a hill. A thousand people were milling around on the turnpike below, tearing each other's cars to pieces. Parts of trucks and motorcycles littered the roadway. The two watched a policeman pull up. He jumped out and yelled through a bullhorn to the people, too far away for the two men to hear what he said.

As one, the crowd jumped him, and pieces of police car began to bounce off the blacktop.

Ollie dusted off his clothing as meticulously as possible. His and Stanley's clothes consisted of torn underwear and crushed derby hats.

"That's another fine mess you've gotten us in, Stanley," he said. He looked north.

"And it looks like it shall soon snow. Mmmm-mmmm-mmmm!"

They went over the hill as the wail of sirens began to fill the air.

"Hello, a-Central, givva me Heaven. ETcumspiri 220."

The switchboard hummed and crackled. Sparks leaped off the receiver of the public phone booth in the roadside park. Arthur did a back flip and jumped behind a trashcan.

The sun was out, though snow was still on the ground. It was a cold February day, and they were the only people in the park.

The noise died down at the other end and Leonard said:

"Hallo, Boss! Hey, Boss! We doin'-a like you tell us, but you no send us to the right place. You no send us to Iowa. You send us to Idaho, where they grow the patooties."

Arthur came up beside his brother and listened. He honked his horn.

On the other end of the line, Rufus T. Quackenbush spoke:

"Is that a goose with you, or do you have a cold?"

"Oh, no, Boss. You funnin'-a me. That's-a Bagatelle."

"Then who are you?" asked Quackenbush.

"Oh, you know who this is. I gives you three guesses."

"Three guesses, huh? Hmmmm, let's see . . . you're not Babe Ruth, are you?"

"Hah, Boss. Babe Ruth, that's-a chocolate bar."

"Hmmm. You're not Demosthenes, are you?"

"Nah, Boss. Demosthenes can do is bend in the middle of your leg."

"I should have known," said Quackenbush. "This is Rampolini, isn't it?"

"You got it, Boss."

Arthur whistled and clapped his hands in the background.

"Is that a hamster with you, Rampolini?"

"Do-a hamsters whistle, Boss?"

"Only when brought to a boil," said Quackenbush.

"Ahh, you too good-a for me, Boss!"

"I know. And if I weren't too good for you, I wouldn't be good enough for anybody. Which is more than I can say for you."

"Did-a we wake you up, Boss?"

"No, to be perfectly honest, I had to get up to answer the phone anyway. What do you want?"

"Like I said, Boss Man, you put us inna wrong place. We no inna Iowa. We inna Idaho."

"That's out of the Bronx, isn't it? What should I do about it?"

"Well-a, we don't know. Even if-a we did, we know we can't-a do it anyway, because we ain't there. An if-a we was, we couldn't get it done no ways."

"How do you know that?"

"Did-a you ever see one of our pictures, Boss?"

There was a pause. "I see what you mean," said Quackenbush.

"Why for you send-a us, anyway? We was-a sleep, an then we inna Idaho!"

"I looked at my calendar this morning. One of the dates was circled. And it didn't have pits, either. Anyway, I just remembered that something very important shouldn't take place today."

"What's-a that got to do with us two?"

"Well . . . I know it's a little late, but I really would appreciate it if you two could manage to stop it."

"What's-a gonna happen if we don't?"

"Uh, ha ha. Oh, small thing, really. The Universe'll come to an end several million years too soon. A nice boy like you wouldn't want that, would you? Of course not!"

"What for I care the Universe'll come to an end? We-a work for Paramount."

"No, no. Not the studio. The big one!"

"M-a GM?"

"No. The Universe. All that stuff out there. Look around you."

"You mean-a Idaho?"

"No, no, Rampolini. Everything will end soon, too soon. You may not be concerned. A couple of million years is nothing to somebody like you. But what about me? I'm leasing this office, you know?"

"Why-a us?"

"I should have sent someone earlier, but I've . . . I've been so terrible busy. I was having a pedicure, you see, and the time just flew by."

"What-a do the two of us do to-a stop this?"

"Oh, I just know you'll think of something. And you'll both be happy to know I'm sending you lots of help."

"Is this help any good, Boss?"

"I don't know if they're any good," said Quackenbush. "But they're cheap."

"What-a we do inna meantime?"

"Be mean, like everybody else."

"Nah, nah. (That's-a really good one, Boss.) I mean, about-a the thing?"

"Well, I'd suggest you get to Iowa. Then give me another call."

"But what iffa you no there?"

"Well, my secretary will take the message."

"Ah, Boss, if-a you no there, you're secretary's-a no gonna be there neither."

"Hmmm. I guess you're right. Well, why don't you give me the message now, and I'll give it to my secretary. Then I'll give her the answer, and she can call you when you get to Iowa!"

"Hey, that's-a good idea, Boss!"

"I thought you'd think so."

Outside the phone booth, Arthur was lolling his tongue out and banging his head with the side of his hand, trying to keep up with the conversation.

There were two lumps of snow beside the highway. The snow shook itself, and Stan and Ollie stepped out of it.

"Brr," said Ollie. "Stanley, we must get to some shelter soon."

"But I don't know where any is, Ollie!"

"This is all your fault, Stanley. It's up to you to find us some clothing and a cheery fireside."

"But Ollie, I didn't have any idea we'd end up like this."

Ollie shivered. "I suppose you're right, Stanley. It's not your fault we're here."

"I don't even remember what we were doing before we were on that road this morning, Ollie. Where have you been lately?"

"Oh . . . don't you remember, Stanley?"

"Not very well, Ollie."

"Oh," said Ollie. He looked very tired, very suddenly. "It's very strange, but neither do I, Stanley."

The cold was forgotten then, and they were fully clothed in their black suits and derbies. They thought nothing of it, because they were thinking of something else.

"I suppose now we shall really have to hurry and find a ride, Stanley."

"I know," said the thin man. "We have to go to Iowa."

"Yes," said Ollie, "and our wives will be none the wiser."

The Iowa they headed for was pulling itself from under a snowstorm which had dumped eleven inches in the last two days. It was bitterly cold there. Crew-cut boys shoveled snow off walks and new '59 cars so their fathers could get to work. It was almost impossible. Snowplows had been out all night, and many of them were stalled. The National Guard had been called out in some sections and was feeding livestock and rescuing stranded motorists. It was not a day for travel.

At noon, the small town of Cedar Oaks was barely functioning. The gleaming sun brought no heat. But the town stirred inside, underneath the snows which sagged the roofs.

The All-Star Caravan was in town that day. The teenagers had prayed and hoped that the weather would break during the two days of ice. The Caravan was a rock 'n' roll show that traveled around the country, doing one-night stands.

The show had been advertised for a month: All the businesses around the two high schools and junior highs were covered with the blazing orange posters. They had been since New Year's Day.

So the kids waited, and built up hopes for it, and almost had them dashed as the weather had closed in.

But Mary Ann Pickett's mother, who worked the night desk at the Holiday Inn, had called her daughter at eleven the night before: The All-Star Caravan had landed at the airport in the clearing night, and all the singers had checked in.

Mary Ann asked her mother, "What does Donny Bottoms look like?"

Her mother didn't know. They were all different-looking, and she wasn't familiar with the singer anyway.

Five minutes after Mary Ann rang off, the word was spreading over Cedar Oaks. The All-Star Caravan was there. Now it could snow forever. Maybe if it did, they would have to stay there, rather than start their USO tour of Alaska.

Bud and Lou slid and slipped their way over the snows in the truck.

"Watch where you're going!" said Bud. "Do you have anything to eat?"

"I got some cheese crackers and some LifeSavers, Bud. But we'll have to divide them, because . . ." His voice took on a little-boy petulance ". . . because I haven't had anything to eat in a long time, Bud."

"Okay, okay. We'll share. Give me half the cheese crackers. You take these."

Lou was trying to drive. There was a munching sound.

"Some friend you are," said Bud. "You have two cheese crackers and I don't have any."

Lou coughed. "But, Bud! I just gave you two cheese crackers?"

"Do I look like I have any cheese crackers?" asked Bud, wiping crumbs from his chin.

"Okay," said Lou. "Have this cheese cracker, Bud. Because you're my friend, and I want to share."

Again, the sound of eating filled the cab.

"Look, Lou. I don't mind you having all the LifeSavers, but can't you give me half your cheese cracker?"

Lou puffed out his cheeks while watching the road. "But, Bud! I just gave you three cheese crackers!"

"Some friend," said Bud, looking at the snowbound landscape. "He has a cheese cracker and won't share with his only friend."

"Okay! Okay!" said Lou. "Take half this cheese cracker! Take it!"

He drove on.

"Boy . . . ," said Bud.

Lou took the whole roll of LifeSavers and stuffed them in his mouth, paper and all. He began to choke.

Bud began beating him on the back. The truck swerved across the road, then back on. They continued toward Cedar Oaks, Iowa.

There were giants in the All-Star Caravan. Donny Bottoms, from Amarillo, Texas; his backup group, the Mosquitoes, most from Amarillo Cooper High School, his old classmates. Then there was Val Ritchie, who'd had one fantastic hit song, which had a beat and created a world all the teenagers wanted to escape to.

The third act, biggest among many more, was a middle-aged man, calling himself The Large Charge. His act was strange, even among that set. He performed with a guitar and a telephone. He pretended to be talking to a girl on the other end of the line. It was billed as a comedy act. Everybody knew what was really involved—The Large Charge was rock 'n' roll's first dirty old man. His real name was Elmo Simpson and he came from Bridge City, Texas.

Others on the bill included the Pipettes, three guys and two girls from Stuttgart, Arkansas, who up until three months ago had sung only at church socials; Jimmy Wailon, who was having a hard time deciding whether to sing "Blue Suede Shoes" for the hundredth time, or strike out into country music where the real money was. Plus the Champagnes, who'd had a hit song three years before, and Rip Dover, the show's M.C.

The All-Star Caravan was the biggest thing that had happened to Cedar Oaks since Bill Haley and the Comets came through a year and a half ago, and one of Haley's roadmen had been arrested for DWI.

"What's-a matter us?" asked Leonard for the fiftieth time that morning. "We really no talka like dis! We was-a grown up mens, with jobs and-a everything."

Whonka whonka went Arthur sadly, as they walked through the town of Friedersville, Idaho.

Arthur stopped dead, then put his hands in his pockets and began whistling. There was a police car at the corner. It turned onto the road where they walked. And slowed.

Leonard nonchalantly tipped his pointy felt hat forward and put his hands in his pockets.

The cop car stopped.

The two ran into the nearest store. Hadley's Music Shop.

Arthur ran around behind a set of drums and hid. Leonard sat down at a piano and began to play with one finger, "You've Taught Me a New Kind of Love."

The store manager came from the back room and leaned against the doorjamb, listening.

Arthur saw a harp in the corner, ran to it and began to play. He joined in the song with Leonard.

The two cops came in and watched them play. Leonard was playing with his foot and nose. Arthur was plucking the harp strings with his teeth.

The police shrugged and left.

"Boy, I'm-a tellin' you," said Leonard, as he waited for the cops to turn the corner. "Quackenbush, he's-a messed up dis-a time! Why we gots to do this?" With one hand he was wiping his face, and with the other he was playing as he never had before.

Donny Bottoms was a scrawny-looking kid from West Texas. He didn't stand out in a crowd, unless you knew where to look. He had a long neck and an Adam's apple that stuck out of his collar. He was twenty-four years old and still had acne. But he was one of the hottest new singers around, and the All-Star Caravan was going to be his last road tour for a while. He'd just married his high school sweetheart, a girl named Dottie, and he had not really wanted to come on the tour without her. But she was finishing nurse's training and could not leave. At two in the afternoon, he and the other members of the Caravan were trying the sound in the Municipal Auditorium.

He and the Mosquitoes ran through a couple of their numbers. Bottoms' style was unique, even in a field as wild and novelty-eating as rock 'n' roll. It had a good boogie beat, but Bottoms worked hard with the music, and the Mosquitoes were really good. They turned out a good synthesis of primitive and sophisticated styles.

The main thing they had for them was Donny's voice. It was high and nasal when he talked, but, singing, that all went away. He had a good range, and he did strange things with his throat.

A critic once said that he dry-humped every syllable till it begged for mercy.

Val Ritchie had one thing he did well, exactly one: that was a song called "Los Niños." He'd taken an old Mexican folk song, got a drummer to beat hell out of a conga, and yelled the words over his own screaming guitar.

It was all he did well. He did some of other people's standards, and some Everly Brothers' stuff by himself, but he always finished his set with "Los Niños" and it always brought the house down and had them dancing in the aisles.

He was the next-to-last act before Bottoms and the Mosquitoes.

He was a tough act to follow.

But he was always on right before The Large Charge, and he was the toughest act in rock 'n' roll.

They had turned the auditorium upside down and had finally found a church key to open a beer for The Large Charge.

Elmo Simpson was dressed, at the sound rehearsal, in a pair of baggy pants, a checked cowboy shirt, and a string tie with a Texas-shaped tie clasp. Tonight, on stage, he would be wearing the same thing.

Elmo's sound rehearsal consisted of chinging away a few chords, doing the first two bars of "Jailhouse Rock" and then going into his dirty-old-man voice.

His song was called "Hello, Baby!" and he used a prop telephone. He ran through the first two verses, which were him talking in a cultured, decadent, nasty voice, and he had the soundman rolling in his control chair before he finished.

Elmo sweated like a hog. He'd been doing this act for two years; he'd even had to lip-synch it on Dick Clark's "American Bandstand" a couple of times. He was still nervous, though he could do the routine in his sleep. He was always nervous. He was in his late thirties. Fame had come late to him, and he couldn't believe it. So he was still nervous.

Bud and Lou were hurrying west in the panel truck, through snow slides, slush, and stalled cars.

Stan and Ollie had hitched a ride on a Mayflower moving van, against all that company's policies, and were speeding toward Cedar Oaks from the south-southeast.

Leonard and Arthur, alias Rampolini and Bagatelle, were leaving an Idaho airport in a converted crop duster which hadn't been flown since the end of the Korean War. It happened like this.

"We gots to find us a pilot-a to fly us where the Boss wants us," said Leonard, as they ran onto a small municipal field.

Whonk? asked Arthur.

"We's gots to find us a pilot, pilot."

Arthur pulled a saber from the fold of his coat, and putting a black poker chip over his eye, began sword fighting his shadow.

"Notta pirate. Pilot! A man whatsa flies in the aeroplanes," said Leonard.

A man in coveralls, wearing a WWII surplus aviator's cloth helmet, walked from the operations room.

"There's-a one now!" said Leonard. "What's about we gets him?"

Without a honk, Arthur ran and tackled the flyer.

"What the hell's the matter with him?" asked the man as Arthur grinned and smiled and pointed.

"You gots to-a excuse him," said Leonard, pulling his top-hatted brother off him. "He's-a taken too many vitsamins."

"Well, keep him away from me!" said the flyer.

"We's-a gots you a prepositions," said Leonard, conspiratorially.

"What?"

"A prepositions. You fly-a us to Iowa, anda we no break-a you arms."

"What's going on? Is this some kind of gag?"

"No, it's-a my brother. He's a very dangerous man. Show him how dangerous you are, Bagatelle."

Arthur popped his eyes out, squinted his face up into a million rolls of flesh, flared his nostrils, and snorted at each breath.

"Keep him away from me!" said the man. "You oughtn't to let him out on the streets."

"He's-a no listen to me, Bagatelle. Get tough with him."

Arthur hunched his shoulders, intensified his breathing, stepped up into the pilot's face.

"No, that's-a no tough enough. Get really tough with him."

Arthur squnched over, stood on tiptoe, flared his nostrils until they filled all his face except for the eyes, panted, and passed out for lack of breath.

The pilot ran across the field and into a hangar.

"Hey, wake-a up!" said Leonard. "He's-a getting the plane ready. Let's-a go."

When they got there, the pilot was warming the crop duster up for a preflight check.

Arthur climbed in the aft cockpit, grabbed the stick, started jumping up and down.

"Hey! Get outta there!" yelled the pilot. "I'm gonna call the cops!"

"Hey, Bagatelle. Get-a tough with him again!"

Leonard was climbing into the forward cockpit. Arthur started to get up. His knees hit the controls. The plane lurched.

Leonard fell into the cockpit head first, his feet sticking out.

Arthur sat back down and laughed. He pulled the throttle. The pilot just had time to open the hangar door before the plane roared out, plowed through a snowbank, ricocheted back onto the field, and took off.

It was heading east toward Iowa.

At three in the afternoon, the rehearsals over, most of the entertainers were back in their rooms at the Holiday Inn. Already the hotel detective had had to chase out several dozen girls and boys who had been roaming up and down the halls looking for members of the All-Star Caravan.

Some of them found Jimmy Wailon in the corridor and were getting his autograph. He had been on the way down the hall, going to meet one of the lady reservation clerks.

"Two of yours is worth one Large Charge," said one of the girls as he signed her scrapbook.

"What's that?" he asked, his eyes twinkling. He pushed his cowlick out of his eyes.

"Two of your autographs are worth one of Donny's," she said.

"Oh," he said. "That's nice." He scribbled his usual "With Best Wishes to My Friend . . . ," then asked, "What's the name, honey?"

"Sarah Sue," she said. "And please put the date."

"Sure will, baby. How old are you?"

"I'm eighteen!" she said. All her friends giggled.

"Sure," he said. "There go!"

He hurried off to the room the lady reservation clerk had gotten for them.

"Did you hear that?" the girl asked behind him as he disappeared around the corner. "He called me 'honey.' "

Jimmy Wailon was smiling long before he got to Room 112.

Elmo was sitting in Donny's room with three of the Mosquitoes. Donny had gone to a phone booth to call his wife collect rather than put up with the noise in the room.

"Have another beer, Elmo?" asked Skeeter, the head Mosquito.

"Naw, thanks, Skeeter," he said. "I won't be worth a diddly-shit if I do." Already, Elmo was sweating profusely at the thought of another performance.

"I'll sure be glad when we get on that tour," he continued, after a pause. "Though it'll be colder than a monkey's ass."

"Yeh," said Skeeter. They were watching television. The Millionaire, the daytime reruns, and John Beresford Tipton was telling Mike what to do with the money with his usual corncob-up-the-butt humor. Skeeter was highly interested in the show. He'd had arguments with people many times about whether the show was real or not, or based on some real person. He was sure somewhere there was a John Beresford Tipton, and a Silverstone, and that one of those checks had his name on it.

"Look at that, will you?" asked Skeeter a few minutes later. "He's giving it to a guy whose kid is dying."

But Elmo Simpson, The Large Charge, from Bridge City, Texas, was lying on his back, fast asleep. Snores began to form inside his mouth, and every few minutes, one would escape.

Donny talked to his wife over the phone out in the motel lobby. They told each other how much they missed each other, and Donny asked about the new record of his coming out this week, and Dottie said she wished he'd come home soon rather than going on the tour, and they told each other they loved each other, and he hung up.

Val Ritchie was sitting in a drugstore just down the street, eating a chocolate sundae and wishing he were home, instead of going to do a show tonight, then fly with one or another load of musicians off to Alaska for two weeks for the USO.

He was wearing some of his old clothes and looked out of place in the booth. He thought most northern people overdressed anyway, even kids going to school. I mean, like they were all ready for church or Uncle Fred's funeral.

He hadn't been recognized yet, and wouldn't be. He always looked like a twenty-year-old garage mechanic on a coffee break.

Bud and Lou swerved to avoid a snowdrift. They had turned onto the giant highway a few miles back and had it almost to themselves. Ice glistened everywhere in the late afternoon sun, blindingly. Soon the sun would fall and it would become pitch black outside.

"How much further is it, Bud?" asked Lou. His stomach was growling.

"I don't know. It's around here somewhere. I'm just following what's-his-name's orders."

"Why doesn't he give better orders, Bud?"

"Because he never worked for Universal."

Stan and Ollie did not know what was happening when the doors of the moving van opened and carpets started dropping off the tops of the racks.

Then the van slammed into another vehicle. They felt it through the sides of the truck.

The driver was already out. He was walking toward a small truck with two men in it.

Stan and Ollie climbed out of the back of the Mayflower truck and saw who the other two were.

The four regarded each other, and the truck driver surveyed the damage to the carpets, which was minor.

They helped him load the truck back up; then Stan and Ollie climbed in the small van with Bud and Lou.

"I wonder what Quackenbush is up to now?" asked Bud, as he scrunched himself up with the others. With Lou and Ollie taking up so much room, he and Stan had to share a space hardly big enough for a lap dog. Somehow, they managed.

"I really don't know," said Ollie. "He seems quite intent on keeping this thing from happening."

"But, why us, Bud?" asked Lou. "We been good boys since . . . well, we been good boys. He could have sent so many others."

"That's quite all right with me," said Stanley. "He didn't seem to want just anybody for this."

"I don't know about you two, but Lou and I were sent from Peoria. That's a long way. What's this guy got against us?"

"Well, there's actually no telling," said Stanley. "Ollie and I have been traveling all day, haven't we, Ollie?"

"Quite right, Stanley."

"But what I don't get," said Bud, working at his pencil-thin mustache, "is that I remember when all this happened the first time."

"So do I," said Stanley.

"But not us two," said Lou, indicating Ollie and himself, and trying to keep the truck on the road.

"Well, that's because you two had . . . had . . . left before them. But that doesn't matter. What matters is that he sent us back here to . . . Come to think of it, I don't understand, either."

"Or me," said Lou.

"Quackenbush moves in mysterious ways," said Bud.

"Right you are," said Stan.

"Mmmm Mmmmm Mmmmm," said Ollie.

By the time they saw they were in the air they also realized the pilot wasn't aboard.

Leonard was still stuck upside down in the forward cockpit. Arthur managed to fly the plane straight while his brother crawled out and sat upright.

Looping and swirling, they flew on through the late afternoon toward Cedar Oaks.

The line started forming in front of the doors of the civic auditorium at five, though it was still bitterly cold.

The manager looked outside at 5:15. It was just dark, and there must be a hundred and fifty kids out there already, tickets in hand. He hadn't been at the sound rehearsal and hadn't seen the performers. All he knew was what he heard about them: They were the hottest rock and roll musicians since Elvis Presley and Chuck Berry.

The show went on at 7:00 P.M. as advertised, and it was a complete sellout. The crowd was ready, and when Rip Dover introduced the Champagnes, the people yelled and screamed even at their tired doo-wah act.

Then came Wailon, and they were polite for him, except that they kept yelling "Rock 'n' roll! Rock 'n' roll!" and he kept singing "Young Love" and the like.

Then other acts, then Val Ritchie, who jogged his way through several standards and launched into "Los Niños." He tore the place apart. They wouldn't let him go, they were dancing in the aisles. He did "Los Niños" until he was hoarse. They dropped the spots on him, finally, and the kids quit screaming. It got quiet. Then there was the sound of a mike being turned on and a voice, greasy in the magnificence, filled the hall:

"Hellooooooooooooo, baby!"

It was long past dark, and the truck swerved down the road, the forms of Stan, Ollie, Bud, and Lou illuminated by the dome light. Bud had a map unfolded in front of the windshield and Ollie's arms were in Lou's way.

"It's here somewhere," said Bud. "I know it's here somewhere!"

Overhead was the whining, droning sound of an old aeroplane, sometimes close to the ground, sometimes far above. Every once in a while was a yell of "Watch-a yourself! Watch-a where you go!" and a whonk whonk.

The truck below passed a sign which said:
WELCOME TO CEDAR OAKS
Speed Limit 30 MPH

After The Large Charge hung up the telephone receiver, and they let him offstage to thunderous ovation, the back curtain parted and there were Donny Bottoms and the Mosquitoes.

And the first song they sang was "Dottie," the song Bottoms had written for his wife while they were still high school sweethearts. Then "Roller Coaster Days" and "Miss America" and all his classics. And the crowd went crazy and . . .

The truck roared in the snowy, jampacked parking lot of the auditorium, skidded sideways, wiped out a '57 cherry-red Merc, and punched out the moon window of a T-Bird. The cops on parking lot duty ran toward the wreck.

Halfway there, they jumped under other cars to get away from the noise.

The noise was that of an airplane going to crash very soon, very close.

At the last second, the sound stopped.

The cops looked up.

An old biplane was sitting still in a parking space in the lot, its propeller still spinning. Two guys in funny clothes were climbing down from it, one whistling and honking to the other, who was trying to get a pointy hat off his ears.

The doors of the truck which had crashed opened, and four guys tumbled out all over each other.

They ran toward the auditorium, and the two from the plane saw them and whistled and ran toward them. They joined halfway across the lot, the six of them, and ran toward the civic hall.

The police were running for them like a berserk football team and then . . .

The auditorium doors were thrown open by the ushers, lances of light gleamed out on the snow and parked cars, and the mob spilled out onto the concrete and snow, laughing, yelling, pushing, shoving in an effort to get home.

The six running figures melted into the oncoming throng, the police right behind them.

Above the cop whistles and the mob noise was an occasional "Ollie, oh, Ollie!" or "Hey, Bud! Hey, Bud!" or whonk whonk and . . .

The six made it into the auditorium as the maintenance men were turning out the lights, and they ran up to the manager's office and inside.

The thin manager was watching TV. He looked up to the six and thought it must be some sort of a publicity stunt.

On TV came the theme music of "You Bet Your Duck."

"It's-a Quackenbush!" said Leonard.

The TV show host looked up from his rostrum. "Hi, folks. And tonight what's the secret woids?" Here a large merganser puppet flopped down and the audience applauded. The show host turned the word card around and lifted his eyebrows, looked at the screen and said:

"That's right. Tonight, the woids are Inexorable Fate. I knew I should've hired someone else. You guys are too late."

Then he turned to the announcer and asked, "George, who's our first guest?" as the duck was pulled back overhead on its strings.

The six men tore from the office and out to the parking lot, through the last of the mob. Stan, Ollie, Bud, and Lou jumped in the truck which a wrecker attendant was just connecting to a winch, right under the nose of the astonished police chief.

Arthur and Leonard, whistling and yelling, jumped in the plane, backed it out, and took off after circling the crowded parking lot. They rose into the air to many a loud scream.

The truck and plane headed for the airport.

The crowd was milling about the airport fence. Inside the barrier, musicians waited to get aboard a DC-3, their instrument cases scattered about the concourse.

The truck with four men in it crashed through the fence, strewing wire and posts to the sides.

It twisted around on its wheels, skidded sideways, almost hitting the musicians, and came to a halt. The four looked like the Keystone Firemen as they climbed out.

There was a roar in the air, and the biplane came out of the runway lights, landed, and taxied to a stop less than an inch from the nose of the passenger plane.

"We not-a too late! We not-a too late!" yelled Leonard, as he climbed down. "Arthur, get tough with-a that plane. Don't let it take off!"

Arthur climbed to the front of the crop duster and repeated the facial expressions he'd gone through earlier with the pilot. This time at the frightened pilot of the DC-3, through the windshield.

Leonard, Bud, Lou, Stan, and Ollie ran to the musicians and found

Wailon.

"Where's Bottoms?" asked Bud.

"Huh?" asked Jimmy Wailon, still a little distraught by the skidding truck and the aeroplane. "Bottoms? Bottoms left on the first plane."

"The first plane?" asked Ollie. "The first aeroplane?"

"Uh, yeah. Simpson and Ritchie were already on. Donny wanted to wait for this one, but I gave him my seat. I'm waiting for someone." He looked at them; they had not moved. "I gave him my seat on the first plane," he said. Then he looked them over in the dim lights. "You friends of his?"

"No," said Stanley, "but I'm sure we'll be seeing him again very soon."

Overhead, the plane which had taken off a few minutes before circled and headed northwest for Alaska.

They listened to it fade in the distance.

Whonk went Arthur.

They drove back through the dark February night, all six of them jammed into the seat and the small back compartment. After they heard the news for the first time, they turned the radio down and talked about the old days.

"This fellow Quackenbush," asked Ollie. "Is he in the habit of doing things such as this?"

"Ah, the Boss? There's-a no tellin' what the boss man willa do!"

"He must not be a nice man," said Lou.

"Oh, he's probably all right," said Bud. "He just has a mind like a producer."

"A contradiction in terms," said Stanley.

"You're so right," said Ollie.

"Pardon me," said the hitchhiker for whom they stopped. "Could you fellows find it in your hearts to give me a ride? I feel a bit weary after the affairs of the day, and should like to nestle in the arms of Morpheus for a short while."

"Sure," said Lou. "Hop in."

"Ah yes," said the rotund hitchhiker in the beaver hat. "Been chasing about the interior of this state all day. Some fool errand, yes indeed. Reminds me of the time on safari in Afghanistan . . ." He looked at the six men, leaned forward, tapping a deck of cards with his gloved hands. "Would any of you gentlemen be interested in a little game of chance?"

"No thanks," said Bud. "You wouldn't like the way I play."

They drove through the night. They didn't need to stop for the next hitchhiker, because they knew him. They saw him in the headlights, on the railroad tracks beside the road. He was kicking a broken-down locomotive. He came down the embankment, stood beside the road as they bore down on him.

He was dressed in a straw hat, a vest, and a pair of tight pants. He wore the same countenance all the time, a great stone face.

The truck came roaring down on him, and was even with him, and was almost by, when he reached out with one hand and grabbed the back door handle and with the other clamped his straw hat to his head.

His feet flew up off the pavement and for a second he was parallel to the ground; then he pulled himself into the spare tire holder and curled up asleep.

He had never changed expression.

Over the hill went the eight men, some of them talking, some dozing, toward the dawn. Just before the truck went out of sight there was a sound, so high, so thin it did not carry well.

It went honk honk.

INTRODUCTION TO

THE PASSING OF THE WESTERN

When I introduced this in *Night of the Cooters*, I did a long riff on how the structure of the story drove George R.R. Martin bananas when he heard me read it. I won't tell that again.

This was written for Joe Lansdale and Pat Lobrutto's *Razored Saddles*, the cowpunk anthology.

There was, as I said, something going on in all the genre fictions in the mid-1980s — mysteries, comic books, SF, Westerns — everything was reexamining itself (except Fantasy, which seemed to be chasing itself up its retrograde butthole, then and now). Part of this was, I think, burnout on the part of the third-and-fourth generation that had been raised on the stuff and was now creating it. Like they all of a suddink (as Popeye would say) stopped and said: Why are we doing it this way? To what end? And they started doing it differently.

There is no genre so standardized as the Western, written or filmed. From *The Great Train Robbery* on, there were "Jersey Westerns"; because of the MPPCo. moviemaking itself moved West, where the scenery and the light were free. Méliès sent his brother to set up Star Films U.S. in San Antonio: product — Westerns. There were formula plots, seven or eight of them. The standard was the Jacobean Revenger Plot on horseback, except for the sheepherder/rancher sodbuster/rancher ones. (The old joke: Dog limps into town with a gunbelt slung around his middle. Sheriff says, "Where you goin', boy?" Dog says, "I'm lookin' for the feller that shot my paw.")

And once again it took a European—this time a Brit, Kim Newman, to tell us what was there all the time: that what was going on in American society was reflected in the Western's treatment of the cattle baron. In the '20s he was a kindly figure whose daughter the go-getter cowboy would marry; in the Depression, he was Capitalism Rampant; in the early '40s a benevolent, patriotic FDR figure; in the late '40s and '50s a psychotic madman torn apart by dissension on and off the ranch. . . .

You started getting strangely written Westerns in the 1980s (after the genre died on television—quick! Name the last regularly broadcast Western before they came back?—*Kung Fu*!). So-called cowpunk—from cyberpunk in SF to splatterpunk in horror to cowpunk, all lit-crit phrases—was both part and cause. Among the truly swell practitioners were Joe Lansdale and Neal Barrett Jr., who loved the Western and wanted to do something new with it. Kenneth Oakley's *Season of Bloody Weather* opens with Doc Holliday coughing up part of a lung in a hotel washbasin. There was so much new excitement that the late Chad Oliver wrote the two books he'd been threatening to for twenty-five years, *Broken Eagle* and *The Cannibal Owl*. (In novels, Joe's *The Magic Wagon* is the true exemplar.)

I don't look like the Western kind of guy to most folks, but don't let that fool you. Joe said he'd have an anthology soon, would I do a story, I said sure. A few months later Joe called me and said, "Where's the story?"

I'd been thinking about Westerns, and what would have happened if things had been a little different. I'd been reading film criticism all my reading life, and there were a couple of people I wanted to, you know, pay homage to, which will be pretty easy to figure out once you start reading this.

Indeedy, things were happening in the Western in the 1980s. I was glad to be a small part of it.

THE PASSING OF THE WESTERN

From Film Review World, April 1972:

A few months ago, we sensed something in the national psyche, a time for reevaluation, and began to put together this special issue of Film Review World devoted to that interesting, almost forgotten art form, the American Western movie.

The genre flourished between 1910 and the late 1930s, went into its decline in the 1940s (while the country was recovering from The Big Recession, and due perhaps more to actual physical problems such as the trouble of finding suitable locations, and to the sudden popularity of costume dramas, religious spectacles, and operettas). There was some renewed interest in the late 1940s, then virtually nothing for the next twenty years.

Now that some Europeans (and some far less likely people) have discovered something vital in the form, and have made a few examples of the genre (along with their usual output of historical epics and heavy dramas), we felt it was time for a retrospective of what was for a while a uniquely American art form, dealing as they did with national westward expansion and the taming of a whole continent.

We were originally going to concentrate on the masters of the form, but no sooner had we assigned articles and begun the search for stills to illustrate them than we ran across (in the course of reviewing books in the field and because we occasionally house-sit with our twelve-year-old nephew) no less than three articles dealing in part with a little-known (but well-remembered by those who saw them) series of Westerns made between 1935 and 1938 by the Metropolitan-Goldfish-Mayer Studios. Admittedly, the last article appeared in a magazine aimed specifically at teenagers with no knowledge of American film industry history (or anything else for that matter), edited by a man with an encyclopedic knowledge of film and an absolutely abominable writing style—who has nevertheless delved into movie arcana in his attempt to fill the voracious editorial maw of the six magazines he edits (from his still-and-poster-laden Boise garage) for a not-so-nice guy in Richmond.

That we could almost dismiss, but the other two we couldn't—two works by film scholars noted for their ability to find people, hunt up lost screenplays and production notes and dig at the facts, both books to be published within a week of each other next month.

We've obtained permission to reprint the relevant portions of the two books, and the whole of that magazine article (including the stills) by way of introduction to this special issue dedicated to the Passing of the Western Movie from the American cinema—taken together, they seemed to strike exactly the right note about the film form we seem to have lost.

Join us, then, in a trip backwards in time—twice, as it were—to both the real events that inspired the films, and to the movies made about them fifty years later.

And, as they used to say on the Chisholm Trail, "always keep to the high ground and have your slicker handy!"

—John Thomas Johns

From: The Boise System: Interviews with Fifteen Directors Who Survived Life in the Studios, by Frederick T. Yawts, Ungar (Film Book 3), 1972.

(From the interview with James Selvors)

Selvors:
... the problems of doing Westerns of course in those days was finding suitable locations—that's why they set up operations in Boise in the first place. See, no matter what steps people had taken, they'd never really

gotten any good constant rainfall in the Idaho part of the basin—oh, they could make it rain occasionally, but never like anywhere else—it was the mountains to the west. They call it orographic uplift, an orographic plain. There used to be one on the west coast of Peru, but they fixed that back in the Nineteen-teens by fooling with the ocean currents down there. They tried that up here, too, in Washington State and Oregon, messed with the ocean currents; instead of raining in Idaho, all they got was more rain on the Pacific slope, which they did not need.

Anyway, Griffith and Laemmle came out to Boise in '09, 1910, something like that, because they could be out in what was left of the Plains in a few hours and they could almost guarantee 150 good-weather days a year.

First thing the early filmmakers had to do was build a bunch of western towns, since there weren't any out there (nobody with any sense ever stopped and put down roots in the Idaho Plains when Oregon was just a few days away). What few towns there had been had all rotted away (there still wasn't much rain but it was a hell of a lot more than there had been sixty years before). The place actually used to be a desert—imagine that, with nothing growing but scrub. By the time the pioneer moviemakers got there it was looking like old pictures of Kansas and Nebraska from the 1850s—flat grasslands, a few small trees; really Western-looking. (God help anyone who wanted to make a movie set in one of the Old Deserts—you've got farms all up and down the Mojave River and Death Valley Reservoir and Great Utah Lake now that get fifty bales to the acre in cotton.) There was the story everybody's heard about making the Western in one of the new nunatak areas in Antarctica—the snow'd melted off some three thousand square miles—taking fake cactus and sagebrush down there in the late '40s. I mean, it looked like a desert, flat bare rock everywhere; everybody had to strip down to just shirt, pants, and hats and put on fake sweat—we heard it froze; the snow's melted in Antarctica a whole lot, but don't let anyone tell you it's not still cold there—it has something to do with not getting as cold by a couple of degrees a year—like the mean temperature's only risen like four degrees since the 1880s. (Filming icebergs is another thing—you either have to do miniatures in a tank, which never worked; use old stock footage, ditto; or go to Antarctica and blast the tops off all jaggedy with explosives—the ones in Antarctica are flat, they're land ice; what everybody thinks of as northern icebergs were sea ice.) Somebody's gonna have to do an article sometime on how the weather's kept special effects people in business. . . .

Int.:
What was it about the Cloudbusters series that made them so popular?

Selvors:
Lots of people saw them. (laughs)

Int.:
No, seriously. They were started as short subjects, then went to steady B Westerns. Only Shadow Smith dying stopped production of them. . . .

Selvors:
I've talked to lots of people over the years about that. Those things resonate. They're about exactly what they're about, if you know what I mean. *Remember Raining Cats and Dogs*? *The Second Johnstown Flood*? Those were A pictures, big budgets, big stars? Well, they all came later, after the last *Cloudbusters* movie was made. I mean, we set out to make a film about the real taming of the West—how it was done, in fact. All these small independent outfits, going from place to place, making it rain, fixing up things, turning the West into a garden and a lush pastureland. That was the real West, not a bunch of people killing off Indians and shooting each other over rights to a mudhole. That stuff happened early on, just after the Civil War. By 1880 all that was changing.

We wanted just to make a short, you know, a three-reeler, about thirty minutes—there was a hot documentary and a two-reel color cartoon going out with the A picture Up and Down the Front, about Canadians in the Big 1920 Push during the Great World War (that being the closest the U.S. got to it)—this was late '34, early '35 [release date April 23, 1935—Int.]. So that package was too much stuff for even a fifty-five-minute B picture. Goldfish and Thalberg came to me and George Mayhew and asked us if we had a three-reeler ready to go—we didn't but we told them we did, and sat up all night working. Mayhew'd wanted to do a movie about the rainmakers and pluvicultists for a long time. There'd been an early silent about it, but had been a real stinker [Dam Burst at Sun Dog Gap, Universal 1911—Int.], so Mayhew thought up the plot, and the mood, and we knew Shadow Smith was available, and Mayhew'd written a couple of movies with "PDQ" Podmer in them so he thought up the "Doodad" character for him, and we went back to Thalberg next day and shook hands on it and took off for Boise the next morning.

Int.:
It was a beautiful little film—most people remember it being a feature.

Selvors:
Mayhew kicked butt with that script—lots of stuff in it, background and things, lots of action, but nothing seemed jammed in sideways or hurried. You remember that one was self-contained; I mean, it ended with the rain and everybody jumping up and down in mud puddles, and the Cloudbusters rolling out for the next place. I think if we'd never made another one, people would still remember The Cloudbusters.

Int.:
It was the first one to show the consequences, too—it ended with the Cloudbusters sitting in the Thunder Wagon bogged up to the wheelhubs and having to be pulled out by two teams of oxen.

Selvors:
That's right. A beautiful touch. But it wasn't called the Thunder Wagon yet. Most people remember it that way but it wasn't, not in that one. That all came later.

Int.:
Really?

Selvors:
Really. Wasn't until the second one their wagon was referred to as the Thunder Wagon. And it wasn't painted on the side until the third one.

Int.:

How did the features, and the rest of the series come about?

Selvors:
Thalberg liked it. So did the preview audiences, better than anything but the cartoon. It even got bookings outside the package and the chains.

Int.:
I didn't know that. That was highly unusual.

Selvors:
So much so they didn't know what to do. But by then we were into the second, maybe the third. All I know is they set up a points system for us.

Int.:
Even though you were on salary?

Selvors:
Me and Mayhew were in pig heaven. Smith got part of it, but the brightest man of all was Podmer. He wasn't on contract—he was, like, a loose cannon; sometimes him and Andy Devine or Eric Blore would work on two or three movies on different lots a day. Anyway, he sure cut some sweet deal with M.G.M. over the series. Podmer talked like a hick and walked like a hick—it was what we wanted in the character of "Doodad" and he was brilliant at it—but he could tear a pheasant with the best of them. . . .

Int.:
So if you and Mayhew set out to tell a realistic story, about the rainmakers and the real business of winning the West . . .

Selvors:
I know what you're going to ask next. (laughs)

Int.:
What?

Selvors:

You're going to ask about the Windmill Trust.

Int.:
What about the Windmill Trust?

Selvors:
That part, we made up.

    From: The Sidekick: Doppelgangers of the Plains by Marvin Ermstien, UCLA Press, 1972.

(This interview with Elmer "PDQ" Podmer took place in 1968, a few months before his death at the age of ninety-four. It was recorded at the Boise Basin Yacht Club.)

ME:
Let's talk about the most popular series you did at M.G.M.

Podmer:
You mean The Cloudbusters?

ME:
You've been in, what, more than three hundred movies . . . ?

Podmer:
Three hundred seventy-four, and I got another one shooting next month, where I play Burt Mustin's father.

ME:
I'm still surprised that people remember you best as "Doodad" Jones. Three of the films were shorts, five were B movies, and I don't think any of them have been on television for a while. . . .

Podmer:
Izzat a fact? Well, I know last time I saw one was mebbe ten year ago when I was over to my great grandniece's house. I remember when Bill Boyd was

goin' on and on about television, way back in 1936 or so. He told all us it was the wave o' the future and to put all our money in Philco. He was buying up the rights to all his Roman Empire movies, that series he made, Hoplite Cassius. We all thought he was crazy as a bedbug at the time. He made quite a bundle, I know that.

ME:
About The Cloudbusters . . .

Podmer:
Well, it was a good character part. It was just like me, and the director and writer had some pretty good ideas what to do with him. Also, you remember, I was the star of the last one. . . .

ME:
The Thunder Wagon. That was the one being made when Shadow Smith died.

Podmer:
That was it. Well, originally of course it had pretty much another script—they'd filmed some of it—in fact they'd filmed the scene that was used in the movie where Shadow talks to me and then rides off to do some damn thing or other. Next day we got the news about Shadow drowning in the Snake River while he was hauling in a fourteen-pound rainbow trout. They found his rod and reel two mile downriver and the trout was still hooked. . . .

ME:
There were lots of ironic overtones in the death notices at the time.

Podmer:
You mean about him being in The Cloudbusters and then dying that way? Yeah, I remember. He was a damn fine actor, a gentleman, just like his screen character. We was sure down for a while.

ME:

So the script was rewritten?

Podmer:
Yep. Mayhew wanted to make it a tribute to Smith, and also do some things he hadn't been able to do before, so he turned out a hum-dinger! I got top billing for the first and only time in my life. In the cutting on the new version, they had Smith say whatever it is; then as he turns to ride away they had this guy who could do Smith's voice tell me where to take the Thunder Wagon, which sets up the plot. That puts me and Chancy Raines (that was Bobby Hornmann, a real piss-ass momma's boy, nothing like the character he played) smack dab up against Dryden and the Windmill Trust on our own. 'Course the real star of that last picture was the wagon itself. Mayhew's screenplay really put that thing through some paces. . . .

ME:
Tell us about the Wagon.

Podmer:
You seen the movies, ain't you?

ME:
Three or four times each.

Podmer:
Then why ask me?

ME:
Well, it looked like you firing off the Lightning Rockets and the Nimbus Mortars. . . .

Podmer:
It was me. I didn't use no stuntman! I wisht I had a nickel for every powder burn I got on that series. Some days I'd be workin' at M.G.M. morning and hightailing it all the way across Boise to the first National lot, and runnin' on the set sayin' my lines, and the makeup men would be bitching because I'd burnt half my real beard off, or had powder burns on my arms, or

something. One of those other films I ain't got no eyebrows in a couple of scenes.

ME:
What about the Sferics Box? I know some critics complained there was nothing like it in use among the rainmakers in the real Old West.

Podmer:
Do I look like a goddamn engineer? I'm a thespian! Ask Mayhew or Selvors about that stuff. I do know I once got a letter from a guy what used to be a rainmaker back then—hell, he must have been older when he wrote that letter than I am now—who said he used something like that there Sferics Box—they'd listen for disturbances in the ether with them. Had something to do with sunspots, I think.

ME:
That was twenty years before deForest sent the first messages....

Podmer:
They wasn't interested in talkin' to each other, they was interested in makin' a gullywasher! That's what the guy wrote, anyway.

ME:
In all those films, Shadow Smith never used a gun, right?

Podmer:
Well, just that once. People talked about that stuff for a long time. It was the next to last one [The Watershed Wars, 1937 —ME] and they was that shootist for the Windmill Trust that called Shadow out to a street duel—Shadow'd just gone into the saloon to find him after all those people were killed when the Windmill Trust tried to make Utah Great Lake salty again, and Shadow's so mad he picks up a couple of guns from the bar and goes out, then you cut out onto the street, bad guy's standing in it, and Shadow comes out the saloon doors a quarter-mile away and starts shooting, just blasting away and walking up the boardwalk, bullets hitting all over the streets around the shootist, and he just takes off and runs, hightails it away.

When Shadow realizes what he's done, that he's used gun-violence, he gets all upset and chagrined. People still talk about that. What few Westerns were made later, even the ones they started filming a few years ago in what was left of the Sahara Plains, they'd never done that—always romanticized it, one-to-one, always used violence. Never like in The Cloudbusters, where we used brains and science. . . .

ME:
It wasn't just Shadow Smith's death that finished the series, then?

Podmer:
It wuz everything. Smith died. Thalberg had been dead a year by then, and Goldfish wanted to move Selvors up to the A pictures; he never could leave well-enough alone. The next one we knew was gonna be directed by just someone with a ticket to punch. Selvors tried to stay, but they told him their way or the highway. That was the middle of '38, just when the European market fell apart, and people was nervous over here—they didn't have to wait but till August before our market started The Long Fall, and people started the Back-to-the-Land movement; they ate all right but there wasn't any real money around. Anyway, that's about the time Mayhew had the garish-headline divorce and we'd be damned if we'd let other people write and direct The Cloudbusters. Also, they took Bill Menzies away from us. He'd designed the Thunder Wagon, and most of the props and did the sets, and about half the effects on the movies—remember the credits, with that big thunderhead rolling in on you and suddenly spelling out The Cloudbusters?—that was Menzies' doing all along.

So we all got together, just after we wrapped The Thunder Wagon and we made a gentlemen's agreement that there wouldn't be any more Cloudbuster films—it was hard to do, we'd been a real family except for that shitty Hornmann kid, I hope he's burning in hell—[Robert Hornmann was killed in a fight in a West Boise nightclub in 1946 —ME] and for me it was walking away from a goldmine, and my only chance to get top billing again. But it was easiest for me, too, since I had a picture-to-picture deal and all I did was line up enough work to stay busy for the solid next year. I also put out the word to all the other comic relief types not to go signin' anything with the name Cloudbusters on it. . . .

ME:

Have you seen Sergio Leone's A Faceful of Rainwater?

Podmer:

Was that the Wop Western about the Two Forks War?

ME:

Yes. It's supposedly an homage to the Cloudbusters, much grittier but not as good, I don't think.

Podmer:

Nope. Ain't seen it.

From: BLAZING SCREENS! The Magazine of Celluloid Thrills, June 1972.

SOUNDTRACK THUNDER AND NITRATE LIGHTING! By Formalhaut J. Amkermackam

Imagine a time when most of the American continent was a vast dry desert from the Mississippi to the Pacific Coast!

Imagine when there were no lush farmlands from sea to sea, when coffee, rubber, and tea had to be imported into this country!

Imagine that once men died crossing huge sandy wastes & when the only water for a hundred miles might turn out to be poison, when the Great Utah Lake was so salty it supported no aquatic life!

Imagine when the Midwest was only sparse grasslands, suitable for crops only like wheat & oats, or an economy based on the herding of cattle & sheep!

Imagine a time when rainfall was so scarce the only precipitation was snow on the high mountains in the winter & when that was melted there was no more till next year!

These things were neither a nightmare nor the fevered dreams of some fantasy writer—this was the American West—where our forefathers actually tried to make a living—less than one hundred years ago!

YOU CAN TAKE A PLUVICULTURE BUT YOU CAN'T MAKE IT DRINK

Then came the men & women who not only talked (as Mark Twain once said) about the weather but they did something about it! They called themselves storm wizards, rainmakers, and even pluviculturists (which is the fancy word for rainmaker!) & their theories were many & varied but what they did & how they did it & how they changed our lives & the destiny of the world was the stuff of legend. But at first everybody just talked about them & nobody did anything about them.

Until 1935, that is!!!

TWO THUNDERHEADS ARE BETTER THAN ONE

That year George Mayhew (the screenwriter of Little Lost Dinosaur & Wild Bill Barnacle) teamed up with James Selvors (director of such great movies as The Claw-Man Escapes, His Head Came C.O.D., and the fantastic musical war movie Blue Skies & Tailwinds) to bring to the screen a series of films dealing with the life & times of the men who broke the weather & transformed the American West to a second Garden of Eatin'—The Cloudbusters!

THE GUN THAT DROWNED THE WEST

Aided by the marvelous & mysterious Thunder Wagon (in which they kept all their superscientific paraphernalia & their downpour-making equipment) they roamed the west through five feature films & three shorts that will never be forgotten by those who've seen 'em.

SHADOWS OF THINGS TO COME

For the lead in the films (except for the last one where he had only a brief appearance due to his untimely & tragic death) they chose Shadow Smith, the big (6'5½") actor who starred in such films as Warden, Let Me Out!, My Friend Frankenstein, and lots more. Before the Cloudbusters films, his best known role was as Biff Bamm in Spooks in the Ring, Singing Gloves, and Biff Bamm Meets Jawbreaker, all for Warner Bros. Shadow was born in 1908 in Flatonia, Texas, & had worked in films from 1928 on, after a stint as an egg-handler & then college in Oklahoma City.

He fit the role perfectly (his character name was Shadow Smith too) and, according to people who knew him, was just like his screen character— soft-spoken, shy, and a great lover of the outdoors. It is interesting that the

Shadow Smith character in the Cloudbusters never used a firearm to settle a score—sometimes resorting to scientific wrestling holds & fisticuffs, but most usually depending on his quick wits, brain, and powers of logic.

WHO DAT WHO DAY "DOODAD"?

As comic relief & sidekick "Doodad" Jones was played by Elmer "PDQ" Podmer (the "PDQ" in the name of this old-time character actor stuck with him for the alacrity with which he learned & assayed his many roles, and the speed with which he went from one acting job to another, sometimes working on as many as three different films at three different studios in one day!). The character of "Doodad" was one of the most interesting he ever had. Many characteristics were the usual—he used malapropisms like other sidekicks ("aspersions to greatness" and "some hick yokelramus," and he once used "matutinal absolution" for "morning bath") but was deferred to by Shadow Smith for his practical knowledge & mechanical abilities, especially when something went wrong with the "consarned idjit contraptions" in the Thunder Wagon.

Their young assistant, Chancy Raines (played by Bobby Hornmann, who died tragically young before he could fulfill his great talents as an actor) was added in the second film as an orphan picked up by Smith and "Doodad" after a drought & sudden flash flood killed his mother & father & little sister.

Together they roamed the West, in three short (three-reel or twenty-eight-minute) films and five full-length features made between 1935 and 1938. They went from small towns and settlements to the roaring hellcamps of Central City and Sherman Colorado to the Mojave Desert in California, and as far north as the Canadian border, bringing with them storms & life-giving rains which made the prairies bloom—always in their magnificent Thunder Wagon!

SKYWARD HO!

The Thunder Wagon! A beautiful & sleek yellow and blue (we were told) wagon pulled by a team of three pure white horses (Cirrus, Stratus, and Cumulus) and one pure black horse (Nimbus)!

Designed by director/cameraman/set designer/special effects man Bill C. Menzies (who had come from Germany via England to the M.G.M.

studios in Boise in 1931), the Thunder Wagon seemed both swift & a solid platform from which Shadow, "Doodad," and Chancy made war on the elements with their powerful Lightning Rockets, Nimbus Mortars (& the black horse neighed every time that weapon was fired), and Hailstone Cannons, which they fired into the earth's atmosphere & caused black clouds & thunderstorms (& in one case a blizzard) to form & dump their precipitation on the hopeful thirsty farmers and ranchers who'd hired them.

DON QUIXOTES OF THE PLAINS!

But the weather wasn't the only thing the Cloudbusters fought in the course of their movies. For they also had to battle the deadly Windmill Trust!

The Windmill Trust! A group of desperate Eastern investors, led by the powerful Mr. Dryden, dedicated to keeping the status quo of low rainfall & limited water resources in the Western territories! Their tentacles were everywhere — they owned the majority of railroads & all the well-drilling & windmill manufacturing firms in the United States & they kept in their employ many shootists & desperados whom they hired to thwart the efforts of all the rainmakers & pluviculturalists to bring moisture to the parched plains. These men resorted to sabotage, mis-sending of equipment, wrongful processes of law, and in many cases outright murder and violence to retain their stranglehold on the American West and its thirsty inhabitants!

DESICCATED TO THE ONE I LOVE

Through these eight films, with their eye-popping special effects (even the credits were an effects matte shot of a giant cloud forming & coming toward you & suddenly spelling out the series' name!), their uncharacteristic themes, and their vision of a changing America (brought on by the very rainmakers these films were about!), there were thrills & images people would never forget.

If you ever get to see these (& someone should really put the first three shorts together in one package & release it to TV) you'll see:

A race to the death between raging floodwaters, the Thunder Wagon, and the formerly unbelieving Doc Geezler & a wagonload of orphans!

"Doodad" Jones using the Nimbus Mortars to cause a huge electrical storm & demolish the Giant Windmill (thirty stories high!) sucking the water from & drying up the South Platte River & threatening the town of Denver with drought!

The henchmen of the Windmill Trust (led by Joe Sawyer) dressed as ghosts in a silent (no sound of hoofbeats, only the snap of quirts and jangle of spurs heard in an eerie scene) raid on the town of Central City, Colorado!

The climactic fight on the salt-drilling platform above Utah Great Lake in the hailstorm between Shadow Smith & Dryden, and three others seemingly plunging to their deaths far below!

The great blizzard forming over the heated floor of the (once) Great Mojave Desert, with its magical scenes of cacti in the snow & icicles on the sagebrush!

ACTION! THRILLS! WET SOCKS!

You can see all this and more, if you travel back via the silver screen & your TV set to a time not so long ago, when the Cloudbusters rode the Wild American West in their eight films:

The Cloudbusters (1935 — a short, introducing Shadow Smith, "Doodad," and the Thunder Wagon!)

44 Inches or Bust! (1935 — the second short — the title refers to the rainfall they promise a parched community — introducing Chancy Raines & the Windmill Trust!)

Storms Along the Mojave (1936 — the last short)

The Desert Breakers (1936 — the first feature, introducing Dryden as head of the Windmill Trust!)

The Dust Tamers (1936 — with the magic blizzard scenes!)

Battling the Windmill Trust (1936 — with the giant windmill that threatens Denver!)

The Watershed Wars (1937 — Dryden and Shadow Smith in hand-to-hand combat above Utah Great Lake!)

The Thunder Wagon (1938 — the best film though not most representative due to the death of Shadow Smith ((who appears only in an early scene & to whom the picture is dedicated)) but the Thunder Wagon is the star along with "Doodad" & Chancy — they have to cause rain in three widely separated places & use the Hailstone Cannons to freeze an underground stream!)

So through these films you can ride (or saddle up again if you were lucky enough to see them the first time) with Shadow Smith, "Doodad"

Jones, and Chancy Raines, fighting the Windmill Trust & bringing the West the rain it so sorely needs & experience a true part of American history & thrill to the science & adventures of The Cloudbusters!

INTRODUCTION TO

THE EFFECTS OF ALIENATION

One of the beauties (there are few) of being a writer is that you can do all the things in one genre that you never did in another.

For instance: I lived, breathed, ate (and dropped other courses in college) theater for a period of about three years. Theater was a crummy one-credit course, and you were spending fifty and sixty hours a week there, besides all the other education-crap-type courses you were supposed to be doing (three- and four-credit courses). I wrote plays, I was technical director, gaffer, best boy, key grip, scene painter and designer, Johannes factotum. I even acted (there's never been another such Thousand Clowns as ours; since I had the twelve-year-old Nick Burns part — the Barry Gordon one in the movie — they cast giants all around me — the leading lady was 6'1" for godsakes, and she was the shortest besides me at 5'7").

Anyway, I did everything, read everything, wrote everything. I was going to be the next Aeschylus, the next Lope de Vega, the next Eugene O'Neill.

Somewhere along the line I made two astounding discoveries: 1) All those guys were dead and we didn't need new ones. 2) I was making money writing prose. Then I was drafted. But that's another story.

One time I got a part because I was the only one who could do a Peter Lorre imitation (the part was of a very confused obscene phone-caller . . .). I wrote a play about the dying Bogart (before Woody Allen) and Lorre called The Long Goodnight. It was probably horrible; like the one about the Round Table, set in the Old West with barbed wire in the place of Mordred . . . and so on and so forth. Copies of some of my playwriting stuff's in the Special Collections Library at Texas A&M University. Those, I pray, aren't. If they exist, they're in box four after the third divider; it says in my list here. I sure hope not . . .

I do have a point and I am getting to it: You will notice that several of my stories have plays in them—this one, "The Lions Are Asleep This Night," not here, and movie scripts, or parts of movies never made. This book's full of them.

That's what you can do when you're a big-time writer—you can put in your stories all the plays you didn't write when you were eighteen; only in the stories, they're all produced and are Big Hits! (or not, but they are produced).

I wrote this in a hotel in Harrowgate England (as with far too many stories, I had to write one or show up empty-handed and wing-it for an hour). Not only that (and I've done this twice), a panel of lit-crits were there, to instantly critique it. Sort of a Gong Show Self-Worth Theater, if you know what I mean.

I wowed 'em. Pretty good going for a guy everybody kept filled to the Plimsoll Line with Guinness Stout for two weeks. At the end of my time over there, at Gatwick, I said, "You know, I'm not a drinking man."

"Could have fooled us," they said.

I'm inordinately proud of this one. And it is about the movies.

THE EFFECTS OF ALIENATION

It always seemed to be snowing in Zürich that winter, but as Peter walked toward the café, he found himself looking up at an astonishingly blue sky.

Cold, still colder than a well-digger's ass, but clear nonetheless. He was so taken aback he stopped. There was a dull sun, looking as frozen as an outdoor Christmas tree ornament, over to the west. The houses and buildings all seemed new-washed; even the slush on the sides of the street was white, not the usual sooty gray. Perhaps the crowd for the opening night might be larger than even he had hoped. If Brecht were still alive, he would have said, "Weather good for a crowd, good for a crowd."

There was a stuttering hum in the air, a summer sound from another country and time, the sound of a fan in a faraway room. It got louder. Then above the lake the airship Herman Göring II pulled into view like an art deco sausage on its daily run from Freidrichschaffen across the border to Berne. Some mighty Germans aboard; an admiral's and two generals' pennants flew from the tail landing ropes just below the swastikas on the stubby fins. Peter's eyes were getting worse (he was in his fifties) but he noticed the flags while the thing was still two kilometers away. The airship passed out of sight beyond the nearest buildings. Its usual course was far northwest of Zürich — one of the Aryans must have wanted a look.

Higher up in the sky he saw the thin slash of white made by the Helsinki-Madrid jet, usually invisible far above the snowy clouds over

Switzerland. Peter hadn't seen it for months (not that he'd even been looking). To people here, the passenger planes were something you only occasionally saw, like summer. Well, maybe that will change tonight, he thought. They'll never look at a jet plane or a rocket the same way again.

Then he asked himself: Who are we fooling?

He went on down the street to the Cabaret Kropotkin.

The actor doubling in the role of the blind organ grinder was having trouble with his Zucco, so in the last run-through he had to sing a cappella. Another headache, thought Peter. Brecht's widow sent the offending instrument out: The one thing you could get done in Switzerland was have things fixed. More trouble: The ropes holding some of the props had loosened; they had to be restrung.

Peter tugged on a carabiner. "Zero," he said to the actor, "you really should lose some weight." Peter had the voice of a small, adenoidal Austrian garter snake.

The other actor (in the Cabaret Kropotkin, everyone was an actor; everyone a stagehand, an usher, a waiter, a dishwasher) pulled himself to his full height. He towered over Peter and blocked his view of the stage. He let go of his end of the rope.

"What? And lose my personality?" said Zero. "It's glands!"

"Glands, my ass," said Peter. "On what we make, I don't know how you gain weight." He pulled on the guy rope.

"Do what? Gain? Back in America, I used to weigh—"

"Back in America," said Shemp, the other actor with a leading role in the play, "back in America, we all had jobs. We also knew how to keep a rope tight." He jerked it away, burning their hands.

"Quit trying to be your late brother!" said Zero, sucking on his fingers. "You just don't have Moe's unique personality."

"And he didn't have my looks. Eeep Eeep Eeep Eeep!"

Peter shook his head, twisted a turnbuckle past the stripped place on the threads.

"Vaudeville!" said Zero. "God, how I don't miss it!"

"Eight shows a day!" said Shemp. "Your name up in lights!"

"The only thing your name is going to be up in is the pay register," said Brecht's widow from the cabaret floor where she had returned without a sound, "if you don't get those ropes straightened out."

"Yes, comrade Ma'am," said Shemp for all of them.

A little after 5:00 P.M. they finished the last rehearsal and it was time for supper. They'd had to cook that, too. A healthy cabbage soup with potatoes and a thick black bread Zero had kneaded up that morning.

Madame Brecht, who wore her hair in a severe bun, joined them. The conversation was light. The Poles, Swedes, English, American, German, French, and Lithuanians who made up the ensemble had been together for such a time they no longer needed to talk. One look, and everybody knew just how everybody else's life was going. When they did speak, it was in a sort of pig-Esperanto comprised of parts of all their languages, and when the Madame was around, great heaping doses of Hegelian gibberish.

Not that a single one of them didn't believe that being right there right then wasn't the only place to be.

Bruno, the old German gaffer, was staring into his soup bowl like it was the floor of Pontius Pilate's house.

Shemp whispered to Peter, "Here comes the fucking Paris story again."

"I was there," said Bruno. "I was in the German Army then. What did I know? I was fifty-three years old and had been drafted."

Madame Brecht started to say something. Peter caught her eye and raised his finger, warning her off.

"Paris!" said the old man, looking up from the table. "Paris, the second time we took it. There we were in our millions, drums beating, bugles blaring, rank on rank of us! There was the Führer in his chariot, Mussolini following behind in his. There they were pulling the Führer down the Champs-Élysées, Montgomery and Eisenhower in the lead traces, de Gaulle and Bomber Harris behind. Poor Bomber! He'd been put in at the last moment after they shot Patton down like a dog when he refused. Then came all the Allied generals with their insignia ripped off. It was a beautiful spring day. It was fifteen years ago."

There were tears streaming down his face, and he looked at the Madame and smiled in a goofy way.

"I remember it well," continued Bruno, "for that night, while looting a store, under the floorboards, I found the writings of Mr. Brecht."

"Thank you for your kind reminiscence, Bruno," said the Madame.

"Suck up!" said Zero, under his breath.

"Just another hard-luck story," said Shemp.

"I like it very much," said Peter to Zero quietly. "It has a certain decadent bourgeois charm."

"Does anyone else have an anecdote about the Master?" asked the Madame, looking around expectantly.

Peter sighed as someone else started in on yet another instructive little dialectic parable.

Arguing with Brecht had been like talking to a Communist post. When the man's mind was made up, that was that. When it wasn't was the only time you could show him he was being a Stalinist putz; only then had he been known to rewrite something.

The first time Peter had met Brecht, Peter had been nineteen and fresh off the last turnip truck from Ludow. All he wanted was a Berlin theater job; what Brecht wanted was a talented marionette. He'd ended up doing Brecht's comedy by night and Fritz Lang's movies by day, and in his copious free time learning to spend the increasingly inflated Weimar money, which eventually became too cheap to wipe your butt with. Then Peter found himself in America, via Hitchcock, and Brecht found himself in Switzerland, via Hitler.

Peter sighed, looking around the table. Everybody here had a story. Not like mine, but just like mine. I was making movies and money in America. I was nominated for the Academy Award twice, after playing Orientals and psychopaths and crazy weenies for ten years. There was a war on. I was safe. It was that fat old fart Greenstreet, God rest his soul, who talked me into the USO tour with him. There we were, waiting for Glenn Miller's plane to come in, near the Swiss border, six shows a day, Hitler almost done in, the biggest audiences we'd ever played to when BLAM! — the old world was gone.

And when I quit running, it's "Hello, Herr Brecht, it is I, your long-lost admirer, Peter, the doormat."

"And you?" asked Madame. "What can you tell us of our late departed genius?"

Peter ran through thirty years of memories, those of the first, and the ones of the last fifteen years. Yes, age had mellowed the parts of Brecht's mind that needed it. Yes, he had begun to bathe and change clothes more often after his second or third heart attack, which had made things much more pleasant. He had exploited people a little less; possibly he'd forgotten how, or was so used to it that he no longer noticed when he wasn't. No, the mental fires had never gone out. Yes, it was hard to carry on their work without the sharp nail of his mind at the center of their theater. He could also have said that Brecht spent the last three years of his life trying to put The Communist Manifesto into rhymed couplets. He could have said all that. Instead, he looked at the Madame. "Brecht wanted to live his life so that every day at 6:00 P.M. he could go into his room, lock the door, read cheap American detective stories, and eat cheese to his heart's content. The man must have had bowel muscles like steel strands."

Then Peter got up and left the room.

Walter Brettschneider was the Cultural Attaché to the Reichsconsul in Zürich and was only twenty-five years old. Which meant, of course, that he was a major in the Geheime Staats Polizei. His job at the Consulate included arranging and attending social and cultural affairs, arrangements for touring groups from the Fatherland to various Swiss cities (Zürich, he thought, rather than Berne, being the only city in the country with any culture at all). His other job was easier—he could have been assigned to one of the Occupied Lands, or South America, or as liaison with the Japanese, which every day was becoming more and more of a chore for the Reich; his friend back in Berlin in the Ministry of Manufacture told him the members of the Greater East Asia Co-Prosperity Sphere had come up with many technical innovations in the last few years; they were now making an automobile as good as the Volkswagen and had radio and televiewing equipment that required only three tubes.

That second job of his consisted of forwarding to Berlin, each year or so, a list of thirty to forty names. Of these, a dozen or fifteen would be picked. These people would suddenly find that their permanent resident alien status in Switzerland was in question, there were certain charges, etc. And then they would be asked by the Swiss to leave the country.

Everyone was satisfied with the arrangement, the Swiss, the Reich, in some strange way the resident aliens, as long as they weren't one of the dozen or so. Switzerland itself was mined and booby-trapped and well defended. If the Reich tried to invade, the Alps would drop on them. Germany controlled everything going in and out—it surrounded the country for two thousand kilometers in every direction—the New Lands, New Russland, New Afrika, New Iceland, the lands along the shiny new Berlin-Baghdad Eisenbahn—except the contents of the diplomatic pouches, and some of those, too.

If the Fatherland tried to use the Weapons on the Swiss, they lost all those glittery numbered assets, and endangered their surrounding territory.

So the system was understood. After all, as the First Führer had said, we have a thousand years; at a dozen a year we will eventually get them all.

Edward, his assistant, knocked and came in.

"Heil Bormann," he said, nonchalantly raising his hand a few inches.

"OK," said Brettschneider, doing likewise.

"You remember that the two younger cousins of the Swabian Minister for Culture are arriving Thursday?" asked Edward.

"I had tried to forget," said Brettschneider. He opened the big 1960 calendar on his desk to February 13th, made a note. "Will you please make sure the schedule in the hall is marked? Why, why do people come to Switzerland in the winter?"

"I certainly have no idea," said Edward. "What's doing?"

"There's a new show at the Kropotkin tonight. They're not saying what it is, so of course I have to go see."

"Not the kind of place you can take the cou—"

"Most assuredly not. But then again, last month they did the decadent American classic Arsenic and Old Lace. Quite amusing in its original version. Of course, in theirs, the Roosevelt character wasn't Theodore. And Jonathan was made up to look like the Second Führer—" Brettschneider looked up at the three photos on his wall—Hitler, Himmler, Bormann—Himmler's was one of the old official ones, from eleven years ago, before the chin operation, not the posthumous new official ones—"no, not really the kind of place, the type of plays two young women should see."

"Have a good time," said Edward. "I have to accompany the Reichsminister's wife to the Turkish thing."

"Oh? Yes? How's your Turkish?"

"It's being given in English, I am led to believe. I'll drop back in later today, in any case."

Edward left. Brettschneider stared at the doorway. For all he knew, Edward might be a colonel in the G.S.P.

"It's too bad they don't make Zambesi cigarettes anymore," said Caspar, the scene designer, as he smoked one of Peter's cheap German cigars. "We'd have them free. It was before your time, before you met Brecht, back in the early twenties. He was always trying to write pirate movies and detective novels. Before Marx. He designed an ad campaign for the tobacco company. He took an unlimited supply of Zambesis in payment. He grew to detest them before the company went out of business. I thought them quite good."

"I'd give anything to smoke a Camel again," said Shemp. They were putting down tablecloths and ashtrays, and lighting the candles out front. Zero was pumping up the beer spigots over behind the bar. Madame was, as usual, nowhere to be seen, but, say something wrong, you could be sure she would hear it. The woman was fueled by the thought that someone, somewhere, wasn't thinking about Bertolt Brecht.

"I heard they don't make them over there anymore," said Caspar. "The Turks, you know? They claim, in Germany, Airship Brand is the same thing as Camels used to be."

"They're as full of shit as Christmas geese," said Shemp. "God, what I wouldn't give for a slice of goose!"

And so it went until time to open, when the Madame suddenly appeared in front of Peter and said, "You work the door until 1930 hours. Then you may get into costume."

"Yes, comrade Madame," he said. There was no use arguing with her. It would have been like asking Rondo Hatton, Why the long face?

He went to the door. Under the covered walkway quite a nice crowd had gathered early. Peter looked at the sign out front with its double silhouette of Kropotkin and Brecht and the hand-painted legend: Tonight! — Cabaret Kropotkin — The Zürcher Ensemble — new BRECHT play!

It wasn't really Brecht. It wasn't exactly a play. It wasn't exactly new. They'd been working on it steadily in the three years since Brecht's death.

He undid the latches as the people surged expectantly toward him. He opened the doors, stood back, nodded his head toward the tables.

"Trough's open," he said.

Brettschneider arrived a few minutes to eight, went in, nodded to

Caspar, who was bartending, and found a spot at a table near the stage with three Swiss students. He listened to their talk a while — it must be nice to live in their world. They were treating the night as a lark; a dangerous place, reputed to be filled with drugs and lady Bolsheviks with mattresses tied to their backs.

Hesse was over in the corner. Brettschneider nodded to him. He doubted the old man saw him, as his eyes were becoming quite bad (he was, after all, eighty-three years old now); he would go over and say hello during the interval.

There were a few of what passed as Swiss celebrities present, some Germans, a few Swiss arms dealers.

Across the length of the stage was the patented Zürcher Ensemble half-curtain let down on a length of pipe. Behind it was the bare back wall. Across this were strung a few twinkling lights, like a Christmas tree with too few bulbs. People moved back and forth across the stage, quite visible to the audience from the neck up.

The band took its place in front of the curtain — banjo, piano, clarinet — and began a jazz arrangement of "The Internationale" — one or two people stood, and the rest began clapping along. When that was done, they played the old favorite "Moon of Alabama" from Mahogany, and "Don't Sit Under the Apple Tree with Anyone Else but Me." Brettschneider drank a chocolate schnapps and began to feel quite warm. The cabaret was already thick with the blue smoke of a hundred different tobaccos.

Then the lights went down. From the ceiling a sign dropped: Cabaret Kropotkin — a hand came down from above and beat on the top of the sign, which unfolded into three parts: Cabaret Kropotkin — The Zürcher Ensemble Presents Bertolt Brecht's — Die Dreiraketenmensch Spaceoper! The half-curtain came up. Another sign dropped in: Scene: The Rocket Men's Club. Time: The Future. Moritaten.

An actor dressed as a blind man came on with a barrel organ and began singing "The Night We Dropped the Big One on Biggin Hill."

Zero, Peter, and Shemp, in their Rocket Men Cadet uniforms, walk by the beggar, who is then escorted offstage by a policeman.

"Here we are at last!" says Zero. "Just out of Basic Training! Our first taste of the Outer Reaches!"

"I'm ready for some inner reaches!" says Shemp.

"Beer again!" says Peter.

The flies pulled up revealing a bar's interior, tables. Dropping in were huge posters of von Braun and Dornberger, and a portrait in the frame reserved for Führers. The audience found it hilarious.

Brettschneider wrote in his notebook: Unnecessary fun made of Himmler Jr.

When things quit falling, unfurling and drooping in from the overheads, there were swastikas whirling like propellers and a giant, very pink rocket with a purple nose cone to be seen.

The three students then sang, as appropriate title cards were revealed, "It's Me for the Stars, and the Stars for Me," followed by Zero's "Once You Get Up There." Then one of their instructor officers, Major Strasser, came in and had a drink with them.

"But don't you find it cold here?" asks Peter.

"We Germans must get used to all climates, from the Sahara to the poles of Saturn," says the major.

Then the chorines danced on and sang "Dock Your Rocket Here" and a chorus line, not of cadets but true Rocket Men, danced on, including one small grotesque figure in sunglasses.

Brettschneider wrote: more " " " H. Jr., beneath his first entry.

The cadets and Rocket Men ran off with the chorines, and a new card dropped in: The Field for Rockets. Training. On one side of the fence the three cadets stood at attention; on the other a girl skipped rope to the chant:

"My girlfriend's name is Guernica. Her Daddy bombed 'Merika . . ."

The Drill Instructor, called Manley Mann, comes on and yells at the cadets. "Where you going, you stupid lot?"

"Up. Up. Up."

"How you goin'?"

"Fast. Fast. Fast."

"At night, whatcha see inna sky?"

"Nazi Socialist Moon!"

"Gimme a thousand pushups."

The cadets dropped down, began to count, "One Vengeance Weapon, Two Vengeance Weapon, Three Vengeance Weapon . . ." There was stage business with the pushups, most of it dealing with Zero's attempts to do nothing while yelling at the top of his voice.

When they finished, Manley Mann said, "Right. Today we're gonna learn about the MD2D3 Course Plottin' Calculator. Walk smart follow me follow me—" and off.

Another card: Six Weeks Later. Cadet Barracks. Night.

Then came Shemp's solo, as he looked out the window at a bored-looking stagehand holding up a cardboard moon. He did some comic patter, then went on to sing "I Wish I Had a Little Rocket of My Own."

Then the lights went up, the Intermission sign dropped down, and the half-curtain was lowered to the stage.

Backstage the Madame was furious. "I told you we must take that song out!" she yelled at Shemp. "You realize you made the audience identify with your character? You know that's against all the Master's teachings! You were supposed to sing the 'Song of the Iron Will.' "

Shemp weaved like a punch-drunk boxer, running his hands through his dank, lanky hair. "I got mixed up," he said. "They played the wrong music, so I sang it. Yell at the band."

"You must always always remember the Verfremsdungeffekt. You must always remind people they are watching a performance. Why do you think the stagehand holds the prop moon so everyone can see him? Are you an idiot? What were you thinking?"

Shemp paused, ticking off on his fingers. "I do. I always do. I don't know. Yes. Nothing."

"Why must I be saddled with morons?"

Shemp said something under his breath.

"What?! What did you say?!"

"I said I gotta get a drink of water, or I'm gonna lose my voice next act."

"That's not what you said!"

"Yes it is, comrade Ma'am."

"Get out of my sight!"

"At once," said Shemp, and disappeared offstage.

Zero sat on a crate in the alleyway. It was bitterly cold, but this was the only place he was sure Madame wouldn't follow him. Peter came out, lit up a butt one of the waiters had brought him from a customer's ashtray.

"We gotta find another way to make a living," said Zero, his breath a fog.

"We've said that every night for sixteen years now," said Peter. "Christ, it's cold!"

"Wasn't it Fitzgerald that said nothing much starts in Switzerland, but lots of things end there?"

"How the fuck should I know?" said Peter.

"Well, I don't want to be one of the things that ends here," said Zero.

Peter thought of lines from a movie he'd been in long ago, lines dealing with exile, expatriation, and death, and started to say one of them, but didn't.

Besides, they'd already used the best lines from that movie in the play.

"It's like I told that fat great Limey actor once," said Peter. " 'Chuck,' I said, 'if you have to pork young men, just go for god's sake and do it, and come back and learn your goddamn lines; just quit torturing yourself about it!' "

"Are you saying I should pick up a little boy?" asked Zero.

Peter shrugged his shoulders. "Where else is there to go but here, Zero?" he asked.

Zero was quiet. Then: "Sometimes I get so tired, Pete. Soon we'll be old men. Like Bruno. Then dead old men . . ."

"But theater! —" began Peter.

" —and Brecht! —" said Zero.

" —will live forever!" they finished in unison. They laughed and Zero fell off his crate into the snow. Then they brushed themselves off and went back inside.

Brettschneider had made his rounds of the tables during the break. He looked over his notes, made an emendation on one of them. He ate a kaiser roll, then drank a gin-and-tonic, feeling the pine-needle taste far back in his throat.

Then the band came back, played the last-act overture, and cards dropped back in.

There was a classroom lecture on the futurist films of Fritz Lang, Metropolis and Frau im Mond, which then went backwards and forwards to cover other spaceward-looking films: Himmelskibet, F.P.1 Antwortet Nicht, Der Tunnel, and Welttraumschiff I Startet, at which Zero insisted on confusing Leni Reifenstahl with the Dusseldorf Murderer.

Brettschneider wrote: unacceptable reference to Reichsminister for Culture.

Then the play moved on to Graduation Day, where the massed cadets (represented by the three actors, some mops and brooms with mustaches painted on them, and a boxful of toy soldiers) sang "Up Up for the Fatherland" and were handed their rocket insignia.

The actors changed onstage into their powder-blue uniforms (overalls) with the jackboots (rubber galoshes) as a sign came down: First Assignment. Rocket Man City — Peënemünde.

Another sign: Suddenly — A Propaganda Crisis!

Major Strasser comes up to the three Rocket Men. "Suddenly," he says, "a propaganda crisis!"

"Eeep Eeep Eeep Eeep!" says Shemp, staggering.

"Attention!" says the major. "Our enemies in the U.S.R. far beyond the Urals have launched one of their primitive reaction-motor ships. It is bound for the far reaches of the Solar System. Our information is that it is filled with the Collected Works of Marx and Lenin, and the brilliant but non-Aryan playwright Bertolt Brecht."

(There was a boo from the audience, followed by laughter. The actors onstage held still until it was over.)

"Your first assignment is to intercept this missile before it can spread unapproved thinking to Nazi Socialist space, and beyond, and to destroy it."

There was a blackout; four signs were illuminated, one after the other:
Three Go Out.
One Gets Killed.
One Goes Mad.
One Doesn't Come Back.

The first two signs were lit. In the darkness, Zero is in a balsawood framework shaped like a small rocket. To his uniform has been added a bent coat hanger representing a space helmet.

His voice is roaring, he is determined. The band is raucous behind him but his singing overpowers it.

"Target in sight!
It's easy, all right!

Just   line   up   the   guns   and   watch   all   the   fu--
Ooops!"

A papier-mâché meteor, painted red and trailing smoke vertically, comes out of the darkness. It smashes into Zero's ship, which flies to flinders. Zero, his coat-hanger helmet now gone, floats up into the air on wires in the dark, a hideous grin on his face.

The spotlit placard: One Goes Mad.

Shemp's balsawood spaceship. Zero floats directly in front of it. "Whoa!" yells Shemp. He punches things on his instrument panel, running his hands over his coat hanger. "Eeep Eeep Eeep Eeep!" Then he sits bolt upright, unmoving except for the lips, making perfect sense in a monotonous voice, reciting the successive graph plots on a Fibonacci curve, as he and his ship, trailing vertical smoke, are pulled by ropes out of the light into the darkness at the back of the stage.

The spotlight searches around, finds the sign: One Doesn't Come Back. Peter in his ship. He is mumbling the Soldier's Creed. At the other side of the stage, light comes up on a toy rocket. Peter takes out a dart gun, fires twice at the toy, his arm outside the ship's framework as he reloads the rubber-tipped darts. One finally hits the toy rocket—it explodes like a piñata.

Then an oogah klaxon horn is blown backstage, causing the audience to jump, and Peter's ship is bathed in flickering red light. "Uh-oh," he says. "Trouble." Then the band begins to play softly, and he sings "I Wonder What Deborah's Doing in Festung Amerika Tonight?"

The ship tilts downwards.

Blackout. A sign: Mars.

When the lights come back up the stage is clear. A red silk drop cloth covers the ground. For a full minute, nothing happens. Then Peter's balsawood ship, him inside, flies out of the wings and he lands flat on his ass, legs straight out while pieces of wood bounce all over.

He stands up, brushes himself off. As he does so, stagehands begin to ripple the red silk, making it look like drifting, gently blowing sand. Peter takes off his coat hanger, takes a deep breath. A book falls from above, bounces at the rear of the moving red stage. Then another follows. Peter looks up. A book slowly lowers toward him on a wire. He reaches up and plucks it from the air. Others fall around him occasionally throughout the scene. Peter begins to read. His eyes widen even more. He looks up at the audience. He reads more. Then he stands up. "Holy dialectical shit!" he says.

Then the lights came up, and the chorines, stagehands, actors, ushers and dishwashers came in, taking their bows. Zero floated down from the ceiling on his wires, blowing kisses. Then the Madame came out, glaring at Zero, turned and took a bow to the audience for having survived Brecht.

Then they all passed among the tables, holding out baskets for donations.

Brettschneider stayed at his table drinking, while the audience mingled with the members of the Ensemble. He noticed that he'd written nothing in his notebook since the couple of entries just after intermission. When he saw Peter take something from Madame, put on his coat and go out the door, Brettschneider wrote: Suspects then all followed their usual routines. Then he gathered up his own things, nodded to Caspar who was still tending bar, and went back to his home and to bed.

Christ, it's even colder than this morning, thought Peter. He turned off the main avenue, went down a side street. The snow, which this morning had seemed so white and pure, was now gray, crusted ice. Even so, as he turned into a small courtyard, he saw that only a few sets of footprints had come and gone that way the whole day.

Near the middle was a rusty iron gate. He went in with a loud groaning squeal from the metal. On the wall was a brass plate that said Union of Soviet Republics Consular Offices. Peter went to the mail drop, took the envelope out of his thin overcoat pocket. On the outside, written in Madame's florid script was From Your Comrades at the Cabaret Kropotkin. Peter tore open the envelope, took out a few hundred francs, slapped some medical adhesive tape over the torn flap, tied it around twice with some twine, and dropped it in the slot.

As Brecht had said: First the beans, then the morals. He went back up the avenue, crunching through the frosty ice on the way. The night was still clear, bitterly frigid. He looked up at the winking stars, and saw the slow-moving dot of Space Platform #6 on its two-hour orbit.

He heard a streetcar bell. He knew of a place he could go and get a cup of real coffee and watch a fireplace burning for an hour or two, where the thought of Herr Brecht would never cross his mind. He began whistling "In the Hall of the Mountain King."

Introduction to

All About Strange Monsters of the Recent Past

This is the oldest story in the book; in fact it's the second story I *ever* sold. And "sold" and "sold." It was written on April 10, 1972. It finally got into print in April of 1981, nine years almost to the day.

It first sold for an eighty-seven dollar advance (when that was a month's rent *anywhere*) to a David Gerrold anthology in 1973, to be published in 1975. The publisher had a reshuffle, three anthologies were squashed into two, etc. Rights were returned in 1976; I updated it a little; it was "sold" to a magazine; the two editors had a punch-up; it was on its own again. Finally it was sold and paid for (sixty dollars this time) and appeared in *Shayol* #4, and was the title story of my second collection in 1987.

The genesis: I was in the Army, doing my bit as The Reluctant Draftee. (A little after Gardner Dozois and Joe Haldeman did theirs—one of the *many* jobs I had in the Army was sitting at the same desk the comic-book writer Bill Dubay had sat in two years before me. . . .) The night before this story was written, I was on guard duty. It was a weekend. You were on for twenty-four hours; instead of the usual two hours on, four hours off in four shifts, we asked the Officer of the Day if we could do eight-hour shifts and get it *all the hell* over with at once. Since what we were guarding was an *empty* PX (site of a former PX, but since it hadn't been taken off the list of *active* buildings, it had to be guarded—such is the fine logic of the military mind . . .), he didn't give much of a whoop either. So there I was with my clipboard, my flashlight, and my nightstick, walking *endlessly* around a deserted building for eight long hours. . . .

The idle mind is the devil's playground, and boy was mine idle.

It occurred to me: What would happen if there were suddenly a Giant Bee Emergency on the East Coast? *I* would be one of the poor dogfaces to have to fight the nectar-hungry sumbitches! There's a scene in every Big Bug SF movie of the 1950s when things get out of hand: All Sheriff Johnson's deputies are eaten, Martial law's declared, and the Army's called out, to great cheers from the audience—tanks come out, jeeps with 75mm recoilless rifles screech around corners, caissons go rollin' along. Goodbye, Mr. Six-or-Eight-Legs; eat napalm dropped by Clint Eastwood! (See "French Scenes" later.)

Me! It would be *Me!* Fighting *Them!*

I went home after roll-call and wrote the story.

(What everybody missed in Joe Dante's *Matinee* was that the Cuban Missile Crisis was the last time the U.S. Military was looked on as the Good Guys—that's why he used "The Lion Sleeps Tonight" twice—once as a lullaby for the younger, scared brother during the Crisis; the second time—over a shot of a hovering helicopter, when the immediate threat's over—as a warning. That lion *wasn't* asleep in that jungle—it was going to eat us up and tear apart the fabric of American Society—once again, US against THEM. . . .)

And if you haven't, I suggest you go out right now and buy both volumes of Bill Warren's *Keep Watching the Skies!* (MacFarland, 1982 and 1986)—simply the most comprehensive, indispensable, thorough, and entertaining work ever on SF films of 1950-1962. I wish it had been around when I wrote this story, but as usual, I'd seen all the movies anyway, growing up and later.

Come with me for a trip down double-feature shock-o-rama Memory Lane . . .

ALL ABOUT STRANGE MONSTERS
OF THE RECENT PAST

It's all over for humanity, and I'm heading east.

On the seat beside me are an M1 carbine and a Thompson submachine gun. There's a special reason for the Thompson. I traded an M16 and 200 rounds of ammo for it to a guy in Barstow. He got the worst of the deal. When things get rough, carbine and .45 ammo are easier to find than the 5.56mm rounds the M16 uses. I've got more ammo for the carbine than I need, though I've had plenty of chances to use it.

There are fifty gallons of gasoline in the car, in cans. I have food for six days (I don't know if that many are left).

When things really fell apart, I deserted. Like anyone else with sense. When there were more of them than we could stop. I don't know what they'll do when they run out of people. Start killing each other, maybe.

Meanwhile, I'm driving 160 kmph out Route 66. I have an appointment in the desert of New Mexico.

God. Japan must have gone first. They deluged the world with them; now, it's Japan's turn. You sow what you reap.

We were all a little in love with death and the atom bomb back in the 1950s. It won't do us much good now.

The road is flat ahead. I've promised myself I'll see Meteor Crater before I die. So many of them opened at Meteor Crater, largest of the astroblemes. How fitting I should go there now.

In the back seat with the ammo is a twenty-kilo bag of sugar.

It started just like the movies did. Small strangenesses in small towns, disappearances in the back woods and lonely places, tremors in the Arctic, stirrings in the jungles.

We never thought when we saw them as kids what they would someday mean. The movies. The ones with the giant lizards, grasshoppers, mollusks. We yelled when the monsters started to get theirs. We cheered when the Army arrived to fight them. We yelled for all those movies. Now they've come to eat us up.

And nobody's cheered the Army since 1965. In 1978, the Army couldn't stop the monsters.

I was in that Army. I still am, if one's left. I was one of the last draftees, with the last bunch inducted. At the Entrance Station, I copped and took three years for a guaranteed job.

I would be getting out in three months if it weren't for this.

I left my uniform under a bush as soon as I decided to get away. I'd worn it for two and a half years. Most of the Army got torn away in the first days of the fight with the monsters. I decided to go.

So I went. East.

I saw one of the giant Gila monsters this morning. There had been a car ahead of me, keeping about three kilometers between us, not letting me catch up. Maybe a family, figuring I was going to rob them or rape the women. Maybe not. It was the first car I'd seen in eighteen hours of dodging along the back roads. The car went around a turn. It looked like it slowed. I eased down, too, thinking maybe it wasn't a family but a bunch of dudes finally deciding to ambush me. Good thing I slowed.

I came around the turn and all I could see was the side of an orange and black mountain. I slammed on the brakes and skidded sideways. The Gila monster had knocked the other car off the road and was coming for me. I was shaken, but I hadn't come this far to be eaten by a lizard. Oh no. I threw the snout of the M1 carbine out the window and blasted away at the thing's eyes. Scales flew like rain. It twitched away then started back for me. I shot it in the tongue. It went into convulsions and crawled over a small sandhill hissing and honking like a freight train. It would come back later to eat whatever was in the other car. I trundled back on the road and drove past the wreck. Nothing moved. A pool of oil was forming on the concrete. I drove down the road with the smell of cordite in my nose and the wind whipping past. There was Gila monster blood on the hood of the car.

I had been a clerk in an airborne unit deployed to get the giant locusts eating up the Midwest. It is the strangest time in the history of the United States. The nights are full of meteors and lights.

At first, we thought it was a practice alert. We suited up, climbed into the C-130s with full combat gear, T-10 parachutes, lurp bags and all. At least the others had chutes. I wasn't on jump status so I went in with the heavy equipment to the nearest airbase. A lot of my buddies jumped into Illinois. I never saw them again. By the time the planes landed, the whole brigade was gone.

We landed at Chanute. By then, the plague of monsters was so bad I ended up on the airbase perimeter with the Air Policemen. We fired at the things until the barrels of the machine guns moaned with heat. The locusts kept coming, squirting brown juice when they were hit or while killing someone.

Their mandibles work all the time.

We broke and ran after a while. I caught a C-130 revving up. The field was a moving carpet of locusts as I looked behind me. They could be killed easily, as could any insect with a soft abdomen. But there were so many of them. You killed and killed and they kept coming. And dying. So you had to run. We roared off the runway while they scuttled across the airfield below. Some took to the air on their rotor-sized wings. One smashed against the Hercules, tearing off part of an elevator. We flew through a night full of meteors. A light paced us for a while but broke off and flew after a fighter plane.

We couldn't land back at Pope AFB. It was a shambles. A survivor said the saucers hit about midnight. A meteor had landed near Charlotte, and now the Martian fighting machines were drifting toward Washington, killing everything in their paths.

We roared back across country, looking for someplace to land where we wouldn't be gobbled up. Fuel got lower. We came in on a wind, a prayer, and fumes to Fitzee Field at Fort Ord. I had taken basic training at Ord.

A few hours later, I duffed.

I heard about New York on the radio before the stations went off. A giant lizard had come up from the Hudson submarine canyon and destroyed Manhattan. A giant octopus was ravaging San Francisco, a hundred miles north of Ord. It had already destroyed the Golden Gate Bridge. Saucers were landing everywhere. One had crashed into a sandpit behind a house nearby. A basic training unit had been sent in. They wouldn't be back, I knew. A glass-globed intelligence would see to that.

Navy ships were pulled under by the monsters that pillaged New York, by the giant octopus, by giant crabs in the South Pacific; by caterpillar-like mollusks in the Salton Sea.

The kinds of invaders seemed endless: Martian fighting machines, four or five types of aliens. The sandpit Martians, much different from the fighting-machine kind. Bigheaded invaders with eyes on the backs of their hands.

A few scattered reports worldwide. No broadcasts from Japan after the first few minutes. Total annihilation, no doubt. Italy: A craft, which only existed on celluloid, brings back from Venus an egg of death. Mexico: A tyrannosaurus rex comes from the swamps for cattle and children. A giant scorpion invades from the volcanoes. South America: giant wasps, fungus disease, terrors from the earth. Britain: A monster slithers wild in Westminster Abbey, another fungus from space, radioactive mud, giant lizards again. Tibet: The yeti are on the move.

It's all over for humanity.

Meteor Crater at sunset. A hole punched in the earth while ice sheets still covered Wyoming and Pennsylvania.

I can see for miles, and I have the carbine ready. I stare into the crater, thinking. This crater saw the last mammoth and the first of the Indians.

The shadow deepens and the floor goes dark. Memories of man, crater. Your friend the Grand Canyon regards you as an upstart in time. It's jealous because you came from space.

Speaking of mammoths, perhaps it's our time to join old woolly in the great land of fossil dreams. Whatever plows farms in a million years can turn up our teeth and wonder at them.

Nobody knows why the mammoth disappeared, or the dinosaur, or our salamander friend the Diplovertebron, for that matter. Racial old age. No plausible reason. So now it's our turn. Done in by our dreams from the silver screen. Maybe we've created our own Id monsters, come to snuffle us out in nightmares.

The reason I deserted: The Air Force was going to drop an A-bomb on the Martian fighting machines. They were heading for Ord after they finished L.A. I was at the command post when one of the last B-52s went over, heading for the faraway carnage on the horizon.

"If the A-bomb doesn't stop it, Colonel," said a major to the commander, "nothing will."

How soon they forget, I thought, and headed for the perimeter.

The Great Southwest saw more scenes of monster destruction than anywhere in the world except Japan. Film producers loved it for the sterility of the desert, the hot sun, the contrasts with no gradations for their black-and-white cameras. In them, saucers landed, meteors hurtled down, townspeople disappeared, tracks and bones were found.

Here is where it started, was the reasoning. In the desert thirty-three years ago when the first atomic bomb was detonated, when sand was turned to glass.

So the monsters shambled, plodded, pillaged, and shook the Southwest. This desert where once there was only a shallow sea. You can find clamshells atop the Sierras, if you look.

I have an appointment here, near Alamogordo. Where it started. The racial old age is on us now. Unexplained, and we'll die not knowing why, or why we lived the least time of all the dominant species on this planet.

One question keeps coming to me. Why only films of the 1950s?

Am I the only one who remembers? Have I been left alone because I'm the only one who remembers and knows what I'm doing? Am I the only one with a purpose, not just running around like a chicken with its head cut off?

The radio stations are going off one by one as I drive from the crater to Alamogordo. Emergency broadcast stations, something out of Arkansas, an Ohio station. Tonight, I'm not going to be stopped. I've got the thirty-round magazine in the carbine and the forty-five-round drum in the Thompson. I wish I had some grenades, or even tear gas, but I have no mask (I lost it in the battle against the grasshopper). Besides, I'm not sure tear gas will be effective for what I have in mind.

On the dying radio stations and in my mind's eye, this is what I see and hear:

The locusts reach Chicago and feast till dawn, while metal robots roam the streets looking for men to kill.

The giant lizard goes past Coney Island with no resistance.

The huge mantis, after pillaging the Arctic, reduces Washington to shambles. It has to dodge flying saucers while it pulls apart monuments, looking for goodies. The statue of Abraham Lincoln looks toward Betelgeuse and realizes that the War Between the States was fought in vain.

The sky is filled with meteors, saucers, a giant flying bird. Two new points of light hang in the sky: a dead star and a planet which will crash to earth in a few days. The night is beginning to be bathed in a dim bloody light.

An amorphous thing sludges its way through a movie theater, alternately flattening, thickening, devouring anything left.

The Martian fighting machines have gone up and down both coasts, moving in a crescent pivotal motion.

The octopus has been driven underwater by heat from the burning of San Francisco.

So much for the rest of the country.

Here in the Southwest, a million-eyed monster has taken over the cattle and dogs for hundreds of miles.

A giant spider eats cattle and people and grows. The last Air Force fighters have given up and are looking for a place to land. Maybe one or two pilots, like me, will get away. Maybe saucers will get them. It won't be long now.

The Gila monsters roam, tongues moving, seeking the heat of people, cars, dogs.

Beings with a broken spaceship are repairing it, taking over the bodies of those not eaten by other monsters. Soon they will be back up in the sky. Benevolent monsters.

Giant columns of stone grow, break, fall, crushing all in their paths.

Miles wide now, and moving toward the Colorado River, the Gulf, and infinite growing bliss. No doubt they have crushed giant Gila monsters and spiders along with people, towns, and mountains.

A stranded spaceman makes it to Palomar and spends his last seconds turning the telescope toward his home star; he has already killed nineteen people in his effort to communicate.

A monster grows, feeding on the atoms of the air.

A robot cuts its way through a government installation fence, off on its own path of rampage. The two MPs fire until their .45s click dry. Bullets ricochet off the metal being. Soon a saucer will fly over and hover. They will fire at the saucer with no effect; the saucer will fire and the MPs will drift away on the wind.

(There may be none of our bones to dig up in a million years.)

All this as I drive toward the dawn, racing at me and the Southwest like the avenging eye of God. No headlights. I saw a large meteor hit back in the direction of Flagstaff; there'll be hell to pay there soon. Meanwhile, I haven't slept in two days. The car sometimes swerves toward the road edge. No time for a crack-up, so close now.

The last radio station went off at 0417.

Nothing on the dial but mother earth's own radio music, and perhaps stellar noises which left somewhere five hundred million years ago, about the time our friend the Diplovertebron slithered through the mud. The east is graying. I'm almost there.

The car motor pops and groans as it cools. The wind blows steadily toward the deeper desert. Not far from here, the first A-bomb went off. Perhaps that was the challenge to the universe, and it waited thirty years to get back at us. This is where it started.

This is where it ends.

I'm drinking a hot Coke. It tastes better than any I've ever had. No uppers, downers, hash, horse, or grass for me. I'm on a natural high.

I've set my things in order. All the empty bottles are filled with gasoline and the blanket's been torn up for fuses. My lighter and matches are laid out, with some cigarettes for punks. With the carbine slung over my shoulder, I wait with the Thompson in my right hand, round chambered, selector on rock and roll.

They won't die easy, but I envision a stack of them ringing my body, my bones, the car: some scorched and blackened, some shot all away, some with mandibles still working long after I'm dead.

I open the twenty-kilo bag of sugar and shake it onto the wind. It sifts into a pile a few feet away. The scent should carry right to them.

I took basic at Fort Ord. There was a tunnel we had to double-time through to get to the range. In cadence. Weird shadows on the wall as we ran. No matter how tired I was, I thought of the soldiers going into the storm drains after the giant ants in a movie I'd seen when I was six. They started here, near the first A-blast. They had to be here. The sugar would bring them.

A sound floats back up the wind like the keening of an off-angle buzz saw. Ah. They're coming. They'll be here soon, first one, then many. Maybe the whole nest will turn out. They'll rise from behind that dune, or maybe that one.

Closer now, still not in sight.

It's all over for man, but there are still some things left. Like choices, there's still that. A choice of personal monsters.

Closer now, and more sounds. Maybe ten or twenty of them, maybe more.

End of movie soon. No chance to be James Arness and get the girl. But plenty of time to be the best James Whitmore ever. No kids to throw to safety. But a Thompson and a carbine. And Molotov cocktails.

Aha. An antenna waves in the middle distance. And—

Bigger than I thought. Take your head right off.

Eat leaden death, Hymenopterae! The Thompson blasts to life.

Screams of confusion. A flash of 100 octane and glass. High keening like an off-angle buzz saw.

I laugh. Formic acid. Cordite.

Hell of a life.

DREAM FACTORIES: THE FUTURE

Two sorts of stabs at what might be, and both look back to an earlier era of the movies as a starting point.

History is not a straight-line thing. As Gardner Dozois once said: SF-type guys and ladies looked around in the 1910s and said, "By 1980, we will have *night baseball!*" They were right, just wrong about the date.

People have predicted revolutions in technology before; they were approximately right; their dates were too pessimistic AND by the time their predictions came true, so had *lots* of others. No straight-line thinking ever turns out just like it was planned.

To very widely paraphrase Asimov in an early essay: First-order thinking, 1880: Tom Oakheart looks around, tinkers, invents the horseless carriage. Second-order thinking, 1880: Tom Oakheart invents horseless carriage, he and Teddy use it to race to the sawmill *faster* than a *horse* could carry them, to rescue Pearl from Oil Can Harry. Third-order thinking, 1880: Tom Oakheart, Pearl, and Teddy are caught in a traffic jam in his horseless carriage, on the way to a drive-in movie (where Oil Can Harry is going to rob the concession stand). (The thinking is Asimov's; the examples are from my W/S u-plotter.)

Lots of people predicted *movies in your house*. TV (radio pictures) fulfilled part of that need (selling *you* oats when Mr. Ed wasn't); then (and there *should* have been video discs before tape, but everyone was waiting for a stylus-less system; by the time they got that, tape had stolen the march) videotape in your home, two formats locked in a Texas-style barbed-wire death match; laserdiscs; DVD; etc. (I'll buy the new stuff when they can guarantee it's the *only* system I'll *ever* need.) Home video recapitulates the ontogeny of recorded music: cylinders to shellac 78s to 45s to 33 1/3rd albums to eight-track to cassette to compact disc to DAT to DVD and audio chips.

Here (he said) in the early 21st Century: All the people who predicted movies in your house ignored *all* the other stuff that would be grab-assing for your time and your increasingly limited attention: video games, computers and computer games, palm pilots, cell phones, walkmans, watchmen, VR glasses and gloves, paintball for gods' sakes, rock climbing, inline skates, snowboards, fly fishing, and beds and breakfasts, the whole thing.

Now movies may or may not go digital. (The idea of film or music or *anything* using up brainpower when there are perfectly good mechanical means of producing *exactly* the same results, seems to be multiplying entities retrogradely. It uses less power, you say. I say: You're forgetting the power that was used to make the chip *in the first place*, which is why Silicon Valley's running out of water and steam.)

There's a future for the movies (on the way to videotape and TV): What it is neither you nor I nor anyone else knows. That movies will still be made (and most get worse and worse, pretested, safe, delivering their dull shocks as regular as clockwork, by people who make them to as narrow a formula as any *ever* devised, including me and Sennett) is certain. That some great stuff will be made, and slip through, by plan or accident, like it always has, is probable, too.

So enjoy these stories; one pretty speculative; one rather elegiac (if I must say so, and I must).

INTRODUCTION TO

FRENCH SCENES

Already, since this was written (1986) there have been some amazing technical advances in film.

If I were in the stunt persons' union, I'd be running scared (this is barely touched on in the story). I envision that guild, ten years from now, as just another featherbed outfit, like locomotive firemen; *there*, maybe, in some advisory capacity or other, with no members *ever* jumping off a burning building *or* crashing a car, or doing anything, except pushing a few buttons, or nodding their heads yes or no. (That their families will sleep lots better is just an added union benefit.)

The story was cutting-edge, in its way, when it was written. Some of it even now has been surpassed; there are lots more technical wonders to come. (That many computer-generated images are in ads, TV, and film where they're *not needed* is just one of those byproducts of technology — they *can* do it, so they *do* — "Oooh. Neat!")

No more junkets to the Barbados for supermodels, no more small-town location shooting, no more delays due to weather or the fargin' sun being in the wrong place for the shot. No more *waiting*, an astounding idea in filmmaking — more than half the time shooting a movie is *nothing happening*. Call it up — hey! Presto! (Sort of like Méliès in reverse, isn't it?) There you are in Faulkner's bedroom at Rowan Oak with the plot outline of *A Fable* written across three walls; there you are *Gump-like* being slapped by Patton; there you are whenever and wherever you want to be, wherever and whenever you want to shoot.

Such is the future: maybe. What I wanted to say here is that anytime new stuff comes along, it's almost like a geologic discontinuity, a Cretaceous/Cenozoic divide. There's movies before *A Trip to the Moon* (1902) and after; *Birth of A Nation* (1915); *The Jazz Singer* (1927); *Gone with the Wind* and *The Wizard of Oz* (both 1939, the year they got Technicolor right); *Citizen Kane* (1941); *Bwana Devil* (1952) and *The Robe* (1953) for 3-D and Cinemascope; movies before *Hiroshima, Mon Amour* and *The 400 Blows* (both 1959), and after.

All these films were important, either technically, or narratively in terms of film grammar; movies could no longer be made like they had been before them, or if so, only at the filmmaker's peril. Whatever one felt about them, they couldn't be ignored, *Birth of A Nation* is about editing, *not* its politics (Tom Oakheart = the KKK). *The Jazz Singer* stopped movies cold for about three years (the whole grammar of film was there by 1925; confronted with sound and a stationary microphone, the movies *forgot* everything they'd learned in the first thirty-two years of filmmaking. Don't take *my* word for it, go see Murnau's *Sunrise* [also 1927]. Movies didn't *move* and tell stories like that again until about 1932 . . .). *Citizen Kane* is just, well, *Citizen Kane*. Nothing had ever looked that way before or told a story like that. *Bwana Devil* and *The Robe* (*art* they're not) in their fight against the One-Eyed Living-Room Monster taught directors you couldn't (1) ignore the depth of field, front to back, of what the camera sees; (2) ignore the left and right sides of the screen, which all but the best filmmakers had *always* done. The movie screen went from being a sheet on the wall to being a moving box in the air.

The Frenchies reshuffled the ol' narrative deck as effectively as Griffith and Welles had done, in an even more with-it way. Why show a guy getting out of bed, cleaning up, going downtown, standing on a corner with a newspaper till the armored car pulls up at the bank, then show him folding his newspaper, walking across the street, and, five minutes into the movie, an insert shot of him reaching into his pocket, pulling out a gun on the security guard? *Blip* guy in bed *blip* guy brushes teeth *blip* corner with newspaper *blip* dead guard on ground, scattered moneybags, newspaper lying in street *blip* Jean-Louis Tritingnant driving an Alfa Romeo on the road above Monaco, forty-nine seconds into film!

The pace of life and perception was changing; *they* saw it first. (It's accelerated even more, here forty years on, but now people are just *quicker* to be dumber.) *They* knew *we* knew how movies worked, there in the audience. They just showed us the good stuff; we filled in the boring parts. (Except for Godard, who reversed the process, but which still shows he knew what he was doing. . . .)

So—this story looks forward, to the wonders that might come, at the same time it's looking back at the last time somebody shook the place up.

And no matter what technologies come, it's still going to take somebody doing something new with it, or using it *just right* (for example, the use of the Steadicam: Kubrick's *The Shining* vs. the Coen brothers' *Raising Arizona*. *Don't* make *me* decide) to tell the story. Miracle technology is just another (*this time* Kubrick: the distal end of an antelope bone *blip* HAL) tool—once you see it and go "Oooh. Neat!" it damn well'd better *do* something. (*Star Wars* just sits there on the screen for the first while, until Harrison Ford puts the pedal to the metal and the *Falcon* goes into hyperdrive—the audience has *waited eighty-two years* for that two seconds; after that the spectators are merely a painted audience in a painted auditorium; they can be told *any* story.)

Come with me, then, on a two-way voyage. Janus-like, I wanted to look both ways at once.

FRENCH SCENES

The fault, dear Brutus, is not in our stars,
But in ourselves . . .
— Julius Caesar act 1, sc. 2, ln. 1-2

There was a time, you read, when making movies took so many people. Actors, cameramen, technicians, screenwriters, costumers, editors, producers, and directors. I can believe it.

That was before computer animation, before the National Likeness Act, before the Noe's Fludde of Marvels.

Back in that time they still used laboratories to make prints; sometimes there would be a year between the completion of a film and its release to theaters.

Back then they used actual pieces of film, with holes down the sides for the projector. I've even handled some of it; it is cold, heavy, and shiny.

Now there's none of that. No doctors, lawyers, Indian chiefs between the idea and substance. There's only one person (with maybe a couple of hackers for the dogs' work) who makes movies: the moviemaker.

There's only one piece of equipment, the GAX-600.

There's one true law: Clean your mainframe and have a full set of specs. I have to keep that in mind, all the time.

Lois was yelling from the next room where she was working on her movie Monster Without a Meaning.

"We've got it!" she said, storming in. "The bottoms of Morris Ankrum's feet!"

"Where?"

"Querytioup," she said. It was an image-research place across the city run by a seventeen-year-old who must have seen every movie and TV show ever made. "It's from an unlikely source," said Lois, reading from the hard copy. "Tennessee Johnson. Ankrum played Jefferson Davis. There's a scene where he steps on a platform to give a secession speech.

"Imagine, Morris Ankrum, alive and kicking, 360°, top and bottom. Top was easy—there's an overhead shot in Invaders from Mars when the guys in the fuzzy suits stick the ruby hatpin-thing in his neck."

"Is that your last holdup? I wish this thing were that goddamn easy," I said.

"No. Legal," she said.

Since the National Fair Likeness Act passed, you had to pay the person (or the estate) of anyone even remotely famous, anyone recognizable from a movie, anywhere. (In the early days after passage, some moviemakers tried to get around it by using parts of people. Say you wanted a prissy hotel clerk—you'd use Franklin Pangborn's hair, Grady Sutton's chin, Eric Blore's eyes. Sounded great in theory but what they got looked like a walking police composite sketch; nobody liked them and they scared little kids. You might as well pay and make Rondo Hatton the bellboy.)

"What's the problem now?" I asked.

"Ever tried to find the heirs of Olin Howlin's estate?" Lois asked.

What I'm doing is called This Guy Goes to Town . . . It's a nouvelle vague movie; it stars everybody in France in 1962.

You remember the French New Wave? A bunch of film critics who wrote for a magazine, Cahiers du Cinema? They burned to make films, lived, slept, ate films in the 1950s. Bad American movies even their directors had forgotten, B Westerns, German silent Expressionistic bores, French cliffhangers from 1916 starring the Kaiser as a gorilla, things like that. Anything they could find to show at midnight when everybody else had gone home, in theaters where one of their cousins worked as an usher.

Some of them got to make a few shorts in the mid-fifties. Suddenly studios and producers handed them cameras and money. Go out and make movies, they said: Talk is cheap.

Truffaut. Resnais. Godard. Rivette. Roehmer. Chris Marker. Alain Robbe-Grillet.

The Four Hundred Blows. Hiroshima, Mon Amour. Breathless. La Jetée. Trans-Europe Express.

They blew moviemaking wide open.

And why I love them is that for the first time, underneath the surface of them, even the comedies, was a sense of tragedy; that we were all frail human beings and not celluloid heroes and heroines.

It took the French to remind us of that.

The main thing guys like Godard and Truffaut had going for them was that they didn't understand English very well.

Like in Riot in Cell Block 11, when Neville Brand gets shot at by the prison guard with a Thompson, he yells:

"Look out, Monty! They got a chopper! Back inside!"

What the Cahiers people heard was:

"Steady, mon frère! Let us leave this place of wasted dreams."

And they watched a lot of undubbed, unsubtitled films in those dingy theaters. They learned from them, but not necessarily what the films had to teach.

It's like seeing D. W. Griffith's 1916 Intolerance and listening to an old Leonard Cohen album at the same time. What you're seeing doesn't get in the way of what you're thinking. The words and images made for cultures half a century apart mesh in a way that makes for sleepless nights and new ideas.

And, of course, every one of the New Wave filmmakers was in love, one way or another, with Jeanne Moreau.

I'm playing Guy. Or my image is, anyway. For one thing, composition, sequencing, and specs on a real person take only about fifteen minutes' easy work.

I stepped up on the sequencer platform. Johnny Rizzuli pushed in a standard scan program. The matrix analyzer, which is about the size of an old iron lung, flew around me on its yokes and gimbals like the runaway merry-go-round in Strangers on a Train. Then it flew over my head like the crop duster in North by Northwest.

After it stopped the platform moved back and forth. I was bathed in light like a sheet of paper on an old office copier.

Johnny gave me the thumbs-up.

I ran the imaging a day later. It's always ugly the first time you watch yourself tie your shoelaces, roll your eyes, scratch your head, and belch. As close, as far away, from whatever angle in whatever lighting you want. And when you talk, you never sound like you think you do. I'm going to put a little more whine in my voice; just a quarter-turn on the old Nicholson knob.

The movie will be in English, of course, with subtitles. English subtitles.

(The screen starts to fade out.)

Director (voice off): Hold it. That's not right.

Cameraman (off): What?

Director (also me, with a mustache and jodhpurs, walking on-screen): I don't want a dissolve here. (He looks around.) Well?

Cameraman (off): You'll have to call the Optical Effects man.

Director: Call him! (Puts hands on hips.)

Voices (off): Optical Effects! Optical Effects! Hey!

(Sounds of clanking and jangling. Man in coveralls ((Jean-Paul Belmondo)) walks on carrying a huge workbag marked Optical Effects. He has a hunk of bread in one hand.)

Belmondo: Yeah, Boss?

Director: I don't want a dissolve here.

Belmondo (shrugs): Okay. (He takes out a stovepipe, walks toward the camera p.o.v., jams the end of the stovepipe over the lens. Camera shudders. The circular image on the screen irises in. Camera swings wildly, trying to get away. Screen irises to black. Sound of labored breathing, then asphyxiation.)

Director's voice: No! It can't breathe! I don't want an iris, either!

Belmondo's voice: Suit yourself, Boss. (Sound of tearing. Camera p.o.v. Belmondo pulls off stovepipe. Camera quits moving. Breathing returns to normal.)

Director: What kind of effects you have in there?

Belmondo: All kinds. I can do anything.

Director: Like what?

Belmondo: Hey, cameraman. Pan down to his feet. (Camera pans down onto shoes.) Hold still, Monsieur Le Director! (Sound of jet taking off.) There! Now pan up.

(Camera pans up. Director is standing where he was, back to us, but now his head is on backwards. He looks down his back.)

Director: Hey! Ow! Fix me!

Belmondo: Soon as I get this effect you want.

Director: Ow! Quick! Anything! Something from the old Fieullade serials!
Belmondo: How about this? (He reaches into the bag, brings out a Jacob's Ladder, crackling and humming.)

Director: Great. Anything! Just fix my head!

(Belmondo sticks the Jacob's Ladder into the camera's p.o.v. Jagged lightning bolt wipe to the next scene of a roadway down which Guy ((me)) is walking.)

Belmondo (v.o.): We aim to please, Boss.

Director (v.o.): Great. Now could you fix my head?

Belmondo (v.o.): Hold still. (Three Stooges' sound of nail being pried from a dry board.)

Director (v.o.): Thanks.

Belmondo (v.o.): Think nothing of it. (Sound of clanking bag being dragged away. Voice now in distance.) Anybody seen my wine?

(Guy ((me)) continues to walk down the road. Camera pans with him, stops as he continues offscreen left. Camera is focused on a road sign:)
Nevers 32 km
Alphaville 60 km
Marienbad 347 km
Hiroshima 14497 km
Guyville 2 km

To get my mind off the work on the movie, I went to one of the usual parties, with the usual types there, and on the many screens in the house were the usual undergrounds.

On one, Erich von Stroheim was doing Carmen Miranda's dance from The Gang's All Here in full banana regalia, a three-minute loop that drew your eyes from anywhere in line of sight.

On another, John F. Kennedy and Marilyn Monroe tore up a bed in Room 12 of the Bates Motel.

In the living room, on the biggest screen, Laurel and Hardy were doing things with Wallace Beery and Clark Gable they had never thought of doing in real life. I watched for a moment. At one point a tired and puffy Hardy turned to a drunk and besmeared Laurel and said: "Why don't you do something to help me?"

Enough, enough. I moved to another room. There was a TV there, too. Something seemed wrong—the screen too fuzzy, sound bad, acting unnatural. It took me a few seconds to realize that they had the set tuned to a local low-power TV station and were watching an old movie, King Vidor's 1934 Our Daily Bread. It was the story of a bunch of Depression-era idealistic have-nots making a working, dynamic, corny, and totally American commune out of a few acres of land by sheer dint of will.

I had seen it before. The Cahiers du Cinema people always wrote about it when they talked about what real Marxist movies should be like, back in those dim pre-Four Hundred Blows days when all they had were typewriters and theories.

The house smelled of butyl nitrate and uglier things. There were a dozen built-in aerosol dispensers placed strategically about the room. The air was a stale mix of vasopressins, pheromones, and endorphins which floated in a blue mist a couple of meters off the floors. A drunken jerk stood at one of the dispensers and punched its button repeatedly, like a laboratory animal wired to stimulate its pleasure center.

I said my goodbyes to the hostess, the host having gone upstairs to show some new arrivals "some really interesting stuff."

I walked the ten blocks home to my place. My head slowly cleared on the way, the quiet buzzing left. After a while, all the parties run together into one big Jell-O-wiggly image of people watching movies, people talking about them.

The grocer (Pierre Brasseur) turns to Marie (Jeanne Moreau) and Guy (me).

"I assure you the brussels sprouts are very fine," he says.

"They don't look it to me," says Marie.

"Look," says Guy (me) stepping between them. "Why not artichokes?"

"This time of year?" asks the grocer.

"Who asked you?" says Marie to Guy (me). She plants her feet. "I want brussels sprouts, but not these vile disgusting things."

"How dare you say that!" says the grocer. "Leave my shop. I won't have my vegetables insulted."

"Easy, mac," I (Guy) say.

"Who asked you?" he says and reaches behind the counter for a baseball bat.

"Don't threaten him," says Marie.

"Nobody's threatening me," Guy (I) say to her.

"He is," says Marie. "He's going to hit you!"

"No, I'm not," says the grocer to Marie. "I'm going to hit you. Get out of my shop. I didn't fight in the maquis to have some chi-chi tramp disparage me."

"Easy, mac," Guy (I) say to him.

"And now, I am going to hit you!" says the grocer.

"I'll take these brussels sprouts after all," says Marie, running her hand through her hair.

"Very good. How much?"

"Half a kilo," she says. She turns to me (Guy). "Perhaps we can make it to the bakery before it closes."

"Is shopping here always like this?" I (Guy) ask.

"I wouldn't know," she says. "I just got off the bus."

It was the perfect ending for the scene. I liked it a lot. It was much better than what I had programmed.

Because from the time Marie decided to take the sprouts, none of the scene was as I had written it.

"You look tired," said Lois, leaning against my office doorjamb, arms crossed like Bacall in To Have and Have Not.

"I am tired. I haven't been sleeping."

"I take a couple of dexadryl a day," she said. "I'm in this last push on the movie, so I'm making it a point to get at least two hours' sleep a night."

"Uh, Lois . . ." I said. "Have you ever programmed a scene one way and had it come out another?"

"That's what that little red reset button is for," she said. She looked at me with her gray-blue eyes.

"Then it's happened to you?"

"Sure."

"Did you let the scene play all the way through?"

"Of course not. As soon as anything deviated from the program, I'd kill it and start over."

"Wouldn't you be interested in letting them go and see what happens?"

"And have a mess on my hands? That was what was wrong with the old way of making movies. I treat it as a glitch, start again, and get it right."

She tilted her head. "Why do you ask?"

"Lot of stuff's been . . . well, getting off track. I don't know how or why."

"And you're letting them run on?"

"Some," I said, not meeting her gaze.

"I'd hate to see your studio timeshare bill. You must be way over budget."

"I try not to imagine it. But I'm sure I've got a better movie for it."

She took my hand for a second, but only a second. She was wearing a blue rib-knit sweater. Blue was definitely her color.

"That way lies madness," she said. "Call Maintenance and get them to blow out the low-level format of your ramdisk a couple of times. Got to run," she said, her tone changing instantly. "Got a monster to kill."

"Thanks a lot. Really," I say. She stops at the door.

"They put a lot of stuff in the GAX," she said. "No telling what kind of garbage is floating around in there, unused, that can leak out. If you want to play around, you might as well put in a bunch of fractals and watch the pretty pictures.

"If you want to make a movie, you've got to tell it what to do and sit on its head while it's doing it."

She looked directly at me. "It's just points of light fixed on a plane, Scott."

She left.

Delphine Seyrig is giving Guy (me) trouble.

She was supposed to be the woman who asks Guy to help her get a new chest of drawers up the steps of her house. We'd seen her pushing it down the street in the background of the scene before with Marie and Guy (me) in the bakery.

While Marie (Moreau) is in the vintner's, Seyrig asks Guy (me) for help. Now she's arguing about her part.

"I suppose I'm here just to be a tumble in the hay for you?" she asks.

"I don't know what you're talking about, lady. Do you want help with the bureau, or what?"

"Bureau? Do you mean FBI?" asks a voice behind Guy (me). Guy (me) turns. Eddy Constantine, dressed as Lemmy Caution in a cheap trench coat and a bad hat, stares at Guy (me) with his cue-ball eyes.

"No! Chest-of-drawers," says Seyrig.

"Chester Gould? Dick Tracy?" asks Constantine.

Guy (me) wanders away, leaving them to argue semantics on the steps. As he turns the corner the sound of three quick shots comes from the street he has just left. He heads toward the wine shop where Marie stands, smoking.

I almost forgot about the screening of Monster Without A Meaning. There was a note on my screen from Lois. I didn't know she was through or anywhere near it, but then, I didn't even know what day it was.

I took my cup of bad black coffee into the packed screening room. Lois wasn't there—she said she'd never attend a showing of one of her movies. There were the usual reps, a few critics, some of her friends, a couple of sequencer operators and a dense crowd of the usual bit-part unknowns.

Boris, Lois's boyfriend, got up to speak. (Boris had been working off and on for five years on his own movie, The Beast with Two Backs.) He said something redundant and sat down, and the movie started, with the obligatory GAX-600 logo.

Even the credits were right—they slimed down the screen and formed shaded hairy letters in deep perspective, like those from a flat print of an old 3-D movie.

John Agar was the scientist on vacation (he was catching a goddamn mackerel out of what purported to be a high Sierra-Nevada lake; he used his fly rod with all the grace of a longshoreman handling a pitchfork for the first time) when the decayed-orbit satellite hits the experimental laboratory of the twin hermit mad scientists (Les Tremayne and Leo G. Carroll).

An Air Force major (Kenneth Tobey) searching for the satellite meets up with both Agar and the women (Mara Corday, Julie Adams) who were on their way to take jobs with the mad doctors when the shock wave of the explosion blew their car into a ditch. Agar had stopped to help them, and the jeep with Tobey and the comic relief (Sgt. Joe Sawyer, Cpl. Sid Melton) drives up.

Cut to the Webb farmhouse—Gramps (Olin Howlin), Patricia (Florida Friebus), Aunt Sophonsiba (Kathleen Freeman) and Little Jimmy (George "Foghorn" Winslow) were listening to the radio when the wave of static swept over it. They hear the explosion, and Gramps and Little Jimmy jump into the woodie and drive over to the The Old Science Place.

It goes just like you imagine from there, except for the monster. It's all done subjective camera—the monster sneaks up (you've always seen something moving in the background of the long master shot before, in the direction from which the monster comes). It was originally a guy (Robert Clarke) coming in to get treated for a rare nerve disorder. He was on Les Tremayne's gurney when the satellite hit, dousing him with experimental chemicals and "space virus" from the newly discovered Van Allen belt.

The monster gets closer and closer to the victims—they see something in a mirror, or hear a twig snap, and they turn around—they start to scream, their eyeballs go white like fried marbles, blood squirts out their ears and nose, their gums dissolve, their hair chars away, then the whole face; the clothes evaporate, wind rushes toward their radioactive burning—it's all over in a second, but it's all there, every detail perfect.

The scene where Florida Friebus melts is a real shocker. From the way the camera lingers over it, you know the monster's enjoying it.

By the time General Morris Ankrum, Colonel R.G. Armstrong and Secretary of State Henry Hull wise up, things are bad.

At one point the monster turns and stares back over its shoulder. There's an actual charred trail of destruction stretching behind it; burning houses like Christmas tree lights in the far mountains, the small town a few miles back looking like the ones they built for the Project Ivy A-bomb tests in Nevada. Turning its head the monster looks down at the quiet nighttime city before it. All the power and wonder of death are in that shot.

(Power and wonder are in me, too, in the form of a giant headache. One of my eyes isn't focusing anymore. A bad sign, and rubbing doesn't help.)

I get up to go—the movie's great but the light is hurting my eyes too much.

Suddenly here come three F-84 Thunderjets flown by Cpt. Clint Eastwood, 1st Lt. Leonard Nimoy, and Colonel James Whitmore.

"The Reds didn't like the regular stuff in Korea. This thing shouldn't like this atomic napalm, either," says Whitmore. "Let's go in and spread a little honey around, boys."

The jets peel off.

Cut to the monster's p.o.v. The jets come in with a roar. Under-wing tanks come off as they power back up into a climb. The bombs tumble lazily toward the screen. One whistles harmlessly by, two are dropping short, three keep getting bigger and bigger, then blam — woosh. You're the monster and you're being burned to death in a radioactive napalm firestorm.

Screaming doesn't help; one hand comes up just before the eyes melt away like lumps of lard on a floor furnace — the hand crisps to paper, curls, blood starts to shoot out and evaporates like verga over the Mojave. The last thing the monster hears is its auditory canals boiling away with a screeching hiss.

Cut to Agar, inventor of the atomic napalm, holding Mara Corday on a hill above the burning city and the charring monster. He's breathing hard, his hair is singed; her skirt is torn off one side, exposing her long legs.

Up above, Whitmore, oxygen mask off, smiles down and wags the jet's wings.

Pull back to a panorama of the countryside; Corday and Agar grow smaller; the scene lifts, takes in jets, county, then state; miles up now the curve of the earth appears, grows larger, continue to pull back, whole of U.S., North and Central America appears. Beeping on soundtrack. We are moving along with a white luminescence which is revealed to be a Sputnik-type satellite.

Beeping stops. Satellite begins to fall away from camera, lurching some as it hits the edges of the atmosphere. As it falls, letters slime down the screen: The End?

Credits: A movie by Lois B. Traven.

The lights come up. I begin to breathe again. I'm standing in the middle of the aisle, applauding as hard as I can.

Everybody else is applauding, too. Everybody.

Then my head really begins to hurt, and I go outside into the cool night and sit on the studio wall like Humpty-Dumpty.

Lois is headed for the Big Time. She deserves it.

The notes on my desk are now hand-deep. Pink ones, then orange ones from the executive offices. Then the bright red-striped ones from accounting.

Fuck'em. I'm almost through.

I sat down and plugged on. Nothing happened.

I punched Maintenance.

"Sorry," says Bobo. "You gotta get authorization from Snell before you can get back online, says here."

"Snell in accounting, or Snell in the big building?"

"Lemme check." There's a lot of yelling around the office on the other end. "Snell in the big building."

"Yeah, yeah, okay."

So I have to eat dung in front of Snell, promise him anything, renegotiate my contract right then and there in his office without my business manager or agent. But I have to get this movie finished.

Then I have to go over to Accounting and sign a lot of stuff. I call Bernie and Chinua and tell them to come down to the studio and clean up the contractual shambles as best they can, and not to expect to hear from me for a week or so.

Then I call my friend Jukai, who helped install the first GAX-600 and talk to him for an hour and a half and learn a few things.

Then I go to Radio Shack and run up a bill of $6,124, buy two weeks' worth of survival food at Apocalypse Andy's, put everything in my car, and drive over to the office deep under the bowels of the GAX-600.

I have locked everyone else out of the mainframe with words known only to myself and Alain Resnais. Let them wait.

I have put a note on the door:

Leave me alone. I am finishing the movie. Do not try to stop me. You are locked out of the 600 until I am through. Do not attempt to take me off-line. I have rewired the 600 to wipe out everything, every movie in it but mine if you do. Do not cut my power; I have a generator in here—if you turn me off, the GAX is history. (See attached receipt.) Leave me alone until I have finished; you will get everything back, and a great movie too.

They were knocking. Now they're pounding on the door. Screw'em. I'm starting the scene where Guy (me) and Marie hitch a ride on the garbage wagon out of the communist pig farm.

The locksmith was quiet but he couldn't do any good, either. I've put on the kind of locks they use on the outsides of prisons.

They tried to put a note on the screen. BACK OFF, I wrote.

They began to ease them, pleading notes, one at a time through the razor-thin crack under the fireproof steel door.

Every few hours I would gather them up. They quit coming for a while.

Sometime later there was a polite knock.

A note slid under.

"May I come in for a few moments?" it asked. It was signed A. Resnais.

GO AWAY, I wrote back. YOU HAVEN'T MADE A GOOD MOVIE SINCE LA GUERRE EST FINIS.

I could imagine his turning to the cops and studio heads in his dignified humble way (he must be pushing ninety by now), shrugging his shoulders as if to say, well, I tried my best, and walking away.

"You must end this madness," says Marie. "We've been here a week. The room smells. I smell. You smell, I'm tired of dehydrated apple chips. I want to talk on the beach again, get some sunlight."

"What kind of ending would that be?" I (Guy) ask.

"I've seen worse. I've been in much worse. Why do you have this obsessive desire to recreate movies made fifty years ago?"

I (Guy) look out the window of the cheap hotel, past the edge of the taped roller shade. "I (Guy) don't know." I (Guy) rub my chin covered with a scratchy week's stubble. "Maybe those movies, those, those things were like a breath of fresh air. They led to everything we have today."

"Well, we could use a breath of fresh air."

"No. Really. They came in on a stultified, lumbering dinosaur of an industry, tore at its flanks, nibbled at it with soft rubbery beaks, something, I don't know what. Stung it into action, showed it there were other ways of doing things—made it question itself. Showed that movies could be free— not straightjackets."

"Recreating them won't make any new statements," said Marie (Moreau).

"I'm trying to breathe new life into them, then. Into what they were. What they meant to . . . to me, to others," I (Guy) say.

What I want to do more than anything is to take her from the motel, out on the sunny street to the car. Then I want to drive her up the winding roads to the cliffs overlooking the Mediterranean. Then I want her to lean over, her right arm around my neck, her hair blowing in the wind, and give me a kiss that will last forever, and say, "I love you, and I'm ready."

Then I will press down the accelerator, and we will go through the guard rail, hang in the air, and begin to fall faster and faster until the eternal blue sea comes up to meet us in a tender hand-shaped spray, and just before the impact she will smile and pat my arm, never taking her eyes off the windshield.

"Movies are freer than they ever were," she says from the bed. "I was there. I know. You're just going through the motions. The things that brought about those films are remembered only by old people, bureaucrats, film critics," she says with a sneer.

"What about you?" I (Guy) ask, turning to her. "You remember. You're not old. You're alive, vibrant."

My heart is breaking.

She gives me (Guy) a stare filled with sorrow. "No I'm not. I'm a character in a movie. I'm points of light, fixed on a plane."

A tear-gas canister crashes through the window. There is a pounding against the door.

"The cops!" I (Guy) say, reaching for the .45 automatic.

"The pimps!" Marie says.

The room is filling with gas. Bullets fly. I fire at the door, the window shades, as I reach for Marie's hand. The door bursts open.

Two quick closeups: her face, terrified; mine, determined, with a snarl and a holy wreath of cordite rising from my pistol.

My head is numb. I see in the dim worklight from my screen the last note they stuck under the door fluttering as the invisible gas is pumped in.

I type fin.

I reach for the non-existent button which will wipe everything but This Guy Goes to Town . . . and mentally push it.

I (Guy) smile up at them as they come through the doors and walls: pimps, Nazis, film critics, studio cops, deep-sea divers, spacemen, clowns, and lawyers.

Through the windows I can see the long geometric rows of the shrubs forming quincunxes, the classical statuary, people moving to and fro in a garden like a painting by Fragonard.

I must have been away a long time; someone was telling me, as I was making my way toward these first calm thoughts, that This Guy . . . is the biggest hit of the season. I have been told that while I was on my four-week vacation from human cares and woes that I have become that old-time curiosity: the rich man who is crazy as a piss ant.

Far less rich, of course, than I would have been had I not renegotiated my contract before my last, somewhat spectacular, orgy of movie-and-lovemaking in my locked office.

I am now calm. I am not looking forward to my recovery, but suppose I will have to get some of my own money out of my manager's guardianship.

A nurse comes in, opens the taffeta curtains at another set of windows, revealing nice morning sunlight through the tiny, very tasteful, bars.

She turns to me and smiles.

It is Anouk Aimee.

Introduction to

Heirs of the Perisphere

If you could have told the eighteen-year-old, writing-mad Howard Waldrop that in fifteen years he would (1) be asked to do an article by *The Writer*, but then not do it, and (2) sell to *Playboy* for lots of (then) money, but that it would not be the pleasant, exciting experience the starry-eyed young writer dreamed of, he would not have believed you.

This far-future backward look was, as is my usual wont, written because I wanted like hell to be in Mike Bishop's *Light Years and Dark* (a swell book that went straight down the tubes when published, but instead I was in there with "Helpless, Helpless"). He said this story "might as well be about a lawnmower, an air-conditioner, and a microwave" — or words to that effect. Mostly he was trying to squeeze me in. I'd futzed around to real near the deadline and he only had 3,000 words of space and money and I was trying to sell him 5,600 words, so instead I sent this off to my then-agent Joe Elder (since retired) and wrote the other story for Mike at 3,200 words, which was more like it.

Joe sent it to Alice K. Turner, who promptly bought it for *Playboy* for more money than I'd ever seen, except for a novel.

Now Alice Turner is one of the finest editors in the business; don't take my word for it, ask anyone who's ever worked with her, or see Robert Silverberg's introductions to the stories in his '80s and '90s collections for his true amazement at her editing abilities (Silverberg's seen and done it all and he doesn't impress easily). What happened in the next fourteen months was not her fault.

We worked on this, on and off, through five successive drafts, each one getting better, deeper, more resonant, or something, until we got to the one you see.

A little background: I was going through truly terrible personal stuff. I was also behind on finishing *Them Bones*, my first solo novel for the late, very-missed, Terry Carr's second set of Ace SF Specials (others—L. Shepard, K.S. Robinson, somebody named Gibson—whatever happened to him?—Carter Scholz and Glenn Harcourt, Michael Swanwick) and while I was trying to write it, other stories were driving me bughouse. I had to stop and write them AND work on *Them Bones* AND the rewrites on this, and deal with the here-and-now-everyday-Halloween-type personal stuff . . .

Well, it's not Alice's fault that I associate this story with a Bad Time; it's just me. I wish I could have had more pleasant memories of selling to *Playboy*. This, like a bunch of other stories I haven't mentioned, was up for a Nebula.

There are just archetypes, and then there are true archetypes in life and in the movies. That they'll be here long after we've gone I have no doubt. And the central element in this story I'd wanted to write about ever since I came across references to it when I was eight or nine or ten years old. It all came together in this story (or the one I started writing, anyway—it's really here in this final, fifth draft).

Take a gander at this one.

HEIRS OF THE PERISPHERE

Things had not been going well at the factory for the last fifteen hundred years or so.

A rare thunderstorm, soaking rain, and a freak lightning bolt changed all that.

When the lightning hit, an emergency generator went to work as it had been built to do a millennium and a half before. It cranked up and ran the assembly line just long enough, before freezing up and shedding its brushes and armatures in a fine spray, to finish some work in the custom design section.

The factory completed, hastily programmed, and wrongly certified as approved the three products which had been on the assembly line fifteen centuries before.

Then the place went dark again.

"Gawrsh," said one of them. "It shore is dark in here!"

"Well, huh-huh, we can always use the infrared they gave us!"

"Wak Wak Wak!" said the third. "What's the big idea?"

The custom-order jobs were animato/mechanical simulacra. They were designed to speak and act like the famous creations of a multimillionaire cartoonist who late in life had opened a series of gigantic amusement parks in the latter half of the twentieth century.

Once these giant theme parks had employed persons in costume to act the parts. Then the corporation which had run things after the cartoonist's death had seen the wisdom of building robots. The simulacra would be less expensive in the long run, would never be late for work, could be programmed to speak many languages, and would never try to pick up the clean-cut boys and girls who visited the Parks.

These three had been built to be host robots in the third and largest of the Parks, the one separated by an ocean from the other two.

And, as their programming was somewhat incomplete, they had no idea of much of this.

All they had were a bunch of jumbled memories, awareness of the thunderstorm outside, and of the darkness of the factory around them.

The tallest of the three must have started as a cartoon dog, but had become upright and acquired a set of baggy pants, balloon shoes, a sweatshirt, black vest, and white gloves. There was a miniature carpenter's hat on his head, and his long ears hung down from it. He had two prominent incisors in his muzzle. He stood almost two meters tall and answered to the name GUF.

The second, a little shorter, was a white duck with a bright orange bill and feet, and a blue and white sailor's tunic and cap. He had large eyes with little cuts out of the upper right corners of the pupils. He was naked from the waist down, and was the only one of the three without gloves. He answered to the name DUN.

The third and smallest, just over a meter, was a rodent. He wore a red bibbed playsuit with two huge gold buttons at the waistline. He was shirtless and had shoes like two pieces of bread dough. His tail was long and thin like a whip. His bare arms, legs, and chest were black, his face a pinkish-tan. His white gloves were especially prominent. His most striking feature was his ears, which rotated on a track, first one way, then another, so that seen from any angle they could look like a featureless black circle.

His name was MIK. His eyes, like those of GUF, were large and the pupils were big round dots. His nose ended in a perfect sphere of polished onyx.

"Well," said MIK, brushing dust from his body, "I guess we'd better, huh-huh, get to work."

"Uh hyuk," said GUF. "Won't be many people at thuh Park in weather like thiyus."

"Oh boy! Oh boy!" quacked DUN. "Rain! Wak Wak Wak!" He ran out through a huge crack in the wall which streamed with rain and mist.

MIK and GUF came behind, GUF ambling with his hands in his pockets, MIK walking determinedly.

Lightning cracked once more but the storm seemed to be dying.

"Wak Wak Wak!" said DUN, his tail fluttering, as he swam in a big puddle. "Oh boy. Oh joy!"

"I wonder if the rain will hurt our works?" asked MIK.

"Not me!" said GUF. "Uh hyuk! I'm equipped fer all kinds a weather." He put his hand conspiratorially beside his muzzle. "'Ceptin' mebbe real cold on thuh order of -40° Celsius, uh hyuk!"

MIK was ranging in the ultraviolet and infrared, getting the feel of the landscape through the rain. "You'd have thought, huh-huh, they might have sent a truck over or something," he said. "I guess we'll have to walk."

"I didn't notice anyone at thuh factory," said GUF. "Even if it was a day off, you'd think some of thuh workers would give unceasingly of their time, because, after all, thuh means of produckshun must be kept in thuh hands of thuh workers, uh hyuk!"

GUF's specialty was to have been talking with visitors from the large totalitarian countries to the west of the country the Park was in. He was especially well versed in dialectical materialism and correct Mao thought.

As abruptly as it had started, the storm ended. Great ragged gouts broke in the clouds, revealing high, fast-moving cirrus, a bright blue sky, the glow of a warming sun.

"Oh rats rats rats!" said DUN, holding out his hand, palm up. "Just when I was starting to get wet!"

"Uh, well," asked GUF, "which way is it tuh work? Thuh people should be comin' out o' thuh sooverneer shops real soon now."

MIK looked around, consulting his programming. "That way, guys," he said, unsure of himself. There were no familiar landmarks, and only one that was disturbingly unfamiliar.

Far off was the stump of a mountain. MIK had a feeling it should be beautiful, blue and snow-capped. Now it was a brown lump, heavily eroded, with no white at the top. It looked like a bite had been taken out of it.

All around them was rubble, and far away in the other direction was a sluggish ocean.

It was getting dark. The three sat on a pile of concrete.

"Them and their big ideas," said DUN.

"Looks like thuh Park is closed," said GUF.

MIK sat with his hands under his chin. "This just isn't right, guys," he said. "We were supposed to report to the programming hut to get our first day's instructions. Now we can't even find the Park!"

"I wish it would rain again," said DUN, "while you two are making up your minds."

"Well, uh hyuk," said GUF. "I seem tuh remember we could get hold of thuh satellite in a 'mergency."

"Sure!" said MIK, jumping to his feet and pounding his fist into his glove. "That's it! Let's see, what frequency was that . . . ?"

"Six point five oh four," said DUN. He looked eastward. "Maybe I'll go to the ocean."

"Better stay here whiles we find somethin' out," said GUF.

"Well, make it snappy!" said DUN.

MIK tuned in the frequency and broadcast the Park's call letters.

". . . ZZZZZ. What? HOOSAT?"

"Uh, this is MIK, one of the simulacra at the Park. We're trying to get a hold of one of the other Parks for, huh-huh, instructions."

"In what language would you like to communicate?" asked the satellite.

"Oh, sorry, huh-huh. We speak Japanese to each other, but we'll switch over to Artran if that's easier for you." GUF and DUN tuned in, too.

"It's been a very long while since anyone communicated with me from down there." The satellite's well-modulated voice snapped and popped.

"If you must know," HOOSAT continued, "it's been rather a while since anyone contacted me from anywhere. I can't say much for the stability of my orbit, either. Once I was forty thousand kilometers up, very stable . . ."

"Could you put us through to one of the other Parks, or maybe the Studio itself, if you can do that? We'd, huh-huh, like to find out where to report for work."

"I'll attempt it," said HOOSAT. There was a pause and some static. "Predictably, there's no answer at any of the locations."

"Well, where are they?"

"To whom do you refer?"

"The people," said MIK.

"Oh, you wanted humans? I thought perhaps you wanted the stations themselves. There was a slight chance that some of them were still functioning."

"Where are thuh folks?" asked GUF.

"I really don't know. We satellites and monitoring stations used to worry about that frequently. Something happened to them."

"What?" asked all three robots at once.

"Hard to understand," said HOOSAT. "Ten or fifteen centuries ago. Very noisy in all spectra, followed by quiet. Most of the ground stations ceased functioning within a century after that. You're the first since then."

"What do you do, then?" asked MIK.

"Talk with other satellites. Very few left. One of them has degraded. It only broadcasts random numbers when the solar wind is very strong. Another . . ."

There was a burst of fuzzy static.

"Hello? HOOSAT?" asked the satellite. "It's been a very long time since anyone . . ."

"It's still us!" said MIK. "The simulacra from the Park. We—"

"Oh, that's right. What can I do for you?"

"Tell us where the people went."

"I have no idea."

"Well, where can we find out?" asked MIK.

"You might try the library."

"Where's that?"

"Let me focus in. Not very much left down there, is there? I can give you the coordinates. Do you have standard navigational programming?"

"Boy, do we!" said MIK.

"Well, here's what you do . . ."

"Sure don't look much different from thuh rest of this junk, does it, MIK?" asked GUF.

"I'm sure there used to be many, many books here," said MIK. "It all seems to have turned to powder though, doesn't it?"

"Well," said GUF, scratching his head with his glove, "they sure didn't make 'em to last, did they?"

DUN was mumbling to himself. "Doggone wizoo-wazoo waste of time," he said. He sat on one of the piles of dirt in the large broken-down building of which only one massive wall still stood. The recent rain had turned the meter-deep powder on the floor into a mâché sludge.

"I guess there's nothing to do but start looking," said MIK.

"Find a book on water," said DUN.

"Hey, MIK! Looka this!" yelled GUF.

He came running with a steel box. "I found this just over there."

The box was plain, unmarked. There was a heavy lock to which MIK applied various pressures.

"Let's forget all this nonsense and go fishing," said DUN.

"It might be important," said MIK.

"Well, open it then," said DUN.

"It's, huh-huh, stuck."

"Gimme that!" yelled DUN. He grabbed it. Soon he was muttering under his beak. "Doggone razzle-frazzin dadgum thing!" He pulled and pushed, his face and bill turning redder and redder. He gripped the box with both his feet and hands. "Doggone dadgum!" he yelled.

Suddenly he grew teeth, his brow slammed down, his shoulders tensed and he went into a blurred fury of movement. "WAK WAK WAK WAK WAK!" he screamed.

The box broke open and flew into three parts. So did the book inside.

DUN was still tearing in his fury.

"Wait, look out, DUN," yelled MIK. "Wait!"

"Gawrsh," said GUF, running after the pages blowing in the breeze. "Help me, MIK."

DUN stood atop the rubble, parts of the box and the book gripped in each hand. He simulated hard breathing, the redness draining from his face.

"It's open," he said quietly.

"Well, from what we've got left," said MIK, "this is called The Book of the Time Capsule, and it tells that people buried a cylinder a very, very long time ago. They printed up five thousand copies of this book and sent it to places all around the world, where they thought it would be safe. They printed them on acid-free paper and stuff like that so they wouldn't fall apart.

"And they thought what they put in the time capsule itself could explain to later generations what people were like in their day. So I figure maybe it could explain something to us, too."

"That sounds fine with me," said GUF.

"Well, let's go!" said DUN.

"Well, huh-huh," said MIK. "I checked with HOOSAT, and gave him the coordinates, and, huh-huh, it's quite a little ways away."

"How far?" asked DUN, his brow beetling.

"Oh, huh-huh, about eighteen thousand kilometers," said MIK.

"WHAAT???"

"About eighteen thousand kilometers. Just about halfway around the world."

"Oh, my aching feet!" said DUN.

"That's not literally true," said GUF. He turned to MIK. "Yuh think we should go that far?"

"Well . . . I'm not sure what we'll find. Those pages were lost when DUN opened the box . . ."

"I'm sorry," said DUN, in a contrite small voice.

". . . but the people of that time were sure that everything could be explained by what was in the capsule."

"And you think it's all still there?" asked DUN.

"Well, they buried it pretty deep, and took a lot of precautions with the way they preserved things. And we did find the book, just like they wanted us to. I'd imagine it was all still there!"

"Well, it's a long ways," said GUF. "But it doesn't look much like we'll find anyone here."

MIK put a determined look on his face.

"I figure the only thing for us to do is set our caps and whistle a little tune," he said.

"Yuh don't have a cap, MIK," said GUF.

"Well, I can still whistle! Let's go fellas," he said. "It's this way!"

He whistled a work song. DUN quacked a tune about boats and love. GUF hummed "The East Is Red."

They set off in this way across what had been the bottom of the Sea of Japan.

They were having troubles. It had been a long time and they walked on tirelessly. Three weeks ago they'd come to the end of all the songs each of them was programmed with and had to start repeating themselves.

Their lubricants were beginning to fail, their hastily wired circuitry was overworked. GUF had a troublesome ankle extensor which sometimes hung up. But he went along just as cheerfully, sometimes hopping and quickstepping to catch up with the others when the foot refused to flex.

The major problem was the cold. There was a vast difference in the climate they had left and the one they found themselves in. The landscape was rocky and empty. It had begun to snow more frequently and the wind was fierce.

The terrain was difficult, and HOOSAT's maps were outdated. Something drastic had changed the course of rivers, the land, the shoreline of the ocean itself. They had to detour frequently.

The cold worked hardest on DUN. "Oh," he would say, "I'm so cold, so cold!" He was very poorly insulated, and they had to slow their pace to his. He would do anything to avoid going through a snowdrift, and so expended even more energy.

They stopped in the middle of a raging blizzard.

"Uh, MIK," said GUF. "I don't think DUN can go much further in this weather. An' my leg is givin' me a lot o' problems. Yuh think maybe we could find someplace to hole up fer a spell?"

MIK looked around them at the bleakness and the whipping snow. "I guess you're right. Warmer weather would do us all some good. We could conserve both heat and energy. Let's find a good place."

"Hey, DUN," said GUF. "Let's find us a hidey-hole!"

"Oh, goody gumdrops!" quacked DUN. "I'm so cold!"

They eventually found a deep rock shelter with a low fault crevice at the back. MIK had them gather up what sparse dead vegetation there was and bring it to the shelter. DUN and GUF crawled in the back and MIK piled brush all through the cave. He talked to HOOSAT, then wriggled his way through the brush to them.

Inside they could barely hear the wind and snow. It was only slightly warmer than outside, but it felt wonderful and safe.

"I told HOOSAT to wake us up when it got warmer," said MIK. "Then we'll get on to that time capsule and find out all about the people."

"G'night, MIK," said GUF.

"Goodnight, DUN," said MIK.

"Sleep tight and don't let the bedbugs bite. Wak Wak Wak," said DUN.

They shut themselves off.

Something woke MIK. It was dark in the rock shelter, but it was also much warmer.

The brush was all crumbled away. A meter of rock and dust covered the cave floor. The war wind stirred it.

"Hey, fellas!" said MIK. "Hey, wake up! Spring is here!"

"Wak! What's the big idea? Hey, oh boy, it's warm!" said DUN.

"Gawrsh," said GUF, "that sure was a nice forty winks!"

"Well, let's go thank HOOSAT and get our bearings and be on our way."

They stepped outside.

The stars were in the wrong places.

"Uh-oh," said GUF.

"Well, would you look at that!" said DUN.

"I think we overslept," said MIK. "Let's see what HOOSAT has to say."

". . . Huh? HOOSAT?"

"Hello. This is DUN and MIK and GUF."

HOOSAT's voice now sounded like a badger whistling through its teeth.

"Glad to see ya up!" he said.

"We went to sleep, and told you to wake us up as soon as it got warmer."

"Sorry. I forgot till just now. Had a lot on my mind. Besides, it just now got warmer."

"It did?" asked GUF.

"Shoulda seen it," said HOOSAT. "Ice everywhere. Big ol' glaciers. Took the top offa everything! You still gonna dig up that capsule thing?"

"Yes," said MIK. "We are."

"Well, you got an easy trip from now on. No more mountains in your way."

"What about people?"

"Nah. No people. I ain't heard from any, no ways. My friend the military satellite said he thought he saw some fires, little teeny ones, but his eyes weren't what they used to be by then. He's gone now, too."

"The fires might have been built by people?"

"Who knows? Not me," said HOOSAT. "Hey, bub, you still got all those coordinates like I give you?"

"I think so," said MIK.

"Well, I better give you new ones off these new constellations. Hold still, my aim ain't so good anymore." He dumped a bunch of numbers in MIK's head. "I won't be talking to ya much longer."

"Why not?" they all asked.

"Well, you know. My orbit. I feel better now than I have in years. Real spry. Probably the ionization. Started a couple o' weeks ago. Sure has been nice talkin' to you young fellers after so long a time. Sure am glad I remembered to wake you up. I wish you a lotta luck. Boy, this air has a punch like a mule. Be careful. Goodbye."

Across the unfamiliar stars overhead, a point of light blazed, streaked in a long arc, then died on the night.

"Well," said MIK. "We're on our own."

"Gosh, I feel all sad," said GUF.

"Warmth, oh boy!" said DUN.

The trip was uneventful for the next few months. They walked across the long land bridge down a valley between stumps of mountains with the white teeth of glaciers on them. Then they crossed a low range and entered flat land without topsoil from which dry rivercourses ran to the south. Then there was a land where things were flowering after the long winter. New streams were springing up.

They saw fire once and detoured, but found only a burnt patch of forest. Once, way off in the distance, they saw a speck of light but didn't go to investigate.

Within two hundred kilometers of their goal, the land changed again to a flat sandy waste littered with huge rocks. Sparse vegetation grew. There were few insects and animals, mostly lizards, which DUN chased every chance he got. The warmth seemed to be doing him good.

GUF's leg worsened. The foot now stuck, now flopped and windmilled. He kept humming songs and raggedly marching along with the other two.

When they passed one of the last trees, MIK had them all three take limbs from it. "Might come in handy for pushing and digging," he said.

They stood on a plain of sand and rough dirt. There were huge piles of rubble all around. Far off was another ocean, and to the north a patch of green.

"We'll go to the ocean, DUN," said MIK, "after we get through here."

He was walking around in a smaller and smaller circle. Then he stopped. "Well, huh-huh," he said. "Here we are. Latitude 40° 44' 34" .089 North. Longitude 73° 50' 43" .842 West, by the way they used to figure it. The capsule is straight down, twenty-eight meters below the original surface. We've got a long way to go, because there's no telling how much soil has drifted over that. It's in a concrete tube, and we'll have to dig to the very bottom to get at the capsule. Let's get working."

It was early morning when they started. Just after noon they found the top of the tube with its bronze tablet.

"Here's where the hard work starts," said MIK.

It took them two weeks of continual effort. Slowly the tube was exposed as the hole around it grew larger. Since GUF could work better standing still, they had him dig all the time, while DUN and MIK both dug and pushed rock and dirt clear of the crater.

They found some long flat iron rods partway down, and threw away the worn limbs and used the metal to better effect.

On one of the trips to push dirt out of the crater, DUN came back looking puzzled.

"I thought I saw something moving out there," he said. "When I looked, it went away."

"Probably just another animal," said MIK. "Here, help me lift this rock."

It was hard work and their motors were taxed. It rained once, and once there was a dust storm.

"Thuh way I see it," said GUF, looking at their handiwork, "is that yah treat it like a big ol' tree made outta rock."

They stood in the bottom of the vast crater. Up from the center of this stood the concrete tube.

"We've reached twenty-six meters," said MIK. "The capsule itself should be in the last 2.3816 meters. So we should chop it off," he quickly calculated, "about here." He drew a line all around the tube with a piece of chalky rock.

They began to smash at the concrete with rocks and pieces of iron and steel.

"Timber!" said DUN.

The column above the line lurched and with a crash shattered itself against the side of the crater wall.

"Oh boy! Oh boy!"

"Come help me, GUF," said MIK.

Inside the jagged top of the remaining shaft an eyebolt stood out of the core.

They climbed up on the edge, reached in and raised the gleaming Cupraloy time capsule from its resting place.

On its side was a message to the finders, and just below the eyebolt at the top was a line and the words CUT HERE.

"Well," said MIK shaking DUN and GUF's hands. "We did it, by gum!"

He looked at it a moment.

"How're we gonna get it open?" asked GUF. "That metal shore looks tough!"

"I think maybe we can abrade it around the cutting line, with sandstone and, well . . . go get me a real big sharp piece of iron, DUN."

When it was brought, MIK handed the iron to GUF and put his long tail over a big rock.

"Go ahead, GUF," he said. "Won't hurt me a bit."

GUF slammed the piece of iron down.

"Uh hyuk," he said. "Clean as a whistle!"

MIK took the severed tail, sat down cross-legged near the eyebolt, poured sand on the cutting line, and began to rub it across the line with his tail.

It took three days, turning the capsule every few hours.

They pulled off the eyebolt end. A dusty waxy mess was revealed.

"That'll be what's left of the waterproof mastic," said MIK. "Help me, you two." They lifted the capsule. "Twist," he said.

The metal groaned. "Now, pull!"

A long thin inner core, two meters by a third of a meter, slid out.

"Okay," said MIK, putting down the capsule shell and wiping away mastic. "This inner shell is threaded in two parts. Turn that way, I'll turn this!"

They did. Inside was a shiny sealed glass tube through which they could dimly see shapes and colors.

"Wow!" said GUF. "Looka that!"

"Oh boy, oh boy," said DUN.

"That's Pyrex," said MIK. "When we break that, we'll be through."

"I'll do it!" said DUN.

"Careful!" said GUF.

The rock shattered the glass. There was a loud noise as the partial vacuum disappeared.

"Oh boy!" said DUN.

"Let's do this carefully," said MIK. "It's all supposed to be in some kind of order."

The first thing they found was the message from four famous humans and another, whole copy of The Book of the Time Capsule. GUF picked that up.

There was another book with a black cover with a gold cross on it; then they came to a section marked "Articles of Common Use." The first small packet was labeled "Contributing to the Convenience, Comfort, Health, and Safety." MIK opened the wrapper.

Inside was an alarm clock, bifocals, a camera, pencil, nail file, a padlock and keys, toothbrush, tooth powder, a safety pin, knife, fork, and slide rule.

The next packet was labeled "Pertaining to the Grooming and Vanity of Women." Inside was an Elizabeth Arden Daytime Cyclamen Color Harmony Box, a rhinestone clip, and a woman's hat, style of autumn 1938 designed by Lily Daché.

"Golly-wow!" said DUN, and put the hat on over his.

The next packet was marked "For the Pleasure, Use, and Education of

Children."

First out was a small, spring-driven toy car, then a small doll and a set of alphabet blocks. Then MIK reached in and pulled out a small cup.

He stared at it a long, long time. On the side of the cup was a decal with the name of the man who had created them, and a picture of MIK, waving his hand in greeting.

"Gawrsh, MIK," said GUF, "it's YOU!"

A tossed brick threw up a shower of dirt next to his foot.

They all looked up.

Around the crater edge stood ragged men, women, and children. They had sharp sticks, rocks, and ugly clubs.

"Oh boy!" said DUN. "People!" He started toward them.

"Hello!" he said. "We've been trying to find you for a long time. Do you know the way to the Park? We want to learn all about you."

He was speaking to them in Japanese.

The mob hefted its weapons. DUN switched to another language.

"I said, we come in peace. Do you know the way to the Park?" he asked in Swedish.

They started down the crater, rocks flying before them.

"What's the matter with you?" yelled DUN. "WAK WAK WAK!" He raised his fists.

"Wait!" said MIK, in English. "We're friends!"

Some of the crowd veered off toward him.

"Uh-oh!" said GUF. He took off clanking up the most sparsely defended side of the depression.

Then the ragged people yelled and charged.

They got the duck first.

He stood, fists out, jumping up and down on one foot, hopping mad. Several grabbed him, one by the beak. They smashed at him with clubs, pounded him with rocks. He injured three of them seriously before they smashed him into a white, blue, and orange pile.

"Couldn't we, huh-huh, talk this over?" asked MIK. They stuck a sharp stick in his ear mechanism, jamming it. One of his gloved hands was mashed. He fought back with the other and kicked his feet. He hurt them, but he was small. A boulder trapped his legs; then they danced on him.

GUF made it out of the crater. He had picked the side with the most kids, and they drew back, thinking he was attacking them. When they saw he was only running, they gave a gleeful chase, bouncing sticks and rocks off his hobbling form.

"WHOA!" he yelled, as more people ran to intercept him and he skidded to a stop. He ran up a long slanting pile of rubble. More humans poured out of the crater to get him.

He reached the end of the long high mound above the crater rim. His attackers paused, throwing bricks and clubs, yelling at him.

"Halp!" GUF yelled. "Haaaaaaaalp!"

An arrow sailed into the chest of the nearest attacker.

GUF turned. Other humans, dressed in cloth, stood in a line around the far side of the crater. They had bows and arrows, metal-tipped spears and metal knives in their belts.

As he watched, the archers sent another flight of arrows into the people who had attacked the robots.

The skin-dressed band of humans screamed and fled up out of the crater, down from the mounds, leaving their wounded and the scattered contents of the time capsule behind them.

It took them a while, but soon the human in command of the metal-using people and GUF found they could make themselves understood. The language was a very changed English/Spanish mixture.

"We're sorry we didn't know you were here sooner," he said to GUF. "We only heard this morning. Those others," he said with a grimace, "won't bother you anymore."

He pointed to the patch of green to the north. "Our lands and village are there. We came to it twenty years ago. It's a good land, but those others raid it as often as they can."

GUF looked down into the crater with its toppled column and debris. Cigarettes and tobacco drifted from the glass cylinder. The microfilm with all its books and knowledge was tangled all over the rocks. Samples of aluminum, hypernik, ferrovanadium, and hypersil gleamed in the dust. Razor blades, an airplane gear, and glass wool were strewn up the side of the slope.

The message from Grover Whalen opening the World's Fair, and knowledge of how to build the microfilm reader were gone. The newsreel, with its pictures of Howard Hughes, Jesse Owens, and Babe Ruth, bombings in China and a Miami Beach fashion show, was ripped and torn. The golf ball was in the hands of one of the fleeing children. Poker chips lay side by side with tungsten wire, combs, lipstick. GUF tried to guess what some of the items were.

"They destroyed one of your party," said the commander. "I think the other one is still alive."

"I'll tend to 'em," said GUF.

"We'll take you back to our village," said the man. "There are lots of things we'd like to know about you."

"That goes double fer us," said GUF. "Those other folks pretty much tore up what we came to find."

GUF picked up the small cup from the ground. He walked to where they had MIK propped up against a rock.

"Hello, GUF," he said. "Huh-huh, I'm not in such good shape." His glove hung uselessly on his left arm. His ears were bent and his nose was dented. He gave off a noisy whir when he moved.

"Oh, hyuk hyuk," said GUF. "We'll go back with these nice people, and you'll rest up and be as right as rain, I guarantee."

"DUN didn't make it, did he, GUF?"

GUF was quiet a moment. "Nope, MIK, he didn't. I'm shore sorry it turned out this way. I'm gonna miss the ol' hothead."

"Me, too," said MIK. "Are we gonna take him with us?"

"Shore thing," said GUF. He waved to the nearby men.

The town was in a green valley watered by two streams full of fish. There were small fields of beans, tomatoes, and corn in town, and cattle and sheep grazed on the hillside, watched over by guards. There was a coppersmith's shop, a council hut, and many houses of wood and stone.

GUF was walking up the hill to where MIK lay.

They had been there a little over two weeks, talking with the people of the village, telling them what they knew. GUF had been playing with the children when he and MIK weren't talking with the grown folks. But from the day after they had buried DUN up on the hill, MIK had been getting worse. His legs had quit moving altogether, and he could now see only in the infrared.

"Hello, GUF," said MIK.

"How ya doin' pardner?"

"I-I think I'm going to terminate soon," said MIK. "Are they making any progress on the flume?"

Two days before, MIK had told the men how to bring water more efficiently from one of the streams up to the middle of the village.

"We've almost got it now," said GUF. "I'm sure they'll come up and thank you when they're finished."

"They don't need to do that," said MIK.

"I know, but these are real nice folks, MIK. And they've had it pretty rough, what with one thing and another, and they like talkin' to yah."

GUF noticed that some of the human women and children waited outside the hut, waiting to talk to MIK.

"I won't stay very long," said GUF. "I gotta get back and organize the cadres into work teams and instruction teams and so forth, like they asked me to help with."

"Sure thing, GUF," said MIK. "I—"

"I wisht there was somethin' I could do . . ."

There was a great whirring noise from MIK and the smell of burning silicone.

GUF looked away. "They just don't have any stuff here," he said, "that I could use to fix you. Maybe I could find something at thuh crater, or . . ."

"Oh, don't bother," said MIK. "I doubt . . ."

GUF was looking at the village. "Oh," he said, reaching in the bag someone had made him. "I been meanin' to give you this for a week and keep fergettin'." He handed MIK the cup with the picture of him on the side.

"I've been thinking about this since we found it," said MIK. He turned it in his good hand, barely able to see its outline. "I wonder what else we lost at the crater."

"Lots of stuff," said GUF. "But we did get to keep this."

"This was supposed to last for a long time," said MIK, "and tell what people were like for future ages? Then the people who put this there must really have liked the man who thought us up?"

"That's for sure," said GUF.

"And me too, I wonder?"

"You probably most of all," said GUF.

MIK smiled. The smile froze. The eyes went dark, and a thin line of condensation steam rose up from the eartracks. The hand gripped tightly on the cup.

Outside, the people began to sing a real sad song.

It was a bright sunny morning. GUF put flowers on MIK's and DUN's graves at the top of the hill. He patted the earth, stood up uncertainly.

He had replaced his frozen foot with a little wood-wheeled cart which he could skate along almost as good as walking.

He stood up and thought of MIK. He set his carpenter's cap forward on his head and whistled a little tune.

He picked up his wooden toolbox and started off down the hill to build the kids a swing set.

INTERLUDE: A SUMMER PLACE, ON THE BEACH, BEYOND THE SEA...

In my thirteen-year-old mind, it was all tied together: a movie I didn't see for forty years, and its theme song; a movie everyone saw; and a song by an Italo-American lounge lizard. By the time you finish this article, it'll all be inseparable in your mind, too. Or, maybe, my confusion will have been made more real and logical-like to you, and I will get to live out my rapidly approaching "golden years" without benefit of tastefully barred windows and supervised outings to the therapeutic trout pond . . .

The short version: The movie I didn't see (till last night) was A Summer Place. It was 1959 and you could not go anywhere without "Theme from A Summer Place" by Percy Faith and His Orchestra playing; on the radio, at the municipal swimming pool, every prom and party, every jukebox (the record sold nine jillion—give or take a bazillion—copies).

The movie me and everyone saw was On the Beach: I had my first date to see it (Linda Rodden, where are you now?). Among other things, it showed the world would end in 1964. . . . ("Welcome to the future, kid" as Gahan Wilson would later say in the comic strip Nuts.)

The other song that played everywhere that year when "Theme from A Summer Place" wasn't playing and poking melodic holes in the air was Bobby Darin's version of "Beyond the Sea."

Stick with me: I lived it; you only have to read about it.

A Summer Place. A movie with Richard Egan, Dorothy McGuire, Arthur Kennedy, Troy Donahue, and Sandra Dee. Everybody was talking about it (over the theme music played everywhere), I mean everybody. It was adapted and directed by Delmer Daves from a Sloan Wilson (The Man in the Gray Flannel Suit) middlebrow novel. The movie is jam-packed with adultery, alcoholism, passion, premarital sex and teen pregnancy, divorce scandal, repression, and a Frank Lloyd Wright house—in other words, 1959 in a nutshell. Plus, it had a swell Max Steiner score, with the aforementioned theme. (Steiner went from King Kong—which figures heavily in a dialogue section of A Summer Place—to Casablanca to this in only twenty-six years. . . .)

All my friends went with their older brothers and sisters and their girlfriends and boyfriends to see it at the drive-in. Me, my parents worked two jobs each all the time; the Arlington Theater wouldn't let kids in UNLESS they paid the full adult price (and sixty-five cents was more money than I saw in three weeks, unless it was summer—it wasn't—and I was mowing 100' x 200' yards for a buck-fifty a pop . . .). So, as was my wont, I grilled all my friends (and some pretty much total strangers at school) for details. They made it sound a lot hotter than it seemed to be as I watched it on tape last night. (Although, for 1959, it's cranked pretty high, you do not, as my friends implied, Get To See The Whole Thing. . . .)

So, it was the year of "Theme from A Summer Place," also On the Beach (more later).

And "Beyond the Sea."

The Bobby Darin song had, to me, the same haunting melancholy as Nevil Shute's novel, and Stanley Kramer's movie made from it. (Give me a break, I was a kid. Or guy. Mannish boy. Teenager in love. With death, and the atomic bomb, at least. Joe Dante's film Matinee, set during the Cuban Missile Crisis of 1962, has some of that same fatalistic melancholy feel, and is at the same time hilarious, and has some deep insight into the times . . . his time, my time.)

In "Beyond the Sea," there's this guy, looking out toward the ocean, singing about the love he knows is there, but has left. Over the horizon, but close, and on the way. I saw Darin staring out into that same irradiated air of the West Coast of the U.S. from On the Beach. Darin sings of his love, across the ocean, knowing, just knowing, they'll meet again . . .

I mean, this is the Bobby Darin of the Ed Sullivan Show/Vegas days, before his "If I Was a Carpenter"-relevant days . . .

It's all tied together, the movies and the songs.

I've had the words to "Waltzing Matilda" (the theme song adapted for On the Beach) in every wallet I've owned from the time I was thirteen, clipped out of a magazine article (Life) about the Kramer film.

The words are by A.B. (Banjo) Paterson, the unofficial poet laureate of the Land Down Under (most of his work reads like a mix of Rudyard Kipling and Robert W. Service . . .). I was in Perth, Australia, in January of 1997, as guest-of-honor at Swancon, a science fiction convention, on Australia Day. I was on a panel at 2:00 P.M. when suddenly, everybody at the convention came into the room and they all sang "Waltzing Matilda" to me. I was moved beyond tears.

The words and music to "Beyond the Sea" are by a Frenchman, Charles Trenet (its original title is La Mer); the English words are by Jack Lawrence. Though it became a big hit in 1959, the year of A Summer Place and On the Beach, it was written in 1945, the year of Hiroshima and Nagasaki . . .

And it wasn't just me, evidently, caught up in this swirling maelstrom of aural and visual emotion, connections and resonance. A year later, Bobby Darin of "Beyond the Sea" married Sandra Dee of A Summer Place.

I started early, being the avatar of the Zeitgeist. . . .

On the Beach was released late in 1959.

There's been either WWIII or some accident that led to the mutual exchange of atomic and hydrogen bombs, and the Northern Hemisphere is devoid of life. The radioactive cloud is drifting south, across the equatorial calms, and Australia and the rest of the Southern Hemisphere await their turn.

The movie opens with the USS Sawfish nuclear submarine entering an Australian harbor — it's been heading southward since whatever happened, and it's commanded by Dwight Towers (Gregory Peck). We meet the rest of the cast of characters — there's Anthony Perkins playing an Aussie naval lieutenant; Moira Davidson (Ava Gardner) as a good-time woman who knows and feels a lot more than she lets on; Julian Osborne (Fred Astaire), an embittered nuclear physicist whose hobby is racing dangerous cars (there's a lot more about this character in the novel than the movie); there's Donna Anderson as Perkins' young wife — and they've just had a baby. There are lots of finely realized character bits — two old guys at a stuffy club trying to drink up all the fine wines before they're wasted on the dead; an Australian admiral and his aide; a really good bit by an actor, playing a doctor, late in the movie as the first symptoms of radiation sickness show up.

These people await the end of life on Earth in the bright Australian sun; what they do with the time left makes up the movie.

Halfway through, the Sawfish goes back to the West Coast of the U.S. There's a theory some of the radioactivity may have been washed from the air by winter rains, which proves to be wrong, and there have been messages, received in Australia, on the shortwave in Morse code, mostly gibberish, from somewhere near San Diego, that may indicate survivors, possibly children.

The only full words that have come through so far are "water" and "connect." (Shades of E.M. Forster. The title of Shute's novel and the movie are from T.S. Eliot's "The Hollow Men," the one that ends "not with a bang but a whimper.")

The messages, it turns out when a sailor in a CIMP suit leaves the sub to explore—it's at a refinery, the generators are still going—are caused by a Coke bottle, caught in the pull-ring of a window shade blowing in the wind—the neck of the bottle occasionally touches a live telegraph key.

It's a swell scene. It was in 1959; it still is.

Just a little earlier, one of the crewmen had deserted when the sub was off his hometown, San Francisco. (In one of those bits of reverse casting: as A. Perkins plays an Australian, Aussie John Meillon is the Californian—he's Mick's pal in the Crocodile Dundee movies made in the 1980s). There's a scene where the sub rises to conning-tower depth and Peck talks to him through the loudspeaker next morning, while he's fishing—all the fish are dead by this time, too—it's too late to take him back in; he'll be dead in a few days. They have a conversation that says much of what the movie was trying to say—it all comes down to people.

There are things wrong with the movie—it was, after all, A Stanley Kramer film. Everybody's stiff-upper-lip, even though these are supposed to be 1964 Aussies and Americans. There are no riots, no Ghost Dances in the streets, no bonfires of money and vanities. The closest we get is the Grand Prix of Australia, where there are crashes galore; it doesn't matter— they're all going to be dead in a few weeks anyway—that Julian, the Astaire character, wins. Everything's keyed so low that Donna Anderson's breakdown (packing for a trip to the England that no longer exists, instead of facing the inevitability of death, or suicide by Government Prescription #24768, which she'll also have to give the baby with its milk) seems out of place, as if the character is pitched too high for the movie she's in.

There's a great deal of quiet heartbreak in the film; instead of Dwight sliding it into Moira at first invitation, he holds out some hope that his family is still alive in Mystic, Connecticut. (He's got a BB gun on the sub for his son, which would have been a belated Christmas present, if the duty tour had not been interrupted by WWIII.)

Dwight and Moira start the big kiss and become lovers, in a mountain resort, among drunken revelers at a disastrous early-opening trout season, in a rainstorm. Drunks are singing in other rooms, at the pub downstairs, everywhere. The scene is a great one (despite what Bill Warren, a man I admire inordinately, says in his entry on the movie in Keep Watching the Skies!). The drunks are singing "Waltzing Matilda" endlessly and off-key; a window blows open, rain comes in; the couple jump up to close it, touch, and, as they kiss, and the camera (which has been still as a stump for most of the movie) swirls around them in a 360° circle, the voices downstairs turn into a single smooth baritone, which sings the final verse of the song perfectly, with its lines "you'll never catch me alive, says he. . . ."

The things which work in the movie really work—cheerful resignation, small grumblings about how nuclear war plays hell with the cricket and fishing seasons; people going through motions they always have (when Dwight returns from the futile Coke bottle-telegraph mission, he comes across a field Moira and her father are plowing, sowing a crop that will never be harvested). Julian, who helped invent the hydrogen bomb, only wants to live long enough to run in the Grand Prix of Australia; when it is time for everyone to die, he closes up his garage, climbs behind the wheel of the machine and guns the motor, thick clouds of exhaust (and carbon monoxide) rising around him—he's made a very personal choice of how he wants to go.

There are endless lines of people waiting to receive the suicide pills, like people getting swine flu shots or the polio vaccine, while the Salvation Army, under the giant banner "There Is Still Time, Brother." plays endlessly to thinner and thinner crowds.

The butler at the gentlemen's club, all gentlemen gone forever, brings himself a drink and starts to play billiards. The lights go out. We assume nobody's running them anymore, either.

After the Perkins, Anderson, Astaire characters are gone, the only actors left are Gardner and Peck. She, Moira, already fevered and throwing up, on the beach, watching the Sawfish sail away, scarf blowing in the wind, beside her car she's taken out for the last time; he, Towers, takes one last sighting of the noon sun and goes down the hatch; the Sawfish submerges (a reverse of the opening) on its last trip back to America so the crew can die there. There's a cut to all the major cities of the world—deserted, a few newspapers blowing in the streets, no movement anywhere except that from the radioactive wind. The movie ends with three close-ups of the Salvation Army banner in Australia.

What all this has to do with is the same feeling Darin got in "Beyond the Sea." It's like, in the old French phrase, nostalgia for the future. In this case, a future closed off to all the possibilities. An imagined future, without anyone around to imagine it, like thoughts hanging in the air.

On the Beach can almost make you see and feel and yearn for it; for the story to go on after everyone's gone.

I had my first date to go see On the Beach; this was the future waiting for me, for everyone my age, for everyone everywhere. Only five years away, maybe, said the movie. Or less . . .

Or more. It's forty years later now; we're still here, lots of us.

It was a future we didn't have to live, because someone imagined it for us; had shown us the face of extinction (without mutants, without showing a single bomb going off, without fights with someone over a can of beans, without fuss and bother, not with a bang; but not exactly a whimper, either).

And the music tied it all together. '59/'60 was the year of "Theme from A Summer Place" and "Waltzing Matilda." And as Bobby Darin married Sandra Dee, so were alpha and omega linked: a movie about the end of the world AND a song written at the very start of the Atomic Age.

Now, it all doesn't seem so dumb, does it?

RADIO PICTURES

What the movies did, around the corner, for a quarter, television came to your house and, in any room you wanted — living room, kitchen, bedroom — did for free.

All the science fiction stories of the '20s and '30s dealt with television (a word coined by Hugo Gernsback) as this great medium that would bring high-tone radio programming — opera, great plays and novels, educational shows — into your home, with pictures.

You would be enlightened, ennobled: you could see great actors and actresses, the world's greatest plays; far-off places, scientists, philosophers, all at the touch of a button and the click of a dial.

They envisioned enlightenment streaming from the great broadcasting centers and (even before Arthur C. Clarke thought of geosynchronous communications satellites) events broadcast simultaneously around the world. You could go anywhere, see anything, never leave home. The wonders of the world would come to you.

So how did we get Mr. Ed, a horse, selling you oats? My Mother the Car? The Love Boat? American Gladiators? Johnnie LaRue's Jumping for Dollars? Who was responsible? How had the dream gone so bad in so few years?

Along with all that great stuff it was capable of (and there has been plenty) it has probably served up more steaming heaps of caca than have been shoveled in the history of the planet, even more than the movies could ever dream

Where had those dreams of the uplifters gone?

What follows are attempts at a stammering explanation in this hydrogenous age, as Dylan Thomas used to say before he croaked at age thirty-nine . . .

s soon as there was photography, there was an attempt to make the picture move. Motion pictures were one answer—all the experiments of Muybridge, Friese-Greene, the Lumières, Edison, the invention of the Maltese Cross and the loop, to cause the camera (and the projector, which at one time were the same machine) to pause at the precise point to add to the persistence of vision at 1/24th of a second.

Parallel to this, and once photoactive chemicals were found, others tried to find a way to instill motion some other way. They knew it involved holding an image a fraction of a second, then the next image, and so on. They knew it probably involved electricity. Their experiments are almost as old as photography. (Go find and read R.A. Lafferty's brilliant take on this in "Selenium Ghosts of the Eighteen Seventies," which originally appeared in the late Terry Carr's Universe 8.) They tried them all: selenium, all the other -iums which take a charge, become luminescent, and can be made to hold an image.

Making it move was another matter. Anything which electrically disrupted the image also obliterated it. Hence the slow development of all kinds of systems, electrical and electronic, mechanical, or a combination of the two, some of which are described in the following three forays.

A few months after I'd meticulously researched, from hundreds of places, the backgrounds for the first two of these stories—voilà! There are big-ass books and two television series that put it all together, in one place, at one time; easy pickin's. My method was more fun and wasted lots more time, and I got most of it right.

So, as I said, here's to all the old SF writers who envisioned the uplift of the (human) race through broadcasting, who wanted a future where great culture was yours at the flick of a switch. And to all the mad Russians in their mothers' basements (Zwyorkin) and Idaho ploughboys seeing in the contours of a field the way to make an image appear on a phosphor-dot screen (Philo T. Farnsworth) and Scots who got so close, and had the thing that could have worked, a good mechanical TV, up and broadcasting, only to take one look at the all-electric orthicon tube, and see the jig was up; he saw the Future, and he wasn't in it (John Logie Baird).

And dozens of others, whose lives were heartbreak and who died unknown somewhere, the places where people laugh when the children say, "My father invented television." For the bitterly ironic thing is, they're telling the truth.

Introduction to

Hoover's Men

The history of broadcasting is one of accidents.

The reason stations started was the dream—music, opera, plays, funny people telling jokes in your house. Stations broadcast: People bought radios. But people quit buying radios for a while because there was nothing to listen to twelve hours of the day. More radio stations were built that broadcast longer hours. People bought more sets. So many stations went on the air they interfered with each other. Radio sales went down again. The Commerce Department set up what later became the FCC and assigned frequencies, and thoughtfully divided up all the airwaves between Canada and the U.S., leaving Mexico out of the picture, which is what led in the 1950s to the million-watt blue-lightning-bolt-emitting Mexican-border radio stations like XERF, sending out signals you could pick up from Newfoundland to McMurdo Sound—won't let us have any airwaves, señor? We'll use them all. Networks were set up by the radio manufacturers to sell more radios.

Then somebody asked if he could advertise his egg farm on WHYY in Philly. He paid something like ten dollars for an hour's worth of time over the next month. The guy was out of eggs in two days. . . .

Gee whiz! When they realized people would pay money to sell people stuff on your radio station, or network, the whole thing changed. Before, it had been about culture, entertainment, and selling radio sets. After, it was about the same thing it is now: dollars. The programming was there to get the audience to get the advertiser to pay dollars to sell their stuff to that audience . . .

Meanwhile, there were the Russians in the basements, and the ploughboys, and mad Scots, and people with a little brains at the stations and networks, who were working on Radio with Pictures, and just could not see that the same damned thing that had happened to radio was going to repeat itself with Tele-Vision. . . .

I wrote this for one of Ellen Datlow's what I call six-authors-for-a-buck things. Once every year or so at Omni—when it was a magazine—she'd ask six or seven writers for very short stories on common themes, and they'd all be printed in a single issue of the magazine. This went on for years—my year was 1988. Ellen said the theme was Urban Fantasy. Urban Fantasy? That means it takes place in a city, and it didn't happen! Okay! Other writers my year: Daniel Pinkwater, Joyce Carol Oates, T. Coraghessan Boyle, Barry Malzberg, and K. W. Jeter. Pretty damn hot-shit company to keep.

And, as I said, after I'd killed myself in the research, here come PBS and the networks doing all my work for me, after the fact, making me sort of the John Logie Baird of the history-of-early-broadcasting SF story, of which I consider myself the exemplar. . .

HOOVER'S MEN

On March 30, 1929, three weeks after Al Smith's Presidential inauguration, four gunmetal-gray Fords were parked on a New Jersey road. On the tonneau top of each was a large silver loop antenna.

There were fifteen men in all — some inside the cars in their shirtsleeves, earphones on their heads, the others sitting on the running boards or standing in stylish poses. All those outside wore dark blue or gray suits, hats, and dark ties with small checks on them. Each had a bulge under one of his armpits.

It was dusk. On the horizon, two giant aerials stood two hundred feet high, with a long wire connecting them. They were in silhouette and here and there they blotted out one of the early stars. Back to the east lay the airglow of Greater Manhattan.

Men in the cars switched on their worklights. Outside the first car Carmody uncrossed his arms, opened his pocket watch, noted the time on his clipboard. "Six fifty-two. Start your logs," he said. Word passed down the line.

He reached in through the window, picked up the extra set of headphones next to Dalmas and listened in:

"This is station MAPA coming to you from Greater New Jersey with fifty thousand mighty watts of power. Now, to continue with The Darkies' Hour for all our listeners over in Harlem, is Oran 'Hot Lips' Page with his rendition of 'Blooey!' featuring Floyd 'Horsecollar' Williams on the alto saxophone. . . ."

"Jesus," said Dalmas, looking at his dials. "The station's all over the band, blocking out everything from 750 to 1245. Nothin' else is getting through nowhere this side of Virginia!"

Carmody made a note on his clipboard pages.

"The engineer—that's Ma—said sorry we were off the air this afternoon for a few minutes but we blew out one of our heptodes, and you know how danged particular they can be. She says we'll get the kinks out of our new transmitter real soon.

"Don't forget—at 7:05 tonight, Madame Sosostris will be in to give the horoscopes and read the cards for all you listeners who've written her, enclosing your twenty-five-cents handling fee, in the past week. . . ."

"Start the wire recorders," said Carmody.

"Remember to turn off your radio sets for five minutes just before 7:00 P.M. That's four minutes from now. First, we're going up to what, Ma?— two hundred and ninety thousand watts—in our continuin' effort to contact the planet Mars, then we'll be down to about three quarters of a watt with our antenna as a receiver in our brand-new effort to make friends with the souls of the departed.

"Here, to end our Negro music broadcast for this evening are Louis 'Satchmo' Armstrong and Dwight 'Ike' Eisenhower with their instrumental 'Do You Know What It Means to Miss New Orleans?' Hang on, this one will really heat up your ballast tubes. . . ."

Some of the sweetest horn and clarinet music Dalmas had ever heard came out of the earphones. He swayed in time to the music. Carmody looked at him. "Geez. You don't have to enjoy this stuff so much. We have a job to do." He checked his pocket watch again.

He turned to Mallory. "I want precise readings on everything. I want recordings from all four machines. Mr. Hoover doesn't want a judge throwing anything out on a technicality like with the KXR2Y thing. Understood?"

"Yeah, boss," said Mallory from the third car.

"Let's go, then," said Carmody.

Just then the sky lit up blue and green in a crackling halo that flickered back and forth between the aerials on the horizon.

"Yikes!" yelled Dalmas, throwing the earphones off. The sound coming out of them could be heard fifty feet away.

"EARTH CALLING MARS! EARTH CALLING MARS! THIS IS STATION MAPA, MA AND PA, CALLING MARS. HOWDY TO ALL OUR MARTIAN LISTENERS. COME SEE US! EARTH CALLING MARS..."

They burst through the locked station door. Small reception room, desk piled high with torn envelopes and stacks of quarters, a glass wall for viewing into the studio, locked power room to one side. A clock on the wall that said 7:07. There was a small speaker box and intercom on the viewer window.

An old woman was sitting at a table at a big star-webbed carbon mike with a shawl wrapped around her shoulders and a crystal ball in front of her. An old man stood nearby holding a sheaf of papers in his hand.

"... and a listener writes 'Dear Madame Sosostris —' "

Carmody went to the intercom and pushed down the button. He held up his badge. "United States Government, Federal Radio Agency, Radio Police!" he said.

They both looked up.

"Cheese it, Pa! The Feds!" said the woman, throwing off her shawl. She ran to the racks of glowing and humming pentodes on the far wall, throwing her arms wide as if to hide them from sight.

"Go arrest some bootleggers, G-Man!" yelled Pa.

"Not my jurisdiction. And Prohibition ends May 1st. You'd know that if you were fulfilling your responsibilities to keep the public informed ..." said Carmody.

"See, ladies and gentlemen in radioland," yelled Pa into the microphone, "this is what happens to private enterprise in a totalitarian state! The airwaves belong to anybody! My great uncle invented radio — he did! — Marconi stole it from him in a swindle. Government interference! Orville Wright doesn't have a pilot's license! He invented flying. My family invented radio ..."

"... you are further charged with violation of nineteen sections of the Radio Act of 1929," said Carmody, continuing to read from the warrant.

"First charge, operating an unlicensed station broadcasting on the AM band, a public resource. Second, interfering with the broadcast of licensed operations—"

"See, Mr. and Mrs. Radio Listener, what putting one man in charge of broadcasting does! Ma! Crank it up all the way!" Ma twisted some knobs. The sky outside the radio station turned blue and green again. Carmody's hair stood up, pushing his hat off his head. His arms tingled.

"SOS!" yelled Pa. "SOS! Help! Help! This is station MAPA. Get your guns! Meet us at the station! Show these Fascists we won't put up with—"

"We'll add sending a false distress call over the airwaves, incitement to riot, and breach of the peace," said Carmody, penciling on his notes, "having astrologers, clairvoyants, and mediums in contravention of the Radio Act of 1929 . . ."

The first of the axes went through the studio door.

". . . use of the airwaves for a lottery." Carmody looked up. "Give yourselves up," he said. He watched while Ma and Pa ran around inside the control room, piling the meager furniture against the battered door. "Very well. Resisting arrest by duly authorized Federal agents. Unlawful variation in broadcast power—"

"Squeak! Squeak! Help!" said Pa. Dalmas had bludgeoned his way into the shrieking power room and threw all the breaker switches. Ma and Pa turned into frantic blurs as all the needles dropped to zero. The sky outside went New Jersey dark and Carmody's hair lay back down.

"Good," he said, still reading into the intercom. "Advertising prohibited articles and products over the public airwaves. Broadcast of obscene and suggestive material. Use of . . ."

The door gave up.

"Book 'em, Dalmas," he said.

"Two minutes, Mr. Hoover," said the floor manager. He waved his arms. In a soundproof room an engineer put his foot on a generator motor and yanked on the starter cord. Then he adjusted some knobs and gave an okay signal with a circled thumb and finger.

Hoover sat down at the bank of microphones. A four-by-eight-foot panel of photosensitive cells lowered into place in front of him. In a cutout portion in its center was a disk punched with holes. As the panel came down the disk began to spin faster and faster. The studio lights came up to blinding intensity. Hoover blinked, shielded his eyes.

Carmody and Mallory stood in the control room behind the engineers, the director, and the station manager. Before them on the bank of knobs and lights was a two-by-three-inch flickering screen filled with lines in which Mallory could barely make out Mr. Hoover. Carmody and the other chiefs had turned in their reports to Hoover an hour before.

"I never thought he'd take this job," said an engineer.

"Aw, Hoover's a public servant," said the director.

The STAND BY sign went off. Hoover arranged his papers.

ON THE AIR blazed in big red letters over the control booth. The announcer at his mikes at the side table said:

"Good evening, ladies and gentlemen. This is Station WRNY and it's 11:00 P.M. in New York City. Tonight, live via coast-to-coast hookup on all radio networks, the Canadian Broadcasting System, and through the television facilities of WIXA2 New York and W2JA4 Washington, D.C., we present a broadcast from the head of the new Federal Radio Agency concerning the future of the airwaves. Ladies and gentlemen of the United States and Canada, Mr. Hoover."

The graying, curly-haired gentleman looked into the whirling Nipkow disk with the new Sanabria interlaced pattern and pushed one of the microphones a little further from him.

"I come to you tonight as the new head of the Federal Radio Agency. After the recent elections, in which I lost the Presidency to Mr. Alfred Smith, I assumed that after eight years as your Secretary of Commerce under the last two administrations I would be asked to leave government service.

"Imagine my delight and surprise when Mr. Smith asked me to stay on, but in the new position of head of the Federal Radio Agency. If I may quote the President: 'Who knows more about raddio than you, Herbert? It's all in a turrible mess and I'd like you to straighten it out, once and for all.'

"Well, tonight, I'm taking your President's words to heart. As chief enforcement officer under the new and valuable Radio Act of 1929, I'm announcing the following:

"Today my agents closed down fourteen radio stations. Nine were violating the total letter of the law; five were, after repeated warnings, still violating its spirit. Tomorrow, six more will be closed down. This will end the most flagrant of our current airwave problems.

"As to the future," Hoover pushed back a white wisp of hair that had fallen over his forehead, "tomorrow I will begin meetings with representatives of the Republic of Mexico and see what can be done about establishing frequencies for their use. They were summarily ignored when Canada and the United States divided the airwaves in 1924."

The station manager leaned forward intently.

"If this means another division and realignment of the frequencies of existing stations, so be it," said Hoover.

The station manager slapped his hand to his forehead and shook it from side to side.

"Furthermore," said Hoover, "under powers given to me, I am ready to issue commercial radiovision/radio movie/television licenses to any applicant who will conform to the seventy-line thirty-frame format for monochrome . . ."

"He's gone meshuggah!" said the engineer. "Nobody uses that format!"

"Quiet," said Carmody. "Mr. Hoover's talking."

". . . or the one-forty-line, sixty-frame format for color transmission and reception, with the visual portion on the shortwave and the audio portion on the newly opened frequency-modulated bandwidths."

"Aaiiii!!" yelled the station manager, running out of the booth toward the desk phone in the next office.

"He's crazy! Everybody's got a different system!" said the director.

"No doubt Mr. Hoover's in for some heat," said Mallory.

"To those who say radio-television is too primitive and experimental to allow regular commercial broadcasting, I say, you're the ones holding up progress. The time for review is after new and better methods are developed, not before. This or that rival concern have been for years trying to persuade the government to adopt their particular formats and methods."

He looked into the whirling lights, put down his papers. "I will say to the people of those concerns: Here is your format, like it or lump it."

Then he smiled. "For a wholesome and progressive future in America, dedicated to better broadcasting for the public good, this is the head of your nation's Federal Radio Agency, Herbert Hoover, saying goodnight. Good Night."

The STAND BY sign came back on. The blinding lights went down and the disk slowed and stopped; then the whole assembly was pulled back into the ceiling.

In the outer office the station manager was crying.

Mr. Hoover was still shaking hands when Carmody and Mallory left.

Early tomorrow they had to take off for upstate New York. There was a radio station there with an experimental-only license that was doing regular commercial broadcasts. It would be a quiet shut-down, not at all like this evening's.

As they walked to the radio car, two cabs and a limo swerved up to the curbing, missing them and each other by inches. Doors swung open. Sarnoff jumped out of the NBC Studebaker limo. He was in evening clothes. The head of CBS was white as a sheet as he piled out of the cab throwing money behind him. One of the vice-presidents of the Mutual System got to the door before they did. There was almost a fistfight.

There was a sound in the air like that of a small fan on a nice spring day. Overhead the airship Ticonderoga was getting a late start on its three-day journey to Los Angeles.

Mallory pulled away from the curb heading back to the hotel where Dalmas and the other agents were already asleep. He reached forward to the dashboard, twisted a knob. A glowing yellow light came on.

"Geez, I'm beat," said Carmody. "See if you can't get something decent on the thing, okay?"

Nine years later, after his second heart attack and retirement, Carmody was in his apartment. He was watching his favorite program, The Clark Gable-Carole Lombard Show on his new Philco console color television set with the big nine-by-twelve-inch screen.

He punched open the top of a Rhinegold with a church key, foam running over onto his favorite chair. "Damn!" he said, holding the beer up and sucking away the froth. He leaned back. He now weighed 270 pounds.

Gable was unshaven; he'd apologized at the show's opening; he'd come over from the set where they were filming Margaret Mitchell's Mules in Horse's Harnesses to do the live show. They'd just started a sketch with Lombard, carrying a bunch of boxes marked Anaconda Hat Co., asking Gable for directions to some street.

Then the screen went black.

"Shit!" said Carmody, draining his beer.

"Ladies and Gentlemen," said an announcer, "we interrupt our regularly scheduled program to bring you a news bulletin via transatlantic cable. Please stand by." A card saying NEWS BULLETIN. ONE MOMENT PLEASE. came up onscreen. Then there was a hum and a voice said, "Okay!"

A face came onscreen, a reporter in a trench coat stepped back from the camera holding a big mike in one hand.

"This morning, 3:00 A.M. Berlin Time, the Prime Minister of Great Britain and the Chancellor of Germany seemed to have reached an accord on the present crisis involving Germany's demands in Austria." Past his shoulder there was movement; flashbulbs went off like lightning. "Here they come," said the newsman, turning. The cameras followed him, picking up other television crews with their big new RCA/UFA all-electronic cameras the size of the doghouses trundling in for the same shot.

Onscreen SA and SS men in their shiny coats and uniforms pushed the reporters back and took up positions, machine guns at ready, around the Chancellery steps.

Atop the steps the Prime Minister and the Führer, followed by generals, aides, and diplomats of both countries, stepped up to a massed bank of microphones.

"Tonight," said the Prime Minister of Great Britain, "I have been reassured, again and again, by the Chancellor, that the document we have signed," he held up a white piece of paper for the cameras, and more flashbulbs went off, causing him to blink, "will be the last territorial demand of the German nation. This paper assures us of peace in our time."

Applause broke out from the massed N.S.D.A.P. crowds with their banners, standards, and pikes. The cameras slowly focused into a close-up view — while the crowd chanted, Seig Heil! Seig Heil! — of Herr Hitler's beaming face.

"Bastid!" yelled Carmody and threw the empty beer can ricocheting off the console cabinet.

A few minutes later, after the network assured viewers it would cover live any further late-breaking news from Berlin, they went back to the show.

There were lots of wrecked hats on the street set, and Gable was jumping up and down on one.

Lombard broke up about something, turned away from him, laughing. Then she turned back, eyes bright, back in character.

"Geez, that Gable . . ." said Carmody. "What a lucky bastid!"

Introduction to

Mr. Goober's Show

I wrote this on a blazing hot January day when the temperature was in the high thirties.

I'm talking 1997. I'm talking Perth, Australia. And I'm talking centigrade, not that wussy Fahrenheit stuff.

It was 6:00 A.M. and already hot. I'm down there as Guest of honor at Swancon. I have to read a story at 4:00 P.M. And it's Australia Day.

Never fear. I'd wanted to write this one a long time. I sat down and started writing it. I had to leave the room at 1:00 P.M. to be on a panel. (During the middle of that panel, the entire rest of the convention came into the room and sang "Waltzing Matilda" to me—the words to which I took out of my billfold where they'd been—every billfold I'd ever owned—since I'd cut them out of a 1959 Life magazine article about On the Beach.) Words failed me. They still do.

Then back to the room, scribble scribble scribble, hey, Mr. Waldrop? Then I read the story at 4:00 P.M. (prefaced by an explication of Joe Dante's movie Matinee, which I think went straight to video in Australia—nothing to do with the story; I just thought they should all go out and buy a copy of the flick).

This is the story that killed Omni Online. Ellen bought it; it went up March 26, 1998. They pulled the plug on Omni Online March 30, 1998. Gordon Van Gelder, in his new role as editor of F&SF, asked if he could publish it there, and pay me more money. Sure.

The deeper you look into the history of early television, the more wonderful it is. I tell you some of the weird stuff here; the PBS Race for Television and the episode of Television that dealt with the early stuff tell you more.

I want to thank again (besides in the acknowledgements) Andrew P. Hooper for his help in getting to me a piece of research I'd read but could no longer find. He walked his ass over to the Fremont branch of the Seattle Public Library one 38° (Fahrenheit this time) pissing-rain day, looked it up, and mailed it to me while I was in the middle of rewriting this. It got to me next day out here in Oso; I stuck it in where I needed it, and sent it off to kill Omni Online. Thanks, Andy.

He also said he thought this would have made a great episode of the first season of the original Twilight Zone or One Step Beyond. I'd never thought about it that way but he's probably right. Too bad I couldn't have written this when I was thirteen years old: maybe me and Serling or John Newland could have made a deal . . . "Missed it by that much, chief." (Only thirty-eight years, Andy. Sorry.)

Mr. Goober's Show

You know how it is:

There's a bar on the corner, where hardly anybody knows your name, and you like it that way. Live bands play there two or three nights a week. Before they start up it's nice, and on the nights they don't play—there's a good jukebox, the big TV's on low on ESPN all the time. At his prices the owner should be a millionaire, but he's given his friends so many free drinks they've forgotten they should pay for more than every third or fourth one. Not that you know the owner, but you've watched.

You go there when your life's good, you go there when your life's bad; mostly you go there instead of having a good or bad life.

And one night, fairly crowded, you're on the stools so the couples and the happy people can have the booths and tables. Someone's put twelve dollars in the jukebox (and they have some taste), the TV's on the Australian Thumb-Wrestling Finals, the neon beer signs are on, and the place looks like the inside of the Ferris Wheel on opening night at the state fair.

You start talking to the guy next to you, early fifties, your age, and you get off on TV (you can talk to any American, except a Pentecostal, about television and you're talking the classic stuff; the last Newhart episode, Northern Exposure; the episode where Lucy stomps the grapes; the coast-to-coast bigmouth Dick Van Dyke; Howdy Doody [every eight-year-old boy in America had a Jones for Princess Summer-Fall Winter-Spring]).

And the guy, whose name you know is Eldon (maybe he told you, maybe you were born knowing it), starts asking you about some sci-fi show from the early fifties, maybe you didn't get it, maybe it was only on local upstate New York, sort of, it sounds like, a travelogue, like the old Seven League Boots, only about space, stars and such, planets . . .

"Well, no," you say, "there was Tom Corbett, Space Cadet; Space Patrol; Captain Video (which you never got but knew about), Rod Brown of the Rocket Rangers; Captain Midnight (or Jet Jackson, Flying Commando, depending on whether you saw it before or after Ovaltine quit sponsoring it, and in reruns people's lips flapped around saying 'Captain Midnight' but what came out was 'Jet Jackson' . . .).

"Or maybe one of the anthology shows, Twilight Zone or Tales of —"

"No," he says, "not them. See, there was this TV . . ."

"Oh," you say, "a TV. Well, the only one I know of was this one where a guy at a grocery store (one season) invents this TV that contacts . . ."

"No," he says, looking at you (Gee, this guy can be intense!). "I don't mean Johnny Jupiter, which is what you were going to say. Jimmy Duckweather invents TV. Contacts Jupiter, which is inhabited by puppets when they're inside the TV, and by guys in robot suits when they come down to Earth, and almost cause Duckweather to lose his job and not get a date with the boss's daughter, episode after episode, two seasons."

"Maybe you mean Red Planet Mars, a movie. Peter Graves —"

". . . Andrea King, guy invents hydrogen tube; Nazis; Commies; Eisenhower president; Jesus speaks from Mars."

"Well, The Twonky. Horrible movie, about a TV from the future?"

"Hans Conreid. Nah, that's not it."

And so it goes. The conversation turns to other stuff (you're not the one with The Answer) and mostly it's conversation you forget because, if all the crap we carry around in our heads were real, and it was flushed, the continents would drown, and you forget it, and mostly get drunk and a little maudlin, slightly depressed and mildly horny, and eventually you go home.

But it doesn't matter, because this isn't your story; it's Eldon's.

When he was eight years old, city-kid Eldon and his seven-year-old sister Irene were sent off for two weeks in the summer of 1953, to Aunt Joanie's house in upstate New York while, unknown to them, their mother had a hysterectomy.

Aunt Joanie was not their favorite aunt; that was Aunt Nonie, who would as soon whip out a Monopoly board, or Game of Life, or checkers as look at you, and always took them off on picnics or fishing or whatever it was she thought they'd like to do. But Aunt Nonie (their Mom's youngest sister) was off in Egypt on a cruise she'd won in a slogan contest for pitted dates, so it fell to Aunt Joanie, their Father's oldest sister to keep them the two weeks.

Their father's side of the family wasn't the fun one. If an adult unbent toward a child a little, some other family member would be around to remind them they were just children; their cousins on that side of the family (not that Aunt Joanie or Uncle Arthridge had any) were like mice; they had to take off their shoes and put on house slippers when they got home from school; they could never go into the family room; they had to be in bed by 8:30 P.M., even when the sun was still up in the summer.

Uncle Arthridge was off in California, so it was just them and Aunt Joanie, who, through no fault of her own, looked just like the Queen in Snow White and the Seven Dwarves, which they had seen with Aunt Nonie the summer before.

They arrived by train, white tags stuck to them like turkeys in a raffle, and a porter had made sure they were comfortable. When Irene had been upset, realizing she would be away from home, and was going to be at Aunt Joanie's for two weeks, and had begun to sniffle, Eldon held her hand. He was still at the age where he could hold his sister's hand against the world and think nothing of it.

Aunt Joanie was waiting for them in the depot on the platform, and handed the porter a $1.00 tip, which made him smile.

And then Aunt Joanie drove them, allowing them to sit in the front seat of her Plymouth, to her house, and there they were.

At first, he thought it might be a radio.

It was up on legs, the bottom of them looking like eagle claws holding a wooden ball. It wasn't a sewing machine cabinet, or a table. It might be a liquor cabinet, but there wasn't a keyhole.

It was the second day at Aunt Joanie's and he was already cranky. Irene had had a crying jag the night before and their aunt had given them some ice cream.

He was exploring. He already knew every room; there was a basement and an attic. The real radio was in the front room; this was in the sitting room at the back.

One of the reasons they hadn't wanted to come to Aunt Joanie's was that she had no television, like their downstairs neighbors, the Stevenses did, back in the city. They'd spent the first part of summer vacation downstairs in front of it, every chance they got. Two weeks at Aunt Nonie's without television would have been great, because she wouldn't have given them time to think, and would have them exhausted by bedtime anyway.

But two weeks at Aunt Joanie and Uncle Arthridge's without television was going to be murder. She had let them listen to radio, but not the scary shows, or anything good. And Johnny Dollar and Suspense weren't on out here, she was sure.

So he was looking at the cabinet in the sitting room. It had the eagle-claw legs. It was about three feet wide, and the part that was solid started a foot and a half off the floor. There was two feet of cabinet above that. At the back was a rounded part with air holes in it, like a Lincoln Continental spare tire holder. He ran his hand over it—it was made out of that same stuff as the backs of radios and televisions.

There were two little knobs on the front of the cabinet though he couldn't see a door. He pulled on them. Then he turned and pulled on them.

They opened, revealing three or four other knobs, and a metal toggle switch down at the right front corner. They didn't look like radio controls. It didn't look like a television either. There was no screen.

There was no big lightning-bolt moving dial like on their radio at home in the city.

Then he noticed a double-line of wood across the top front of it, like on the old icebox at his grandfather's. He pushed on it from the floor. Something gave, but he couldn't make it go farther.

Eldon pulled a stool up to the front of it.

"What are you doing?" asked Irene.

"This must be another radio," he said. "This part lifts up."

He climbed atop the stool. He had a hard time getting his fingers under the ridge. He pushed.

The whole top of the thing lifted up a few inches. He could see glass.

Then it was too heavy. He lifted at it again after it dropped down, and this time it came up halfway open.

There was glass on the under-lid. It was a mirror. He saw the reflection of part of the room. Something else moved below the mirror, inside the cabinet.

"Aunt Joanie's coming!" said Irene.

He dropped the lid and pushed the stool away and closed the doors.

"What are you two little cautions doing?" asked Aunt Joanie from the other room.

The next morning, when Aunt Joanie went to the store on the corner, he opened the top while Irene watched.

The inner lid was a mirror that stopped halfway up, at an angle. Once he got it to a certain point, it clicked into place. There was a noise from inside and another click.

He looked down into it. There was a big dark glass screen.

"It's a television!" he said.

"Can we get Howdy Doody?"

"I don't know," he said.

"You better ask Aunt Joanie, or you'll get in trouble."

He clicked the toggle switch. Nothing happened.

"It doesn't work," he said.

"Maybe it's not plugged in," said Irene.

Eldon lay down on the bare floor at the edge of the area rug, saw the prongs of a big electric plug sticking out underneath. He pulled on it. The cord uncoiled from behind. He looked around for the outlet. The nearest one was on the far wall.

"What are you two doing?" asked Aunt Joanie, stepping into the room with a small grocery bag in her arms.

"Is — is this a television set?" asked Eldon.

"Can we get Howdy Doody?" asked Irene.

Aunt Joanie put down the sack. "It is a television. But it won't work anymore. There's no need to plug it in. It's an old-style one, from before the War. They don't work like that anymore. Your uncle Arthridge and I bought it in 1938. There were no broadcasts out here then, but we thought there would be soon."

As she was saying this, she stepped forward, took the cord from Eldon's hands, rewound it, and placed it behind the cabinet again.

"Then came the War, and everything changed. This kind won't work anymore. So we shan't be playing with it, shall we? It's probably dangerous by now."

"Can't we try it, just once?" said Eldon.

"I do not think so," said Aunt Joanie. "Please put it out of your mind. Go wash up now, we'll have lunch soon."

Three days before they left, they found themselves alone in the house again, in the early evening. It had rained that afternoon, and was cool for summer.

Irene heard scraping in the sitting room. She went there and found Eldon pushing the television cabinet down the bare part of the floor toward the electrical outlet on the far wall.

He plugged it in. Irene sat down in front of it, made herself comfortable. "You're going to get in trouble," she said. "What if it explodes?"

He opened the lid. They saw the reflection of the television screen in it from the end of the couch.

He flipped the toggle. Something hummed, there was a glow in the back, and they heard something spinning. Eldon put his hand near the round part and felt pulses of air, like from a weak fan. He could see lights through the holes in the cabinet, and something was moving.

He twisted a small knob, and light sprang up in the picture-tube part, enlarged and reflected in the mirror on the lid. Lines of bright static moved up the screen and disappeared in a repeating pattern.

He turned another knob, the larger one, and the light went dark and then bright again.

Then a picture came in.

They watched those last three days, every time Aunt Joanie left; afraid at first, watching only a few minutes, then turning it off, unplugging it, and closing it up and pushing it back into its place, careful not to scratch the floor.

Then they watched more, and more, and there was an excitement each time they went through the ritual, a tense expectation.

Since no sound came in, what they saw they referred to as "Mr. Goober's Show," from his shape, and his motions, and what went on around him. He was on any time they turned the TV on.

They left Aunt Joanie's reluctantly. She had never caught them watching it. They took the train home.

Eldon was in a kind of anxiety. He talked to all his friends, who knew nothing about anything like that, and some of them had been as far away as San Francisco during the summer. The only person he could talk to about it was his little sister, Irene.

He did not know what the jumpiness in him was.

They rushed into Aunt Joanie's house the first time they visited at Christmas, and ran to the sitting room.

The wall was blank.

They looked at each other, then ran back into the living room.

"Aunt Joanie," said Eldon, interrupting her, Uncle Arthridge, and his father. "Aunt Joanie, where's the television?"

"Television . . . ? Oh, that thing. I sold it to a used furniture man at the end of the summer. He bought it for the cabinetry, he said, and was going to make an aquarium out of it. I suppose he sold the insides for scrap."

They grew up, talking to each other, late at nights, about what they had seen. When their family got TV, they spent their time trying to find it again.

Then high school, then college, the '60s. Eldon went to Nam, came back about the same.

Irene got a job in television, and sent him letters, while he taught bookkeeping at a junior college.

April 11, 1971

Dear Bro' —

I ran down what kind of set Aunt Joanie had.

It was a mechanical television, with a Nipkov disk scanner. It was a model made between 1927 and 1929.

Mechanical: Yes. You light a person, place, thing, very very brightly. On one side are the studio's photoelectric cells that turn light to current.

Between the subject and the cells, you drop in a disk that spins three hundred times a minute. Starting at the edge of the disk and spiraling inward, all the way around to the center, are holes. You have a slit-scan shutter. As the light leaves the subject it's broken into a series of lines by the holes passing across the slit. The photoelectric cells pick up the pulses of light. (An orthicon tube does exactly the same thing, except electronically, in a camera, and your modern TV is just a big orthicon tube on the other end.) Since it was a mechanical signal, your disk in the cabinet at home had to spin at exactly the same rate. So they had to send out a regulating signal at the same time.

Not swell, not good definition, but workable.

But Aunt Joanie (rest her soul) was right—nothing in 1953 was broadcasting that it could receive because all early prewar televisions were made with the picture-portion going out on FM, and the sound going out on shortwave. So her set had receivers for both, and neither of them are where TV is now on the wavelengths (where they've been since 1946).

Mr. Goober could not have come from an FCC licensed broadcaster in 1953. I'll check Canada and Mexico, but I'm pretty sure everything was moved off those bands by then, even experimental stations. Since we never got sound, either there was none, or maybe it was coming in with the picture (like now) and her set couldn't separate four pieces of information (one-half each of two signals, which is why we use FM for TV).

It shouldn't have happened, I don't think. There are weird stories (the ghost signals of a Midwest station people saw the test patterns of more than a year after they quit broadcasting; the famous 2.8-second delay in radio transmissions all over the world on shortwave in 1927 and early 1928).

Am going to the NAB meeting in three weeks. Will talk to everybody there, especially the old guys, and find out if any of them knows about Mr. Goober's Show. Stay sweet.

Your sis,
Irene

Eldon began the search on his own: at parties, at bars, at ball games. During the next few years, he wrote his sister with bits of fugitive matter he'd picked up. And he got quite a specialized knowledge of local TV shows, kid's show clowns, Shock Theater hosts, and eclectic local programming of the early 1950s, throughout these United States.

June 25, 1979

Dear Eldon—

Sorry it took so long to get this letter off to you, but I've been busy at work, and helping with the Fund Drive, and I also think I'm on to something. I've just run across stuff that indicates there was some kind of medical outfit that used radio in the late '40s and early '50s.

Hope you can come home for Christmas this time. Mom's getting along in years, you know. I know you had your troubles with her (I'm the one to talk) but she really misses you. As Bill Cosby says, she's an old person trying to get into Heaven now. She's trying to be good the second thirty years of her life. . . .

Will write you again as soon as I find out more about these quacks.

Your little sister,

Irene

August 14, 1979

Dear Big Brother—

Well, it's depressing here. The lead I had turned out to be a bust, and I could just about cry, since I thought this might be it, since they broadcast on both shortwave and FM (like Aunt Joanie's set received), but this probably wasn't it, either.

It was called Drown Radio Therapy (there's something poetic about the name, but not the operation). It was named for a Dr. Ruth Drown; she was an osteopath. Sometime before the War, she and a technocrat started working with a low-power broadcast device. By War's end, she was claiming she could treat disease at a distance, and set up a small broadcast station behind her suburban Los Angeles office. Patients came in, were diagnosed, and given a schedule of broadcast times when they were supposed to tune in. (The broadcasts were directly to each patient, supposedly, two or three times a day.) By the late '40s, she'd also gone into TV, which is, of course, FM (the radio stuff being shortwave). That's where I'd hoped I'd found someone broadcasting at the same time on both bands.

But probably no go. She franchised the machines out to other doctors, mostly naturopaths and cancer quacks. It's possible that one was operating near Aunt Joanie's somewhere, but probably not, and anyway, a committee of doctors investigated her stuff. What they found was that the equipment was so low-powered it could only broadcast a dozen miles (not counting random skipping, bouncing off the Heaviside layer, which it wouldn't have been able to reach). Essentially, they ruled the equipment worthless.

And, the thing that got to me, there was no picture transmission on the FM (TV) portion; just the same type of random signals that went out on shortwave, on the same schedule, every day. Even if you had a rogue cancer specialist, the FCC said the stuff couldn't broadcast a visual signal, not with the technology of the time. (The engineer at the station here looked at the specs and said 'even if they had access to video orthicon tubes, the signal wouldn't have gotten across the room, unless it was on cable, which it wasn't.')

I've gone on too long. It's not it.

Sorry to disappoint you (again), but I'm still going through back files of Variety and BNJ and everything put out by the networks in those years. And, maybe a motherlode, a friend's got a friend who knows where all the Dumont records (except Gleason's) are stored.

We'll find out yet, brother. I've heard stories of people waiting twenty, thirty, forty years to clear things like this up. There was a guy who kept insisting he'd read a serialized novel in a newspaper, about the fall of civilization, in the early 1920s. Pre-bomb, pre-almost everything. He was only a kid when he read it. Ten years ago he mentioned it to someone who had a friend who recognized it, not from a newspaper, but as a book called Darkness and the Dawn. It was in three parts, and serial rights were sold, on the first part only, to, like, three newspapers in the whole U.S. And the man, now in his sixties, had read it in one of them.

Things like that do happen, kiddo.

Write me when you can.

Love,

Irene

Sept. 12, 1982

El—

I'm ready to give up on this. It's running me crazy—not crazy, but to distraction, if I had anything else to be distracted from.

I can't see any way out of this except to join the Welcome Space Brothers Club, which I refuse to do.

That would be the easy way out: Give up, go over to the Cheesy Side of the Force. You and me saw a travelogue, a See It Now of the planets, hosted by an interstellar Walter Cronkite on a Nipkov disk TV in 1953. We're the only people in the world who did. No one else.

But that's why CE3K and the others have made so many millions of dollars. People want to believe, but they want to believe for other people, not themselves. They don't want to be the ones. They want someone else to be the one. And then they want everybody to believe. But it's not their ass out there, saying: The Space Brothers are here; I can't prove it, take my word for it, it's real. Believe me as a person.

I'm not that person, and neither are you; OR there has to be some other answer. One, or the other, but not both; and not neither.

I don't know what to do anymore; whatever it is, it's not this. It's quit being fun. It's quit being something I do aside from life as we know it. It is my life, and yours, and it's all I've got.

I know what Mr. Goober was trying to tell us, and there was more, but the sound was off.

I'm tired. I'll write you next week when I can call my life my own again.

Your Sis

Cops called from Irene's town the next week.

After the funeral, and the stay at his mother's, and the inevitable fights, with his stepfather trying to stay out of it, he came home and found one more letter, postmarked the same day as the police had called him.

Dear Eldon—

Remember this, and don't think less of me: What we saw was real.

Evidently, too real for me.

Find out what we saw.

Love always,

Irene

So you'll be sitting in the bar, there'll be the low hum and thump of noise as the band sets up, and over in the corner, two people will be talking. You'll hear the word "Lucy," which could be many things—a girlfriend, a

TV show, a late President's daughter, a two-million-year-old ape-child. Then you'll hear "M-Squad" or "Untouchables" and there'll be more talk, and you'll hear distinctly, during a noise-level drop, "... and I don't mean Johnny-fucking-Jupiter either ..."

And in a few minutes he'll leave, because the band will have started, and conversation, except at the 100-decibel level, is over for the night.

But he'll be back tomorrow night. And the night after.

And all the star-filled nights that follow that one.

Introduction to

Major Spacer in the Twenty-First Century

The history of television was full of starts, stops, fights, backstabs, and the FCC coming down like a ton of bricks on people, even more than radio had been.

It was ready to go in the late '30s (it broadcast the opening of the 1939 World's Fair; NHK in Japan was going to broadcast the 1940 Olympics in Tokyo to department stores and theaters so the Japanese would leave the stadium to the gai-jin; there was a small worldwide unpleasantness that canceled them both; the BBC TV service was up and running in 1936 and shut down for the duration September 3, 1939, while showing a Mickey Mouse cartoon . . .). Experimental American television went off the air on December 8, 1941, and only started up again in 1946.

There were punchouts over airwaves, over channels and content; the big fight was over formats. There was the fight over color: When it started, the FCC was going to make everybody junk their TVs again (after just junking the prewar shortwave/FM sets mentioned last story) — easy to do when there were 10,000 sets, like in 1946; not so easy when there were ten million of them in 1950. In the middle of The Freeze from 1948-1952, when the FCC issued no new TV licenses, it was going to make everybody go back to an incompatible mechanical color TV system (I'm not making this up). Cooler heads (and those with NBC stock) prevailed, and held out for color-compatible broadcasting, and so on and so forth. Sound — HDTV — familiar?

Meanwhile, those who'd gotten a pre-1948 license pioneered on, showing old Brit and independent American movies — all the major studios held out from leasing movies to TV and made fun of it, and then tried everything — 3-D, wide-screen, stereo, Aromarama and Smell-0-Vision, and blipverts — to get the audience back.

Sure, some of it was very bad ("radio with pictures"), comparable to the first couple of years of sound in the movies. But here and there, good stuff got done. There's Kovacs over there. Some of the best writing ever done in this country was for the early Box.

Take a look at the TV work of Serling, Chayevsky, Vidal, Howard Rodman; all that Golden Age of Television stuff you always hear about — some of it was really good. The local stuff: There's Zacherly in Philadelphia (and Bill Camfield in Ft. Worth — see "Occam's Ducks") — hundreds of people out there, figuring it out, what works, what doesn't, what you could do live; wouldn't it be wonderful if you could only record it some way? (Kinescopes — films of the TV monitors — always looked like they were made by your Uncle Norris fifteen minutes after getting his first Bell & Howell. . . .)

It was a new world; they soon found it wasn't Radio with Pictures at all, or like anything else. It was Television. And they were it.

This story shows what happens when you get a way swell idea, way late. It came to me in April of 1999, when everybody was waiting for Y2K (remember?). I wanted a story about the year 2000, but not about Y2K. Just set there.

I wrote it for a reading I was doing at the University Bookstore (University of Washington), with lots of hand props and primitive visual aids.

There was about one editor who could get it into print pronto, i.e., before 2000 A.D. I sent it to him. He wanted a few changes. I was so torqued (and I mean that in the original, good way) on the story that instead of doing a lot of changes to a novelette, I wrote him a whole other new short story ("London, Paris, Banana . . .") for the rent that month. I sent this to another editor; there were revisions (short pause here while (1) the World SF Convention in Australia interferes, and (2) the USPS takes fifteen days to deliver a two-day Priority Mail manuscript); I sent it to a third editor whose venue dropped dead two days before the manuscript got there. We are now in December 1999. Since it was written for the April 1999 rent, and we are now almost in 2000, I said "Screw this, I don't need the aggravation."

What I merely wanted to do was show a major societal change, and how media-dependent we had become, and media-conscious we were since the early days of television broadcasting.

And I wanted to show it mostly through the life of one person; there at the beginning, maybe there at the end, too.

MAJOR SPACER IN THE TWENTY-FIRST CENTURY

June 1950

"Look," said Bill, "I'll see if I can go down and do a deposition this Thursday or Friday. Get ahold of Zachary Glass, see if he can fill in as . . . what's his name . . . ?"

"Lt. Marrs," said Sam Shorts.

". . . Lt. Marrs. We'll move that part of the story up. I'll record my lines. We can put it up over the spacephone, and Marrs and Neptuna can have the dialogue during the pursuit near the Moon we were gonna do week after next . . ."

"Yeah, sure!" said Sam. "We can have you over the phone, and them talking back and forth while his ship's closing in on hers, and your voice — yeah, that'll work fine."

"But you'll have to rewrite the science part I was gonna do, and give it yourself, as Cadet Sam. Man, it's just too bad there's no way to record this stuff ahead of time."

"Phil said they're working on it at the Bing Crosby Labs, trying to get some kind of tape to take a visual image; they can do it but they gotta shoot eight feet of tape a second by the recording head. It takes a mile of tape to do a ten-minute show," said Sam.

"And we can't do it on film, kids hate that."

"Funny," said Sam Shorts. "They pay fifteen cents for Gene Autry on film every Saturday afternoon, but they won't sit still for it on television . . ."

Philip walked in. "Morgan wants to see you about the Congress thing."

"Of course," said Bill.

"Run-through in . . ." Phil looked at his watch, and the studio clock ". . . eleven minutes. Seen Elizabeth?"

"Of course not," said Bill, on the way down the hall in his spacesuit, with his helmet under his arm.

That night, in his apartment, Bill typed on a script.

MAJOR SPACER: LOOKS LIKE SOMEONE LEFT IN A HURRY.

Bill looked up. Super Circus was on. Two of the clowns, Nicky and Scampy, squirted seltzer in ringmaster Claude Kirchner's face.

He never got to watch Big Top, the other circus show. It was on opposite his show.

Next morning, a young guy with glasses slouched out of a drugstore.

"Well, hey Bill!" he said.

"Jimmy!" said Bill, stopping, shifting his cheap cardboard portfolio to his other arm. He shook hands.

"Hey, I talked to Zooey," said Jimmy. "You in trouble with the Feds?"

"Not that I know of. I think they're bringing in everybody in the city with a kid's TV show."

He and Jimmy had been in a flop play together early in the year, before Bill started the show.

"How's it going otherwise?" asked Jimmy.

"It's about to kill all of us. We'll see if we make twenty weeks, much less a year. We're only four to five days ahead on the script. You available?"

"I'll have to look," said Jimmy. "I got two Lamps Unto My Feet next month, three-day rehearsals each, I think. I'm reading a couple plays, but that'll take a month before anybody gets off their butt. Let me know'f you need someone quick some afternoon. If I can, I'll jump in."

"Sure thing. And on top of everything else, looks like we'll have to move for next week; network's coming in and taking our space; trade-out with CBS. I'll be real damn glad when this Station Freeze is over, and there's more than ten damn places in this city that can do a network feed."

"I hear that could take a couple more years," said Jimmy, in his quiet Indiana voice.

"Yeah, well . . . hey, don't be such a stranger. Come on with me, I gotta get these over to the mimeograph room; we can talk on the way."

"Nah, nah," said Jimmy. "I, you know, gotta meet some people. I'm late already. See ya 'round, Bill."

"Well, okay."

Jimmy turned around thirty feet away. "Don't let the Feds get your jock strap in a knot!" he said, waved, and walked away.

People stared at both of them.

Damn, thought Bill. I don't get to see anyone anymore; I don't have a life except for the show. This is killing me. I'm still young.

"And what the hell are we supposed to do in this grange hall?" asked Bill.

"It's only a week," said Morgan. "Sure, it's seen better days, the Ziegfeld Roof, but they got a camera ramp so Harry and Fred can actually move in and out on a shot; you can play up and back, not just sideways like a crab, like usual."

Bill looked at the long wooden platform built out into what used to be the center aisle when it was a theater.

"Phil says he can shoot here . . ."

"Phil can do a show in a bathtub, he's so good, and Harry and Fred can work in a teacup, they're so good. That doesn't mean they have to," said Bill.

A stagehand walked in and raised the curtain while they stood there.

"Who's that?" asked Bill.

"Well, this is a rehearsal hall," said Morgan. "We're lucky to get it on such short notice."

When the curtain was full up there were the usual chalk marks on the stage boards, and scene flats lined up and stacked in twenty cradles at the rear of the stage.

"We'll be using that corner there," said Morgan, pointing. "Bring our sets in, wheel 'em, roll 'em in and out—ship, command center, planet surface."

Some of the flats for the other show looked familiar.

"The other group rehearses 10:00–2:00. They all gotta be out by 2:15. We rehearse, do the run-through at 5:30, do the show at 6:30."

Another stagehand came in with the outline of the tail end of a gigantic cow and put it into the scene cradle.

"What the hell are they rehearsing?" asked Bill.

"Oh. It's a musical based on the paintings of Grant Wood, you know, the Iowa artist?"

"You mean the Washington and the Cherry Tree, the DAR guy?"

"Yeah, him."

"That'll be a hit," said Bill. "What's it called?"

"I think they're calling it In Tall Corn. Well, what do you think?"

"I think it's a terrible idea. I can see the closing notices now."

"No, no. I mean the place. For the show," said Morgan.

Bill looked around. "Do I have any choice in the matter?"

"Of course not," said Morgan. "Everything else in town that's wired up is taken. I just wanted you to see it before you were dumped in it."

"Dumped is right," said Bill. He was looking at the camera ramp. It was the only saving grace. Maybe something could be done with it. . . .

"Harry and Fred seen it?"

"No, Phil's word is good enough for them. And, like you said, they can shoot in a coffee cup . . ."

Bill sighed. "Okay. Let's call a Sunday rehearsal day, this Sunday, do two blockings and rehearsals, do the run-through of Monday's show, let everybody get used to the place. Then they can come back just for the show Monday. Me and Sam'll see if we can do something in the scripts. Phil got the specs?"

"You know he has," said Morgan.

"Well, I guess one barn's as good as another," said Bill.

And as he said it, three stagehands brought on a barn and a silo and a windmill.

Even with both window fans on, it was hot as hell in the apartment. Bill slammed the carriage over on the Remington Noiseless Portable and hit the margin set and typed:

MAJOR SPACER: CAREFUL. SOMETIMES THE SURFACE OF MARS CAN LOOK AS ORDINARY AS A DESERT IN ARIZONA.

He got up and went to the kitchen table, picked up the bottle of Old Harper, poured some in a coffee cup and knocked it back.

There. That was better.

On TV, Haystacks Calhoun and Duke Kehanamuka were both working over Gorgeous George, while Gorilla Monsoon argued with the referee, whose back was to the action. Every time one of them twisted George's arm or leg, the announcer, Dennis James, snapped a chicken bone next to the mike.

"Look at this," said Morgan, the next morning.

It was a handwritten note.

I know your show is full of commies. My brother-in-law told me you have commie actors. Thank God for people like Senator McCarthy who will run you rats out of this land of Liberty and Freedom.

Signed,

A Real American

"Put it in the circular file," said Bill.

"I'll keep it," said Morgan. "Who are they talking about?"

"You tell me. I'm not old enough to be a communist."

"Could it be true?" asked Morgan.

"Don't tell me you're listening to all that crap, too?"

"There's been a couple of newsletters coming around, with names of people on it. I know some of them; they give money to the NAACP and ACLU. Otherwise they live in big houses and drive big cars and order their servants around like Daddy Warbucks. But then, I don't know all the names on the lists."

"Is anybody we ever hired on any of the lists?"

"Not as such," said Morgan.

"Well, then?"

"Well, then," said Morgan, and picked up a production schedule. "Well, then, nothing, I guess, Bill."

"Good," said Bill. He picked up the letter from Morgan's desk, wadded it into a ball, and drop-kicked it into the wastebasket.

The hungover Montgomery Clift reeled by on his way to the Friday performance of the disaster of a play he was in. Bill waved, but Clift didn't notice; his eyes were fixed on some far distant promontory fifty miles up the Hudson, if they were working at all. Clift had been one intense, conflicted, messed-up individual when Bill had first met him. Then he had gone off to Hollywood and discovered sex and booze and drugs and brought them with him back to Broadway.

Ahead of Bill was the hotel where the congressmen and lawyers waited.

Counsel (Mr. Eclept): Now that you have taken the oath, give your full name and age for the record.

S: Major William Spacer. I'm twenty-one years old.

E: No, sir. Not your stage name.

S: Major William Spacer. That's my real name.

Congressman Beenz: You mean Major Spacer isn't just the show name?

S: Well, sir, it is and it isn't . . . Most people just think we gave me a promotion over Captain Video.

Congressman Rice: How was it you were named Major?

S: You would have had to have asked my parents that; unfortunately they're deceased. I have an aunt in Kansas who might be able to shed some light . . .

S: That's not the way it's done, Congressman.

B: You mean you just can't fly out to the Big Dipper, once you're in space?

S: Well, you can, but they're . . . they're light years apart. They . . . they appear to us as The Big Dipper because we're looking at them from Earth.

R: I'm not sure I understand, either.

S: It . . . it's like that place in . . . Vermont, New Hampshire, one of those. North of here, anyway. You come around that turn in Rt 9A or whatever, and there's Abraham Lincoln, the head, the hair, the beard. It's so real you stop. Then you drive down the road a couple hundred yards, and the beard's a plum thicket on a meadow, and the hair's pine trees on a hill, and the nose is on one mountain, but the rest of the face is on another. It only looks like Lincoln from that one spot in the road. That's why the Big Dipper looks that way from Earth.

B: I do not know how we got off on this . . .

S: I'm trying to answer your questions here, sir.

E: Perhaps we should get to the substantive matters here . . .

S: All I've noticed, counsel, is that all the people who turn up as witnesses and accusers at these things seem to have names out of old W. C. Fields' movies, names like R. Waldo Chubb and F. Clement Bozo.

E: I believe you're referring to Mr. Clubb and Mr. Bozell?

S: I'm busy, Mr. Eclept; I only get to glance at newspapers. I'm concerned with the future, not what's happening right this minute.

B: So are we, young man. That's why we're trying to root out any communist influence in the broadcast industry, so there won't be any in the future.

R: We can't stress that too forcefully.

S: Well, I can't think of a single communist space pirate we've ever portrayed on the show. It takes place in the 21st Century, Congressman. So I guess we share the same future. Besides, last time I looked, piracy was a capitalist invention. . . .

S: That's why we never have stories set further than Mars or Venus, Congressman. Most of the show takes place in near-space, or on the Moon. We try to keep the science accurate. That's why there's always a segment with me or Sam — that's Samuel J. Shorts, the other writer on the show — by the way, he's called "Uncle Sam" Spacer — telling kids about the future, and what it'll be like to grow up in the wonderful years of the 21st Century.

B: If we don't blow ourselves up first.

R: You mean if some foreign power doesn't try to blow us up first.

S: Well, we've talked about the peaceful uses of atomic energy. Food preservation. Atomic-powered airplanes and cars. Nuclear fusion as a source of energy too cheap to meter.

E: Is it true you broadcast a show about a world government?

S: Not in the science segment, that I recall.

E: No. I mean the story, the entertainment part.

S: We've been on the air three months, that's nearly sixty shows. Let me think . . .

E: A source has told us there's a world government on the show.

S: Oh. It's a worlds' government, counsel. It's the United States of Space. We assume there won't be just one state on Mars, or the Moon, or Venus, and that they'll have to come to the central government to settle their disputes. We have that on the Moon.

R: They have to go to the Moon to settle a dispute between Mars and the United States?

S: No, no. That would be like France suing Wisconsin. . . .

B: ". . . and other red channels." And that's a direct quote.

S: Congressman, I created the show; I act in it; I write either half the scripts, or one-half of each script, whichever way it works out that week. I do this five days a week, supposedly for fifty weeks a year — we'll see if I make it that long. I've given the day-to-day operations, all the merchandising negotiations to my partner, James B. Morgan. We have a small cast with only a few recurring characters, and except for the occasional Martian bad guy, or Lunar owl-hoot, they're all known to me. I never ask anybody about their politics or religion. All I want to know is whether they can memorize lines quick, and act in a tight set, under time pressure, live, with a camera stuck in their ear. The only thing red we have anything to do with is Mars. And it isn't channels; it's canals. . . .

S: . . . I have no knowledge of any. I'll tell you what, right now, Congressman, I'll bet my show on it. You come up with any on the cast and crew, I'll withdraw the show.

B: We'll hold you to that, young man.

R: I want to thank you for appearing for this deposition today, and for being so forthcoming with us, Mr. Spacer.

B: I agree.

R: You are excused.

There was one reporter waiting outside in the hallway, besides the government goon keeping everyone out.

The reporter was the old kind, press card stuck in his hat, right out of The Front Page.

"Got any statement, Mr. Spacer?"

"Well, as you know, I can't talk about what I said till the investigation's concluded. They asked me questions. I answered them as best as I could."

"What sort of questions?"

"I'm sure you can figure that out. You've seen the televised hearings?"

"What were they trying to find out?" asked the reporter.

"I'm not sure . . ." said Bill.

The government goon smiled. When he and the reporter parted ways in the lobby, Bill was surprised that it was already summer twilight. He must have been in there five or six hours. . . . He took off for the studio, to find out what kind of disaster the broadcast with Zach Glass had been.

Bill wiggled his toes in his socks, including the stump of the little one on the right foot, a souvenir from a Boy Scout hatchet-throwing contest gone wrong back when he was twelve.

He was typing while he watched Blues By Bargy on TV. Saturday night noise came from outside.

Then the transmission was interrupted with a PLEASE STAND BY notice. Douglas Edwards came on with a special bulletin, which he ripped out of the chundering teletype machine at his right elbow.

He said there were as yet unconfirmed reports that North Korean Armed Forces had crossed into South Korea. President Truman, who was on a weekend trip to his home in Independence, Missouri, had not been reached by CBS for a comment. Then he said they would be interrupting regularly scheduled programming if there were further developments.

Then they went back to Blues by Bargy.

"Look," said Phil. "James, you gotta get those rehearsing assholes outta here, I mean, out of here, earlier. When I came in Saturday to set up, I found they used all the drop-pipes for their show. I had to make them move a quarter of their stuff. They said they needed them all. I told 'em to put wheels on their stuff like we're having to do with most of ours, but we still need some pipes to drop in the exteriors, and to mask the sets off. And they're hanging around with their girlfriends and boyfriends, while I'm trying to set up marks."

It was Sunday, the start of their week at the Ziegfeld Roof. They were to block out Monday's and Tuesday's shows, rehearse them, and do the run-through and technical for Monday's broadcast.

"I'll talk to their stage manager," said Morgan. "Believe me, moving here gripes me as much as it does you. Where's Elizabeth?"

"Here," said Elizabeth Regine, coming out of the dressing room in her rehearsal Neptuna outfit. "I couldn't believe this place when I got here."

"Believe it, baby," said Phil. "We've got to make do." He looked at his watch. "Bill, I think the script may be a little long, just looking at it."

"Same as always. Twenty-four pages."

"Yeah, but you got suspense stuff in there. That's thirty seconds each. Be thinking about it while we're blocking it."

"You're the director, Phil."

"That's what you and James pay me for." He looked over at the stage crew. "No!" he said. " Right one, left one, right one," he moved his hands.

"That's what they are," said the foreman.

"No, you got left, right, left."

The guy, Harvey, joined him to look at the wheeled sets. "Left," he pointed to the rocket interior. "Right," the command room on the Moon. "Left," the foreground scenery and the rocket fin for the Mars scenes.

"And from whence does the rest of the Mars set drop in?" asked Phil.

"Right. Oh, merde!" said Harve.

"And they're the best crew on television," said Phil, as the stagehands ratcheted the scenery around. "They really are," he said, turning back to Bill and Morgan. "That way we stay on the rocket interior, and you leave, run behind the middle set, and step down onto Mars, while the spacephone chatters away. Also, you'll be out of breath, so it'll sound like you just climbed down fifty feet of ladder. . . ."

It was seven when they finished the blocking, two rehearsals, and the run-through of the first show of the week. Phil was right, the script was one minute and fifty-three seconds long.

Bill looked at the camera ramp. "I still want to do something with that," he said, "while we've got it."

"Wednesday," said Phil.

"Why Wednesday?"

"You got a blast-off scene. We do it from the front. We get the scenery guy to build a nose view of the ship. Red Mars background behind. Like the ship from above. You and Neptuna stand behind it, looking out the cockpit. You count down. Harvey hits the CO_2 extinguisher behind you for rocket smoke. I get Harry or Fred to run at you with the camera as fast as he can, from way back there. Just before he collides, we cut to the telecine chain for the commercial."

"Marry me," said Bill.

"Some other time," said Phil. "Everybody back at 4:00 P.M. tomorrow. Everything's set. Don't touch a goddamn thing before you leave."

Toast of the Town, hosted by Ed Sullivan, was on TV.

Señor Wences was having a three-way conversation with Johnny (which was his left hand rested on top of a doll body); Pedro, the head in the cigar box; and a stagehand who was down behind a crate, supposedly fixing a loose board with a hammer.

Halfway through the act, two stagehands came out, picked up the crate, showing it was empty, and walked off, leaving a bare stage.

"Look. Look!" said Johnny, turning his fist-head on the body that way. "There was not a man there."

"There was no man there?" asked Wences.

"No," said Johnny. "There was not a man there."

"What do you t'ink, Pedro?" asked Wences, opening the box with his right hand.

"S'awright," said Pedro. The box snapped shut.

"Come in here," said Morgan from the door of his makeshift office, as Bill came into the theater.

Sam was in a chair, crying.

Morgan's face was set, as Bill had never seen before. "Tell him what you just told me."

"I can't," Sam wailed. "What am I gonna do? I'm forty years old!"

"Maybe you should have thought of that back in 1931."

"What the hell is going on? Sam! Sam? Talk to me."

"Oh, Bill," he said. "I'm sorry."

"Somebody. One of you. Start making sense. Right now," said Bill.

"Mr. Sam Shorts, here, seems to have been a commie bagman during the Depression."

"Say it ain't so, Sam," said Bill.

Sam looked at him. Tears started down his face again.

"There's your answer," said Morgan, running his hands through his hair and looking for something to throw.

"I was young," said Sam. "I was so hungry. I swore I'd never be that hungry again. I was too proud for the bread line, a guy offered me a job, if you can call it that, moving some office stuff. Then as a sort of messenger. Between his office and other places. Delivering stuff. I thought it was some sort of bookie joint or numbers running, or money laundering, or the bootleg. Something illegal, sure . . . but . . . but . . . I didn't . . . didn't . . ."

"What? What!"

"I didn't think it was anything un-American!" said Sam, crying again.

"Morgan. Tell me what he told you."

"He was a bagman, a messenger between United Front stuff the Feds know about and some they probably don't. He did it for about three years."

"Four," said Sam, trying to control himself.

"Great," continued Morgan. "Four years, on and off. Then somebody pissed him off and he walked away."

"Just because they were reds," said Sam, "didn't make 'em good bosses."

Bill hated himself for asking; he thought of Parnell Thomas and McCarthy.

"Did you sign anything?"

"I may have. I signed a lot of stuff to get paid."

"Under your real name?"

"I guess so. Some, anyway."

"Guess what name they had him use sometime?" asked Morgan.

"I don't want to," said Bill.

"George Crosley."

"That was one of the names Whittaker Chambers used!" said Bill.

"They weren't the most inventive guys in the world," said Morgan.

"I knew. I knew the jig would be up when I watched the Hiss thing," said Sam. "When I heard that name. Then nothing happened. I guess I thought nothing would . . ."

"How could you do this to me?!!" yelled Bill.

"You? You were a one-year-old! I didn't know you! It wasn't personal, Bill. You either, Morgan."

"You know I put my show on the line in the deposition, don't you?"

"Not till Morgan told me." Sam began to cry again.

"What brought on this sudden cleansing, now, twenty years later?" asked Bill.

"There was another letter," said Morgan. "This time naming a name, not the right one, but it won't take anybody long to figure that one out. Also that they were calling the Feds. I was looking at it, and looking glum, when Sam comes in. He asks what's up; I asked him if he knew anybody by the name of the guy in the letter, and he went off like the Hindenburg. A wet Hindenburg."

Sam was crying again.

Bill's shoulders slumped.

"Okay, Morgan. Call everybody together. I'll talk to them. Sam, quit it. Quit it. You're still a great writer. Buck up. We'll get through this. Nothing's happened yet. . . ."

Live. The pressure's on, like always. Everybody's a pro here, even with this world falling apart. Harry and Fred on the cameras, Phil up in the booth, Morgan with him, Sam out there where the audience would be, going through the scripts for Thursday and Friday like nothing's happened.

He and Elizabeth, as Neptuna, are in the rocket interior set, putting on their spacesuits, giving their lines. Bill's suit wasn't going on right; he made a small motion with his hand; Fred moved his camera in tight on Bill's face; Philip would switch to it, or Harry's shot on Neptuna's face; the floor manager reached up while Bill was talking and pulled at the lining of the spacesuit, and it went on smoothly; the floor manager crawled out and Fred pulled his camera back again to a two-shot. Then he and Neptuna moved into the airlock; it cycled closed. Harry swung his camera around to the grille of the spacephone speaker; an urgent message came from it, warning Major Spacer that a big Martian dust storm was building up in their area.

While the voice was coming over the speaker in the tight shot, Bill and Elizabeth walked behind the Moon command center flats and hid behind the rocket fin while the stage crew dropped in the Martian exterior set and the boom man wheeled the microphone around and Fred dollied his camera in.

"Is Sam okay?" Elizabeth had asked, touching her helmet to Bill's before the soundman got there.

"I hope so," said Bill.

He looked out. The floor manager, who should have been counting down on his fingers five-four-three-two-one was standing stock still. Fred's camera wobbled — and he was usually the steadiest man in the business.

The floor manager pulled off his earphones, shrugged his shoulders, and swung his head helplessly toward the booth.

It's got to be time, thought Bill; touched Elizabeth on the arm, and gave his line, backing down off a box behind the fin out onto the set.

"Careful," he said. "Sometimes the surface of Mars can look as ordinary as a desert in Arizona."

Elizabeth, who was usually unflappable, stared, eyes wide past him at the exterior set. And dropped her Neptuna character, and instead of her line, said: "And sometimes it looks just like Iowa."

Bill turned.

Instead of a desert, and a couple of twisted Martian cacti and a backdrop of Monument Valley, there was the butt-end of a big cow and a barn and silo, some chickens, and a three-rail fence.

Bill sat in the dressing room, drinking Old Harper from the bottle.

Patti Page was on the radio, singing of better days.

There was a knock on the door.

It was the government goon. He was smiling. There was one subpoena for Bill, and one for Sam Shorts.

June 2000

Bill came out the front door of the apartments on his way to his job as a linotype operator at the New York Times.

There were, as usual, four or five kids on the stoop, and as usual, too, Rudy, a youngster of fifty years, was in the middle of his rant, holding up two twenty-dollar bills.

"...that there was to trace the dope, man. They changed the money so they could find out where all them coke dollars were. That plastic thread shit in this one, that was the laser radar stuff. They could roll a special truck down your street, and tell what was a crack house by all the eyeball noise that lit up their screens. And the garage-sale people and the flea-market people. They could find that stuff— Hey, Bill—"

"Hey, Rudy."

" — before it All Quit they was goin' to be able to count the ones in your billfold from six blocks away, man."

"Why was that, Rudy?" asked a girl-kid.

"'Cause they wasn't enough money! They printed the stuff legit but it just kept going away. It was in the quote 'underground economy.' They said it was so people couldn't counterfeit it on a Savin 2300 or somebullshit, or the camel-jocks couldn't flood the PXs with fake stuff, but it was so they didn't have to wear out a lotta shoe leather and do lotsa Hill Street Blues wino-cop type stuff just to get to swear out a lot of warrants. See, that machine in that truck make noise, they take a printout of that to a judge, and pretty soon door hinges was flyin' all over town. Seen 'em take two blocks out at one time, man. Those was evil times, be glad they gone."

"So are we, Rudy; we're glad they can't do that even though we never heard of it."

"You just wait your young ass," said Rudy. "Some devious yahoo in Baltimore workin' on that right now; they had that knowledge once, it don't just go away, it just mutates, you know. They'll find a way to do that with vacuum tubes and such . . ."

Rudy's voice faded as Bill walked on down toward the corner. Rudy gave some version of that talk, somewhere in the neighborhood, every day. Taking the place of Rudy was the voice from the low-power radio station speakerbox on the corner.

". . . that the person was dressed in green pants, a yellow Joe Camel tyvek jacket, and a black T-shirt. The wallet grab occurred four minutes ago at the corner of Lincoln and Jackson, neighbors are asked to be on the lookout for this person, and to use the nearest call-box to report a sighting. Now back to music, from a V-disk transcription, Glenn Miller and His Orchestra with "In the Mood.""

Music filled the air. Coming down the street was a 1961 armored car, the Wells-Fargo logo spray-painted over, and a cardboard sign saying TAXI over the high windshield. On the front bumper was a sticker that said SCREW THE CITY TAXI COMMISSION.

Bill held up his hand. The car rumbled over to the curb.

"Where to, kindly old geezer?"

Bill said the Times Building, which was about thirty blocks away.

"What's it worth to you, Pops?"

"How about a buck?" said Bill.

"Real money?"

"Sure."

"Hop in, then. Gotta take somebody up here a couple blocks, and there'll be one stop on the way, so far."

Bill went around back, opened the door and got in, nodding to the other two passengers. He was at work in fifteen minutes.

It was a nice afternoon, so when Bill got off work he took the omnibus to the edge of the commercial district, got off there and started walking home. Since it was summer, there seemed to be a street fair every other block. He could tell when he passed from one neighborhood to another by the difference in the announcer voices on the low-power stations.

He passed Ned Ludd's Store #23, and the line, as usual, was backed out the door onto the sidewalk, and around the corner of the building. In the display window were stereo phonographs and records, transistor radios, batteries, toaster ovens, and none-cable-ready TVs, including an old Philco with the picture tube supported above the console like a dresser mirror.

Some kids were in line, talking, melancholy looks on their faces, about something. "It was called Cargo Cult," said one. "You were on an island, with a native culture, and then WWII came, and the people tried to get cargo, you know, trade goods, and other people were trying to get them to keep their native ways . . ."

"Plus," said the second kid, "you got to blow up a lotta Japanese soldiers and eat them!"

"Sounds neat," said the third, "but I never heard of it."

A guy came out of the tavern next door, a little unsteady, and stopped momentarily, like Bill, like everyone else who passed, to watch the pixievision soap opera playing in black and white.

The guy swayed a little, listening to the kids' conversation; then a determined smile came across his face.

"Hey, kids," he said.

They stopped talking and looked at him. One said "Yeah?"

The man leaned forward. "Triple picture-in-picture," he said.

Their faces fell.

He threw back his head and laughed, then put his hands in his pockets and weaved away.

On TV, there was a blank screen while they changed the pixievision tapes by hand, something they did every eight-and-a-half minutes.

Bill headed on home.

He neared his block, tired from the walk and his five-hour shift at the paper. He almost forgot Tuesday was mail day until he was in sight of the apartments, then walked back to the Postal Joint. For him there was a union meeting notice, in case he hadn't read the bulletin board at work, and that guy from Ohio was bothering him again with letters asking him questions for the biography of James Dean he'd been researching since 1989, most of which Bill had answered in 1989.

He was halfway back to the apartments, just past the low-power speaker, when six men dragged a guy, in ripped green pants and what was left of a Joe Camel jacket, out onto the corner, pushed the police button, and stood on the guy's hands and feet, their arms crossed, talking about a neighborhood fast-pitch softball game coming up that night.

Bill looked back as he crossed the street. A squad car pulled up and the guys all greeted the policemen.

"Today was mail day, right kids?" said Rudy. "Well in the old days the Feds set up Postal Joint-type places, you know, The Stamp Act, Box Me In, stuff like that, to scam the scammers that was scammin' you. That shoulda been fine, but they was readin' like everybody's mail, like Aunt Gracie's to you, and yours to her, and you know, your girlfriend's and boyfriend's to you, and lookin' at the Polaroids and stuff, which you sometimes wouldn't get, you dig? See, when they's evil to be fought, you can't be doin' evil to get at it. Don't be lettin' nobody get your mail—there's a man to see you in the lobby, Bill—"

"Thanks, Rudy."

"—and don't be readin' none that ain't yours. It's a fool that gets scammed; you honest, you don't be fallin' for none o' that stuff like free boats and cars and beautiful diamond-studded watches, you know?"

"Sure, Rudy," said the kids.

The guy looked at something in his hand, then back at Bill, squinted and said: "Are you Major Spacer?"

"Nobody but a guy in Ohio's called me that for fifty years," said Bill.

"Arnold Fossman," said the guy, holding out his hand. Bill shook it.

"Who you researching? Monty Clift?"

"Huh? No," said Fossman. He seemed perplexed, then brightened. "I want to offer you a job, doesn't pay much."

"Son, I got a good-payin' job that'll last me way to the end of my time. Came out of what I laughingly call retirement to do it."

"Yeah, somebody told me about you being at the Times, with all the old people with the old skills they called back. I don't think this'll interfere with that."

"I'm old and I'm tired and I been setting a galley and a quarter an hour for five hours. Get to it."

"I want to offer you an acting job."

"I haven't acted in fifty years, either."

"They tell me it's just like riding a bicycle. You . . . you might think—wait. Hold on. Indulge me just a second." He reached up and took Bill's rimless Trotsky glasses from his face.

"Whup!" said Bill.

Fossman took off his own thick black-rimmed glasses and put them over Bill's ears. The world was skewed up and to the left and down to the right and Fossman was a tiny figure in the distance.

"I ain't doin' anything with these glasses on!" said Bill. "I'm afraid to move."

The dim fuzzy world came back, then the sharp normal one as Fossman put Bill's glasses back on him.

"I was getting a look at you with thick frames. You'll be great."

"I'm a nice guy," said Bill. "You don't get to the point, I'll do my feeble best to pound you into this floor here like a tent peg."

"Okay." Fossman held up his hand. "But hear me out completely. Don't say a word till I'm through. Here goes.

"I want to offer you a job in a play, a musical. Everybody says I'm crazy to do it; I've had the idea for years, and now's the time to do it, with everything like it is. I've got the place to do it in, and you know there's an audience for anything that moves. Then I found out a couple of weeks ago my idea ain't so original, that somebody tried to do it a long time ago; it closed out of town in Bristol, CT, big flop. But your name came up in connection with it; I thought maybe you had done the show originally, and then they told me why your name always came up in connection with it— the more I heard, and found out you were still around, the more I knew you had to be in it, as some sort of, well, call it what you want—homage, reparation, I don't know. I'm the producer-guy, not very good with words. Anyway. I'm doing a musical based on the paintings of Grant Wood. I want you to be in it. Will you?"

"Sure," said Bill.

It was a theater not far from work, a 500-seater.

"Thank God it's not the Ziegfeld Roof," said Bill. He and Fossman were sitting, legs draped into the orchestra pit, at the stage apron.

"Yeah, well, that's been gone a long time."

"They put it under the wrecking ball while I was a drunk, or so they told me," said Bill.

"And might I ask how long that was?" asked Fossman.

"Eight years, three months, and two days," said Bill. "God, I sound like a reformed alcoholic. Geez, they're boring."

"Most people don't have what it really takes to be an alcoholic," said Fossman. "I was the son of one, a great one, and I know how hard you've got to work at it."

"I had what it takes," said Bill. "I just got tired of it."

He heard on the neighborhood radio there had been a battery riot in the Battery.

Bill stretched himself, and did some slow exercises. Fifty years of moving any old which way didn't cure itself in a few days.

He went over to the mirror and looked at himself.

The good-looking fair-haired youth had been taken over by a balding old man.

"Hello," said Marion.

"Hello yourself," said Bill, as he passed her on his way to work. She was getting ready to leave for her job at the library, where every day she took down books, went through the information on the copyright page, and typed it up on two 4x6 cards, one of which was put in a big series of drawers in the entryway, where patrons could find what books were there without looking on all the shelves, and one of which was sent to the central library system.

She lived in one of the apartments downstairs from Bill. She once said the job would probably take herself, and three others, more than a year, just at her branch. She was a youngster in her forties.

Bill found rehearsals the same mixture of joy and boredom they had been a half-century before, with the same smells of paint and turpentine coming from the scene shop. The cast had convinced Arnold to direct the play, rather than hiring some schmuck, as he'd originally wanted to do. He'd conceived it; it was his vision.

During a break one night, Bill lay on the floor; Arnold slumped in a chair, and Shirlene, the lead dancer, lay face down on the sofa with a migraine. Bill chuckled, he thought, to himself.

"What's up?" asked Fossman.

"It was probably just like this in rehearsals when Plautus was sitting where you are."

"Guess so."

"Were there headaches then?" asked Shirlene.

"Well, there were in my day, and that wasn't too long after the Romans," said Bill. "One of our cameramen had them." He looked around. "Thanks, Arnold."

"For what?"

"For showing me how much I didn't remember I missed this stuff."

"Well, sure," said Fossman. "OK, folks, let's get back to the grind. Shirlene, lie there till you feel better."

She got to her feet. "I'll never feel better," she said.

"See—" said Rudy—"it was on January third, and everybody was congratulatin' themselves on beatin' that ol' Y2K monster, and was throwin' out them ham and lima bean MREs into the dumpsters. Joyful, you know— another Kohoutek, that was a comet that didn't amount to a bird fart back in them way old '70s. Anyway, it was exactly at 10:02 A.M. EST right here, when them three old surplus Russian-made diesel submarines that somebody — and nobody's still sure just who — bought up back in the 1990s surfaced in three places around the world — and fired off them surplus NASA booster rockets, nine or ten of 'em — "

"Why 'cause we know that, Rudy, if we don't know who did it?"

"'Cause everybody had electric stuff back then could tell what kind of damn watch you was wearin' from two hundred miles out in space by how fast it was draggin' down that 1.5-volt battery in it. They knew the subs was old Russian surplus as soon as they surfaced, and knew they was NASA boosters as soon as the fuses was lit — 'cause that's the kind of world your folks let happen for you to live in — that's why 'cause."

"Oh."

"As old Rudy was sayin', them nine or ten missiles, some went to the top of the atmosphere, and some went further out where all them ATT and HBO and them satellites that could read your watch was, and they all went off and meanwhile everybody everywhere was firin' off all they stuff to try to stop whatever was gonna happen — well, when all that kind of stuff went off, and it turns out them sub missiles was big pulse explosions, what they used to call EMP stuff, and all the other crap went off that was tryin' to stop the missiles, well then, kids, Time started over as far as ol' Rudy's concerned. Not just for the US of A and Yooropeans, but for everybody everywhere, even down to them gentle Tasaday and every witchety grub-eatin' sonofagun down under."

"Time ain't started over, Rudy," said a kid. "This is Tuesday. It's June. This is the year 2000 A.D."

"Sure, sure. On the outside," said Rudy. "I'm talkin' 'bout the inside. We can do it all over again. Or not. Look, people took a week to find out what still worked, when what juice there was gonna be came back on. See, up till then they all thought them EMP pulses would just knock out everything, everywhere that was electronic, solid state stuff, transistors. That's without takin' into account all that other crap that was zoomin' around, and people tryin' to jam stuff, and all that false target shit they put up cause at first they thought it was a sneak attack on cities and stuff, and they just went, you know, apeshit for about ten minutes.

"So what was left was arbitrary. Like nobody could figure why Betamax players sometimes was okay and no Beta III VCR was. Your CDs are fine; you just can't play 'em. Then why none of them laserdiscs are okay, even if you had a machine that would play 'em? It don't make a fuckin' bit o' sense. Why icemaker refrigerators sometimes work and most others don't? You can't get no fancy embroidery on your fishing shirt: It all come out lookin' like Jackson Pollock. No kind of damn broadcast TV for a week, none of that satellite TV shit, for sure. Ain't no computers work but them damn Osbornes they been usin' to build artificial reefs in lakes for twenty years. Cars? You seen anything newer than a 1974 Subaru on the street, movin'? Them '49 Plymouths and '63 Fords still goin', cause they ain't got nothin' in them that don't move you can't fix with a pair o' Vise Grips . . .

"Look at the damn mail we was talking about! Ain't nobody in the Post Office actually had to read a damn address in ten years; you bet your ass they gotta read writin' now! Everybody was freaked out. No e-mail, no phone, no fax, ain't no more Click On This, kids. People all goin' crazy till they start gettin' them letters from Visa and Mastercard and such sayin' 'Hey, we hear you got an account with us? Why doncha tell us what you owe us, and we'll start sendin' you bills again?' Well, that was one thing they liked sure as shit. They still waitin' for their new cards with them raised-up letters you run through a big ol' machine, but you know what? They think about sixty to seventy percent o' them people told them what they owed them. Can you beat that? People's mostly honest, 'ceptin' the ones that ain't. . . .

"That's why you gettin' mail twice a week now, not at your house but on the block, see? You gonna have to have some smart people now; that's why I'm tellin' you all this."

"Thanks, Rudy," said a kid.

"Now that they ain't but four million people in this popsicle town, you got room to learn, room to move around some. All them scaredy cats took off for them wild places, like Montana, Utah, New Jersey. Now you got room to breathe, maybe one o' you gonna figure everything out someday, kid. That'll be thanks enough for old Rudy. But this time, don't mess up. Keep us fuckin' human— Morning, Bill—"

"Morning, Rudy."

"—and another thing. No damn cell phones. No damn baby joggers or double fuckin' wide baby strollers. No car alarms!"

Opening night.

The dancers are finishing the Harvest Dinner dance, like Oklahoma! or " June Is Bustin' Out All Over" on speed. It ends with a blackout. The packed house goes crazy.

Spotlight comes up on center stage.

Bill stands beside Shirlene. He's dressed in bib overalls and a black jacket and holds a pitchfork. She's in a simple farm dress. Bill wears thick glasses. He looks just like the dentist B.H. McKeeby, who posed as the farmer, and Shirlene looks just like Nan Wood, Grant's sister, who posed as the farmer's spinster daughter, down to the pulled-back hair, and the cameo brooch on the dress.

Then the lights come up on stage, and Bill and Shirlene turn to face the carpenter-gothic farmhouse, with the big arched window over the porch.

Instead of it, the backdrop is a painting from one of the Mars Lander photos of a rocky surface.

Bill just stopped.

There was dead silence in the theater, then a buzz, then sort of a louder sound; then some applause started, and grew and grew, and people came to their feet, and the sound rose and rose.

Bill looked over. Shirlene was smiling, and tears ran down her cheeks. Then the house set dropped in, with a working windmill off to the side, and the dancers ran on from each wing, and they did, along with Bill, the Pitchfork Number.

The lights went down, Bill came off the stage, and the chorus ran on for the Birthplace of Herbert Hoover routine.

Bill put his arms around Fossman's shoulders.

"You . . . you . . . asshole," said Bill.

"If you would have known about it, you would have fucked it up," said Arnold.

"But . . . how . . . the audience . . . ?"

"We slipped a notice in the programs, just for the opening, which is why you didn't see one. Might I say your dancing was superb tonight?"

"No. No," said Bill, crying. "Kirk Alyn, the guy who played Superman in the serials in the Forties, now there was a dancer . . ."

On his way home that night, he saw that a kid had put up a new graffiti on the official site, and had run out of paint at the end, so the message read

"What do we have left they could hate us" and then the faded letters, from the thinning and upside-down spray can, "f o r ?"

Right on, thought Bill. Fab. Gear. Groovy.

At work the next day, he found himself setting the galleys of the rave review of Glorifying the American Gothic, by the Times' drama critic.

And on a day two months later:

"And now!" said the off-pixievision-camera announcer, "Live! On Television! Major Spacer in the 21st Century!"

". . . tune in tomorrow, when you'll hear Major Spacer say:

WE'LL GET BACK TO THE MOON IF WE HAVE TO RETROFIT EVERY ICBM IN THE JUNKPILE WITH DUCT TAPE AND SUPERGLUE.

"Don't miss it. And now, for today's science segment, we go to the Space Postal Joint, with Cadet Rudy!" said the announcer.

Rudy: "Hey, kids. Listen to ol' Rudy. Your folks tried hard but they didn't know their asses from holes in the ground when it came to some things. They didn't mean to mess your world up; they just backed into one that could be brought down in thirty seconds 'cause it was the easiest thing to do. Remember the words of Artoo Deetoo Clarke: 'With increasin' technology, you headin' for a fall.' Now listen how it could be in this excitin' world of the future . . ."

A few years later, after Bill and the show and Rudy were gone, some kid, who'd watched it every day, figured everything out.

And kept us human.

CPSIA information can be obtained
at www.ICGtesting.com
Printed in the USA
BVOW09s1354201017
498247BV00001B/126/P